Going the Other Way

Going the Other Way

LESSONS FROM A LIFE IN AND OUT OF MAJOR-LEAGUE BASEBALL

Billy Bean
with Chris Bull

MARLOWE & COMPANY
NEW YORK

GOING THE OTHER WAY:
Lessons from a Life in and out of Major-League Baseball

Published by
Marlowe & Company
An Imprint of Avalon Publishing Group Incorporated
161 William Street, 16th Floor
New York, NY 10038

Some names of people in this account have been changed to protect their privacy.

Frontispiece: *Putting It Together, 1982* ~ Center fielder/pitcher for the Santa Ana Saints, my high school varsity baseball team; we won that year's state championship.

Library of Congress Cataloging-in-Publication Data

Bean, Billy, 1964–
Going the other way : lessons from a life in and out of major-league baseball / by Billy Bean with Chris Bull.
p.cm.
ISBN 1-56924-486-3
1. Bean, Billy, 1964– 2. Baseball players—United States—Biography.
3. Gay athletes—United States—Biography. I. Bull, Chris, 1963– II. Title.

GV865.B336A3 2003
796.357'092—dc21
[B]
2003041266

9 8 7 6 5 4 3 2 1

Designed by Simon M. Sullivan
Printed in the United States of America
Distributed by Publishers Group West

To my mom, Linda

*For too long, I made the terrible mistake of leaving you
out of my life. This time around, you're coming along for the ride.*

Contents

Introduction

~

For Love of the Game

I T WAS MY SUREFIRE cure for the blues. Around noon, I threw on my tank top, shorts, and Nike training shoes and headed to the seashore, where the cloudless sky and the vast expanse of blue-green Atlantic—along with the endorphins coursing through my body—usually acted as Valium to my nerves, no matter how frayed. My body took on the rhythm of the velvet-voiced companion on my Walkman, Natalie Merchant. A cool breeze swept off the ocean. I watched cruise ships, veritable floating cities, head out of port for Caribbean fun.

It was March 1996, my first spring without Cactus or Grapefruit League training camp. The clock of my life was set to baseball's schedule, and I was lost without it. As I turned around and headed back home, my shirt already drenched, I switched on the radio and turned the dial to 560 WQAM, the Florida Marlins' radio station, thinking maybe a little baseball was what I needed.

The Marlins' Robb Nen was facing the Braves' Chipper Jones in the ninth inning. As I listened to the sounds of the game, the crack of bat against ball, the shouts of fans, the banter of the play-by-play announcers, I saw myself standing on second base after lining one into the gap.

I could still do that, I thought. *I should still be out there mixing it up with the greatest players around. I'm no quitter.*

I wanted to race over to Space Coast Stadium, the Marlins' training facility, and beg the team to let me suit up and take my familiar position in center field. Even the bench, the source of so much frustration during my playing days, suddenly seemed like the best seat in the house. After ten years with the Tigers, Dodgers, and Padres, any team would do, as long as I could be back in the show.

Had I left too soon? At the age of thirty-one, I was haunted by the notion that I still had many years of baseball left in me. On the beach, the length of my stride increased as I tried to stifle the voice of regret in my head.

I reminded myself of why it had to be this way. I'd sacrificed my love of the game to another kind of love. Four months earlier I'd fallen for a wonderful man, Efraín Veiga. We were building a life together. I'd finally achieved the sense of security and stability I lacked while locked in the big-league closet. There was no way I was going back to hiding. I just couldn't bear any longer the constant fear of exposure, the anti-gay remarks of teammates and coaches, and the exhausting, grinding pressure of being someone I wasn't.

Baseball, I knew, wasn't ready for a guy like me, no matter how well I played. The game wasn't mature enough to deal with a gay ballplayer, and I wasn't in an emotional state to take it on by myself. It was time to change course. I had a good life. I had my health. I had a partner who loved me. I wasn't a victim or a hero, but I was tired of being a pawn.

My last conversation with my agent, Dennis Gilbert, just a few weeks earlier, ran through my head like a scene from a horror flick. Despite the fact that I'd torn up the Pacific Coast League the previous season in between three trips back and forth to the majors, he was having no luck securing a major-league contract. Six teams were offering minor-league contracts with a chance to make the big club out of spring training. This was standard for a reserve like me, basically an inexpensive insurance policy for a team, but this year I was determined not to settle for so little.

"Dennis, if I don't get a good deal, I'm not going back," I told him. "I'm sick of the bushes."

I was sick of a lot more than that. Dennis was puzzled by my attitude, and he let me know it. He wasn't afraid to point out that I was inconsistent at the big-league level and that I'd created my own problems. Every ballplayer is told to play until he drops. It's a testament to our commitment for the game and how lucky we are to get paid to play it. I was about to break a cardinal rule.

My anger and frustration got the best of me, and I just couldn't listen to him.

"Dennis, you just don't know how hard it's been," I said. "You can't even imagine."

It was true. I hadn't confided my secret to him, and a baseball guy like Dennis never would've guessed what I was harboring. This was uncharted territory. There was no map by which a gay ballplayer could navigate toward stardom and happiness.

I wanted my agent to fight for me and for my career, but it really wasn't his fight. He'd heard me complain bitterly for years about the uncertainty of my status in the game, and the constant ups and downs.

"You've got to put up some numbers," he said. "If you put up some numbers on the field, I can get you some numbers in your contract."

Fair enough. But just then I was looking to him to talk me out of quitting. I wanted him to persuade me to stay in the game. But all Dennis could come up with was a limp, "Do whatever makes you happy."

My triple-A manager Tim Flannery, a terrific baseball guy who'd also played in the big leagues, was the one guy who had really leaned on me to give it another shot.

"Make them rip the uniform off your back, Beaner," he'd said. "You can't give it up now." But then Tim didn't know about my facade either.

On the radio, Robb Nen threw a slider. Chipper Jones went down on strikes. Game over.

I slowed to a jog as I reached Efraín's house in Coral Gables. I walked around to the backyard to cool down from my run and sat on the steps. Since I was eight, I'd always had a baseball season to look forward to. I buried my face in my hands and had my first real cry since I'd retired. *What am I gonna do now?*

It would be three more years before the story I was determined to keep private made national headlines. The truth is I'd never wanted to be a star anywhere but on the field. I never set out to be a role model for gay ballplayers or for anyone else. I couldn't figure out why all the attention had come to me.

For twenty-five years, I had only wanted to play ball. But something surprising had happened along the way. I discovered there was more to life than hitting .300. Perhaps my life was meant for other things.

With the perspective the last several years had provided, I felt ready to tell my story, in my own words, so that others might avoid the cruel dilemma I'd faced. *Going the Other Way* is not just a ballplayer's story. It's for anyone who has ever wanted to make their parents proud, play for the team, reach a goal, and be their best. It's for parents who want to understand the struggles faced by their children. It's for athletes who are not sure they can deal with a gay teammate. It's for gay athletes who may feel, as I did, that no one else walked in their cleats or high-tops.

My story is about feeling alone in a crowded room. It's about embracing the notion that our lives don't always turn out the way we thought they would. It's about realizing that while we may not all be alike, or come from the same place, we can survive and thrive as long as we learn to play together as a team.

This is the chronicle of a journey, an arduous voyage made possible by the great game of baseball. To take you on this trip, I must start at the beginning, on the dusty playing fields of my youth.

Going
the Other
Way

Part One

Suiting Up

1 *Fields of My Dreams*

ACTION HEROES AND SUPERMOM ~ FATHER IN A FAR-
AWAY LAND ~ MUDVILLE ~ NOTHING MORE THAN A BULLY
~ THE SILKIEST ATHLETE ~ SLURPEES AND FRED LYNN ~
NEVER LET US DOWN

E VEN AS A KID, I lived to wear a uniform. But my first choice
might have been a little ambitious. At my fourth birthday party,
I'm tearing open a present from Mom, a full-body Superman
outfit. Pulling it on over my clothes, I race out of the house and around
the block, hoping the momentum will lift me off the pavement and into
the blue sky. Why can't I take off? I scamper back into the house,
jumping from couch to armchair to floor.

Starting with this first conscious memory, my childhood fantasy life
revolved around action heroes. I never cared about toy guns or cars like
other boys. I couldn't wait for the comic books Mom would bring
home. When I got home from school each day, I'd plop myself down in
front of the television with a glass of chocolate milk to watch the
Dynamic Duo.

On weekends, Mom let me watch SuperFriends cartoons, and I'd
spend the rest of the day mimicking my heroes. I ran like Flash, swam
like Aquaman, flew like Superman. I imagined myself having the

strength of Popeye, the courage and guile of Batman, the loyalty of Robin. When rescuing someone from danger, I morphed back into Superman. Unlike the other kids, I wasn't satisfied with admiring my heroes from afar. I actually strove to acquire a fantastic amalgam of their powers, and as a result I was always running headfirst into walls, jumping off the highest point I could climb, and generally causing havoc. I never slowed down. Remember those old newspaper stories about kids eating canned spinach like Popeye, and then standing in front of speeding trains?

Well, I wasn't that stupid. But I was a daredevil. In one crazy stunt, my friends and I would stand on the cement wall in our back-yard and jump into the small pool just before the train that ran behind our house rumbled by. Then there was the time I took a run-ning start and leapt off grandpa's truck, hands outstretched, trying to fly. Catching some major air, but a lot more pavement, I shattered my collarbone.

Mom says I taught myself to read before my fourth birthday by devouring those dog-eared comic books. I created elaborate scenarios in which I saved the day, winning the undying love and affection I always longed for. Even though I was just a pint-sized kid, I always managed to kill the intruder, foil the bad guys, and save Mom from danger.

~

LINDA JANE ROBERTSON and William Joseph Bean grew up on Camile Street in Santa Ana, just three houses from each other. Massive oak trees shaded manicured lawns and yes—quite literally—picket fences.

They met in junior high. Two years later, in tenth grade, they began dating. Mom has often described the strong physical attraction between the two, and by her senior year in high school, when she was seventeen, she'd become pregnant with me. It was an ominous start to a relationship in an era when premarital sex was taboo.

The trouble began, as it often does, with religion. My dad's mother, Carmela Caruso Bean, converted to the Church of Jesus Christ of Latter-Day Saints and kept strict tabs on her five children. The Robertsons, who weren't particularly religious, were skeptical of the Mormon faith. I remember Mom angrily dismissing it as a "cult."

After learning about the pregnancy, the Bean family hastily arranged a marriage at a local mortuary, presided over by a Mormon bishop. The morgue became a running family joke, but at the time it was anything but funny. Carmela refused to embrace the union, perhaps because I was conceived before vows were exchanged, at least of the official kind.

Grandma wanted to name me after her husband, Joseph William Bean, and to baptize me in her newfound faith. But even at an impressionable age and under intense pressure, Mom stayed true to herself.

"Over my dead body," she said succinctly, adding that I would be christened Timothy John Bean, if only to spite her overbearing mother-in-law.

They eventually compromised on William Daro Bean, after my father and my mom's father, Daro Robertson. I hadn't even been born, and hardly anyone was on speaking terms.

By the time I arrived, on May 11, 1964, my grandmother had barred her daughter-in-law from the Bean home. When I was still an infant, under the guise of taking me to the park, she smuggled me into the temple for baptism. When Mom found out about this, it marked the last time I got to see Carmela for a long, long time.

The baptism stuck for about as long as my parents' marriage. I consider myself a spiritual person, but I grew up viewing organized religions as hypocritical. In my childhood at least, religion gave people an excuse to mistreat others and then take refuge in the church's teaching. There were plenty of human failings as well. My father failed to defend and protect his wife and newborn. After about a year of marriage, at his mother's urging, he left on a two-year assignment as a Mormon missionary in Canada. It would be years before he reemerged in my life.

~

I HAD PLENTY of time to daydream about a father in a faraway land. Working two jobs, Mom was rarely around. After school, I stayed home alone or with her mother, Dottie Arnett, who left me to my own devices. I understood why Mom was gone while the other kids' households were filled with parents and grandparents and toys and sports gear. Even so, I didn't quite accept it.

I'd be in the park with friends and notice someone else's father playing catch or Frisbee with his kid. I'd stand and stare, wondering what it would be like to play catch with my dad. Later, back home, just what I was missing would hit me, and I'd beg Mom to tell me stories about the man she'd loved. Mom did her best to reassure me. But not knowing any better, I attributed his abandonment to some grave flaw. If I were a better kid, wouldn't Dad have stayed? Wouldn't I be surrounded by friends?

I developed some unusual habits to compensate. When I was in third grade, Mom noticed that I'd started laying out my clothing in neat piles, picking out just the right combination of colors for the next school day. Then I'd wake up before everyone else, make my bed, shower, and comb and blow-dry my hair in front of the bathroom mirror. Before long, I was giving Mom fashion tips.

"Honey, where in the world did you come from?" she would say, patting me on the backside as I scurried out the door.

Being the son of a single mother *did* have its advantages. Mom and I developed an intense attachment. I slept in her bed in our one-bedroom apartment until I was five. The men Mom dated, jealous of our bond, accused her of coddling me. The implication was clear: there was something wrong with loving your firstborn too much.

"The boy will never grow up to be a *man*," I remember one insisting.

Of course, these men never bothered to ask my opinion. If they had, I would have said that I loved every second of my life with Mom. I adored her. She was smart and strong, tall and pretty—with curly brown hair that fell over her shoulders like a cape. She treated me as an equal in every way, making me feel important. I was so proud of her determination to make a life for us despite all the obstacles thrown in her way.

Since we were always on the move, from one cheap apartment to another, I attended a different school every year from preschool until fourth grade. On my first day, Mom, hoping to ward off another awkward transition and questions about our financial status, dressed me in jacket and tie. I hated changing schools because it meant I'd have to endure another round of hazing when the teacher called on "Billy Bean," which kids thought was the funniest name they'd ever heard. I wished Mom would change our name back to Robertson, which sounded much more normal. I wished Dad had taken the name with him.

The few friends I had were the kids of Mexican immigrants. Like us, they didn't have much money, and both parents worked all the time. They never looked down on the dirty little speed demon with the funny name, the bad suit, and the single mom. Jessie Rodriguez and I became inseparable. The youngest of six kids, he showed me how to avoid getting caught doing the naughty things your mother doesn't want you to do.

~

A CHAIN-LINK FENCE enclosed the diamond of dirt in the small green lot. In the late afternoon sun, a two-story press box, which doubled as a hot-dog stand, cast a long shadow on the field. Home-run clouts of a mere 200 feet, still Herculean for boys, sailed over a hedge that served as the center-field fence and smacked into the side of a brown stucco house in a residential neighborhood where many of the Little Leaguers lived. More than a few balls dove clean through kitchen windows. On the other side of the field, behind the backstop, lay gravel parking lots and asphalt basketball courts. A Catholic church loomed in the background.

This diamond was little different from thousands of ragged fields across the nation. Yet the moment I stepped onto it, I knew I'd found the place I belonged. I was eight, and so scrawny that everyone called me "Little Billy." I was the last child anyone would pick for any team.

But for some inexplicable reason I was drawn to the crack of the bat, the trajectory of the ball through the summer sky, the early days of spring when the morning dew turns the outfield grass damp and slippery. Who can say why we get involved in the things we do as kids? Who can connect the dots between these passions and the adults we become? At the time, it seemed like a wonderful accident. Looking back, it seems as if I didn't have a choice at all.

I nearly didn't set foot on any field. It was 1972, and local favorite Richard Nixon had just been reelected president. Mom and I were squeezed together in another small apartment, in Tustin, just 30 minutes south of Los Angeles. This land of strip malls, tract houses, and blazing heat bordered the city of Santa Ana. Mom struggled to get by in a succession of low-wage jobs, and there was never enough money.

She took the jobs available to women at the time—meter maid, police dispatcher, clerk. She worked long and hard to put a roof over our heads and food on the table. At the supermarket, Mom returned items to the shelves as quickly as I tossed them into the basket. She was always telling me we couldn't afford the stuff other kids got.

Eager for action, my friend Tommy and I faced a major childhood dilemma: choosing between baseball and karate. We discovered that something called Little League, of which I'd never heard, would set us back $10; karate, $15. At first Mom was adamant that both activities were too expensive. Fearing for the safety of her undersized boy and holding a low opinion of organized sports, she discouraged me from taking up any game at all.

What was a rambunctious kid to do? Innocently, I explained the situation to Tommy's father. A few nights later during dinner, we heard a knock on the front door. It was Tommy's dad. I feigned surprise as best an eight-year-old could.

"Mrs. Bean," he said politely. "Can Billy play baseball if I agree to drive the boys to the field every day?"

My plan had worked. Charmed, Mom relented, and I became the littlest Little Leaguer.

~

IT TURNED OUT that superhero skills were more than aspirations for a lonely kid. They were also the building blocks of competitive sports. I wasn't satisfied with admiring my heroes, whose common attribute seemed to be fearlessness. Off the field, I might have worried about everything from life without my biological father to Mom's financial straits. I wondered what my father was like. Did he like sports, too? Did I look anything like him?

On the field, I left all the worries behind. The moment I stepped on a baseball or football field or a basketball court, I was transformed into a daring competitor. I longed for the chance to take the winning shot or hurl a last-second touchdown with defenders bearing down on me. I ached to bat in a clutch situation, with the go-ahead run on base, and, in the final inning, make the spectacular diving catch to save the game. Other kids feared failure; I lived for the opportunity to fail because it meant the opportunity to be the hero.

Coaches trained players to visualize positive scenarios, but I had already spent years unconsciously developing the habit. Excelling under pressure had become part of my earliest mindset. I willed myself to succeed, and, because I believed it would happen, it usually did. I took my best shot, guiding the ball through the hoop, into the end zone, or, best of all, over the outfield fence. I wondered where this part of me came from. So did my family. Did my biological father have some gene we were unaware of? Or was it his absence that brought it out in me?

"My little action hero," Mom would say with a combination of surprise and affection in her voice. "What'll become of you?"

Other kids ran track, swam competitively, or played golf—more solitary athletic pursuits. But I wanted to be an indispensable part of a team, to be in the middle of the action. Surrounded by other kids who relied upon me and looked up to me, I felt warm and wanted.

Kickball and dodgeball were the first sports I'd ever played, at recess in grade school. They led naturally to baseball, basketball, and football. In the heavily black and Latino environment I grew up in, tennis, golf, and swimming were considered "country club," whereas "real" boys played hoops, football, and baseball. I also enjoyed the feeling of representing the school, and the popularity became intoxicating. The brotherhood of teammates is something individual-sport athletes rarely experience.

Then there was the pure pleasure of athleticism. I loved mastering the coordination required to hit a baseball on the screws or thread a touchdown pass over the arms of defenders to my target. I loved the feel of the laces on a basketball rotating off my fingertips, up into the air, and into the hoop.

It wasn't enough to be quick and strong, you had to have hand-eye coordination and perfect timing. You had to understand what my coaches called "fundamentals," the techniques that underlie the game. You had to anticipate where the action would lead. Like Superman, you had to sense the disaster about to occur to your team and dash in fast to avert it. You had to leap tall buildings in a single bound.

~

LIKE CLARK KENT, I thought I should have a bookish side. School came easily, and, just as in sports, excelling brought me the attention I sought. I loved math and science, but writing was my strongest suit. I wasn't afraid to express myself in words, and this helped me sail through school.

Once again, a gift became a means to an end. The other kids seemed indifferent to this eager puppy in their midst. So I provided answers on exams to anyone who asked. They were relieved to breeze through their exams. Cheating seemed a small price to pay for affection.

When I reached second grade, class met in the same room as third-graders. An older kid, Bobby, was a bully. But as an undersized, insecure kid, I envied his power. The best way to befriend him, I quickly figured out, was to do third-grade work. He loved the attention, and before long I was completing his assignments for him. There was only one thing we hadn't considered. Bobby's test scores took off, and the teacher noticed the similarities in our work. We were hauled into the principal's office for a lecture. The silver lining was that my desire to please my friends revealed a hidden intelligence. I was placed in a new class for advanced kids.

In third grade, I developed a crush on my teacher, Ms. Evans. Every month, she handed out citizenship awards. One day she told us that she would be giving out "citizen of the year" awards, one for boys and one for girls. The way I went after it, you'd have thought I was competing for a batting title. After Christmas vacation, Ms. Evans returned to class and introduced herself as Mrs. Lightner. She had gotten married over the break. I sat at my desk with tears rolling down my cheeks.

It was even harder to imagine sharing my teacher than it was my mom. After class, Mrs. Lightner ushered me into the hallway. I looked into her big brown eyes. What could she possibly say to reassure me?

"You're not going to be a little boy forever, Billy," she said. "And someday, you will meet someone who loves you so much it will make everything seem better."

I started crying again.

"Why do I have to grow up for that?"

She put her arm around my shoulder.

Our private moment cheered me up. By noticing my hurt, she'd consoled me and made me feel special at the same time. And, yes, it wasn't long before she presented me with the citizen of the year award. All was well in Mudville.

~

IT DIDN'T TAKE LONG for our little family to expand. Mom had a wild streak, and she wasn't going to stop looking for love simply because she'd picked one bad apple. Mom would discuss her many suitors, allowing me a fair amount of say. It made me feel like I was the man of the house and softened the impact of the competition for her affection.

For a while, Mom dated a man named Bruce Briggs. At first, I wasn't big on him, a smooth-talking Santa Ana policeman. Mom, however, was convinced she was pregnant again, so the two got hitched, this time in a more traditional ceremony. In fact, she wasn't pregnant at all; she had a tumor in her uterus the size of a grapefruit. Thinking she was nearly five months pregnant, she had gone about her business before collapsing at work. After removing the growth, her doctors told her she was lucky to be alive.

She struggled to make the marriage work, and the young couple had a son, my half-brother Brian. They were divorced a year or so later. Bruce Briggs turned out to be a good role model. He was so concerned about the absence of a male figure in my life that he talked my mother into changing my last name to Briggs so he could play a larger role in my life.

I finally got my wish for a "normal name." Bruce never legally adopted me; we just changed it. From the age of six to thirteen, I was known as Billy Briggs, even though the Briggses were no more. It was all very confusing, especially for my teachers. At least I shared a surname with my little brother. (At fourteen, as I was starting high school, we changed it back to Bean. It was time to stop the charade that Bruce Briggs was my father.)

In 1973, Mom started working as dispatcher for the Tustin Police Department. She was promoted to undercover investigator after becoming the first woman to graduate from the police academy. It was at the PD that she met "Number Three," as I privately nicknamed her third husband. Ed Kovac was a brawny police sergeant and former Marine. At the time, he was in an unhappy marriage that had produced three children—Colette, Joseph, and Tommy.

At the ripe old age of nine, I tried to be the voice of wisdom. I didn't want to accept Ed, whose wife came over to our apartment to threaten my mother. I wanted to turn back the clock.

"Three kids," I kept saying to her, shaking my head as gravely as I could.

But Mom was tired of being alone. Being twice divorced with two kids and low-paying jobs was no picnic. Now she had found a principled man who loved her and offered her stability. She loved him, too, and Ed's kids were just part of the package.

Mom told me she would marry Ed only if I agreed to give her away. She rented me a white tuxedo and a black felt tie, and I walked her down the aisle. In another year, I gained my second half-brother, Jason Kovac. I went from being an only child at the age of five to the oldest of six kids at the age of eleven.

~

If I played like Superman, I discovered, I'd be treated like him. In 1976 Jimmy Carter was elected president. More importantly, I made the Northeast Santa Ana Little League all-star squad. We traveled to diamonds up and down the California coast, winning thirteen in a row, and sending us to the Western Regional Championship game in San Bernadino.

The bleachers were packed with buzzing fans. Before the game against the northern California finalists, Campbell, I looked around in disbelief that all these adults were here to watch a bunch of twelve-years-olds running around the bases. California Angels third baseman Doug DeCinces threw out the first pitch.

I was hardly the best player. That distinction went to Floyd Jensen, a six-foot-two right-hander who blew the ball past hitters. He was one of those "man-childs" you find in every Little League World Series, the guy who puts the entire team on his back and carries them for as long as his legs hold out. But like many early achievers, he had trouble living up to the expectations attached to him so early in life. By high school, he had dropped out of sports and become one of the Pink Floyd burnouts who hung out in the parking lot making fun of us goody-goodies.

I was still the smallest guy on the team, wondering whether I'd ever grow up. Floyd already had a dozen homers when I hit my first ball out of the park. As I watched the ball disappear over the fence, I stood at the plate in shock as my teammates yelled at me to run around the bases. I played catcher, pitcher, and shortstop, a rarity for a left-hander. My coach, Hershel Musick, a Kansas City Royals scout, realized he should use my speed and arm in the outfield. But I thought that was where you stow the losers who can't catch anything.

Hershel took me to watch Fred Lynn of the Boston Red Sox play against the Angels in Anaheim. Lynn was one of the silkiest athletes I'd ever seen, gliding around center field like a cheetah. His smooth left-handed swing made opposing pitchers weep. He used a slick black bat, and he could hit the ball out of the park on a line.

I couldn't keep my eyes off him. Lynn was the kind of athlete who made everything look easy. Before long I was imitating his every move, from his crouch in center to the way he massaged the length of the bat as he stood in at the plate. From watching Lynn, I learned how to slide on the outfield grass in preparation for a running catch of a ball dropping at my feet.

Back at the Little League field, Coach Musick would stand at the plate, blue KC cap shielding the bright sun, and hit hundreds of soaring fungoes to the outfield, moving me in and out, left and right. No matter how hot it got, I couldn't get enough. I'd strip off my shirt in the blazing California sun and chase madly after the ball, trying my best to impress my coach.

"Remember to keep your head level as you run," he'd shout. "Run to the spot and then pick up the ball." When I'd accomplished one of his commands, he'd hold the bat high and yell, "Way to go, Billy. Way to go."

When our team made fifteen tough catches in a row, he'd take us out for Slurpees, and then drop me off at home, tired, sweaty, and happy.

I was ready for some serious ball. Back then, Little League tournaments tended to be single-elimination, making every game a cliffhanger. Fourteen teams, representing the western region of the United States, bunked in dorms at the stadium and fought it out for the ultimate: a berth in the Little League World Series in Williamsport, Pennsylvania.

It was such a big deal that our coach at this point, Dick Prospero, rented limousines to make the two-hour drive to San Bernadino—complete with police escort. We felt like rock stars, far higher up in the hierarchy than mere ballplayers. Floyd hurled a no-hitter and blasted a tremendous home run over the flagpole in center field. He was living up to legend as the best Little Leaguer in the nation. I stroked line drives every time up, and we walloped New Mexico 6-0. As I was walking off the field, the last out clutched safely in my glove, I looked into the stands to see my whole family cheering.

Next up was Pearl City, Hawaii. It was traditional for each team to present the other team with a gift in a ceremony before the game. We received Hawaiian leis from the other team. They got California oranges.

Since he'd just pitched six innings, Floyd couldn't go again. Pat Simms, our second-best pitcher, struggled in the early innings.

Prospero made the walk to the mound. I was playing center when he motioned me in.

"Just throw to the mitt, kid," he said, flipping me the ball. "You'll do fine."

I hardly needed his encouragement. In my white uniform with blue and red lettering, I felt like I was in my Superman outfit again. I was hardly throwing speeding bullets, but I caught enough of the plate to pitch two scoreless innings. We squeaked by in a close one.

We made it to the finals, squaring off against Campbell under the lights. After a week of pillow fights, junk food, late-night stories, homesickness, and tense games, we were a close-knit crew. But as our achievement sunk in, we got a little uptight. We looked at each other for support. No one stepped forward. For the first time all season, I could see fear in my teammates' eyes, and there was nothing I could do about it. Floyd was not sharp this time around, and we got beaten up pretty good, losing 7-3. Trying bravely to fight back tears, we walked off the field, heads held high.

I learned that no one can take away your achievements as a team, even if you don't go all the way. In our hearts, we were champs, even though our name wasn't etched on the trophy that night. It softened the blow when Campbell went on to win the Little League World Series. The best team in the country had defeated us.

Back at school, we were greeted like conquering heroes.

"Hey, Billy, you look great out there," other kids, parents, and even teachers would tell me. "A .620 batting average. Amazing. Way to go."

People even began to credit me for the collective success. "The team played great," they'd say. "Keep it up. We know you'll never let us down."

2 *Myth of the Golden Boy*

Up in the sky ~ Go little Billy ~ Pleasures of
free throws ~ Back to San Francisco ~ It's you
against him ~ Best Friend's girlfriend ~ David vs.
Goliath ~ Two boys sitting together

Santa Ana High is not your typical suburban public school. With its Mission-style arches and Spanish tile roof, expansive lawns and giant eucalyptus trees, it could pass for a monastery, at least from the outside.

On my first day, Mom dropped me off in the parking lot in front of the school, which she had graduated from only fourteen years earlier. She had apparently been applying her "biology" lessons when I was conceived, so I guess I really was a product of the school.

"I know you're going to be the best," she said, kissing me on the cheek before driving off to work. "Don't let anyone put you down."

Knapsack slung over my shoulder, I walked through the double doors into a scene that was anything but monastic. I was shocked by the flurry of three thousand kids, of every conceivable color and nationality, racing every which way. Endless rows of red metal lockers lined the halls.

I spotted a few of my old Willard Junior High buddies and hunted for my homeroom among the maze of classrooms. As I listened to the teacher take roll, learning the names of my new classmates, I gazed out the windows. I was already far more interested in what lay on the other side of the glass: a hulking indoor basketball arena that far outshone the rest of the school and, beyond that, acres of lush green playing fields.

"So you'll be leading off this year, right?" one of my teammates from our old school said, seeing me staring out the window. "But I get to pitch and bat third," he added. We both smiled.

Sports at Santa Ana were a huge cut above Little League and Pop Warner football league. The best athletes from all over the area clustered at the school, and dozens of kids would vie for a few spots on the junior varsity and varsity teams. I drew a big red, yellow, and blue "S" in my notebook. *There, up in the sky, it's a bird, it's a plane, it's, it's Superman.*

~

ONLY ONE THING stood in the way of my dream of three-sport stardom: my body, all five feet, 105 pounds of it. Even by ninth grade, I was still one of the smallest boys.

I reacted the only way I knew: by outworking everyone else. I hit the bench presses like a boy possessed. My body may have looked like Jimmy Olsen's, but I was determined to sculpt it into Superman's. It's a good thing steroids didn't become popular for another decade or so. I was just saying no to drugs, and I'd never heard of Nancy Reagan. But I would have been sorely tempted by their promise of bulk.

With its emphasis on brute force, football presented the biggest challenge. I'd played tailback in Pop Warner since fourth grade. But on the first day of practice my freshman year, a couple of weeks before classes began, I made a point of crashing through the line, throwing myself into the huge defensive linemen like a child trying to push a refrigerator across the ice, my legs pumping furiously. I wanted to prove that I could gain the tough extra yardage.

The freshman coach, Carl Rosetti, was a short, muscular guy whose gentle manner belied a fierce will. I begged him to let me run the ball.

"Come on, Coach, give me a chance," I'd say. "I know I can do it. I'm gonna go all the way."

He would shake his head and flash a bemused smile.

During one practice later that year, varsity coach Tom Meiss stood on the sidelines, sizing up varsity prospects.

"Who is the crazy little guy causing all sorts of problems for the defense?" he asked Rosetti.

My desire far outstripped my fourteen-year-old ability. My best friend, Yale Riley, was the star. He stood six-foot-three with a rocket arm. I looked up to him as though he were an uncle. That didn't stop me from secretly coveting his starting-quarterback job. I settled for the tailback slot.

As I went to bed every night, I said a silent prayer.

"Please, God, make me as big as Yale Riley. I promise to be a good boy."

Rosetti wasn't convinced of my future on the gridiron. He seemed certain about everything, so I struggled not to look very hurt when he said I should go out for the wrestling team after football season ended.

"Son," he explained as gently as he could, "in wrestling you can compete against kids closer to your size. You could probably qualify for the 103-pound division."

Wrestling? Was that even a sport? That's what rug rats did on the front lawn or living room carpet when they were bored. I tried out for the team despite my misgivings. Even I realized that basketball would have to wait.

To compete in the 103-pound division I needed to drop five pounds. This was not easy for a growing boy with a workout regimen and a huge appetite for Mom's spaghetti and meatballs. I went from having one of the biggest sack lunches in school to eating only carrots and celery, washed down by apple juice. Mom couldn't believe a fourteen-year-old could be so disciplined. Dropping below my already low three percent body fat, I made the varsity team as a freshman.

I earned a varsity letter by beating everyone who tried out. But after a month it became clear that dieting at such a young age wasn't beneficial to my health. It broke my heart to tell Rosetti I had to quit. But the next day I was wearing a basketball uniform and playing on the freshman team. After the first practice we went out for pizza, and I must have consumed an entire pie by myself.

I was an odd combination of imp and adult, adolescent and athlete, boyish yet skilled enough to play with the best of my age level. The other kids didn't know what to make of me. After practice one day, I was in the locker room getting ready to shower. I was always shocked to see thick hair sprouting on the other kids' bodies like weeds in the spring, while mine remained smooth and underdeveloped. The locker room became traumatizing, and I always waited until everyone was done to find a shower.

That day, two football teammates, Enrique Espinosa and Armando Gomez, arrived in the shower at the same time I did.

Enrique was already a nemesis. A couple years earlier we'd vied for the same girl, so we were wary of each other. As they approached, it became painfully obvious I wasn't in their league—at least not yet.

"Go, Billy, go," they taunted as they surrounded me. "Go little Billy with his little dick."

The boys repeated the refrain over and over. As other kids looked on, joining the derision, I realized there was nowhere to hide, nothing to say. I just stood there shivering, covering myself with my hand. Ducking under them, I darted for my locker, dressed, and raced home as fast as I could.

The hazing didn't intimidate me for long. It put a chip on my shoulder the size of Texas. I determined to bury those oafs on the field.

~

THE DESIRE TO be liked was one of my defining characteristics. But my need to please my coaches bordered on the pathological, and looking back it seems pretty obvious it was a vehicle for winning the approval I'd been denied by my biological father. By senior year, I'd become close to Coach Meiss, who I thought walked on water.

After practice one day, the coach's oldest daughter, Paula, stopped by for a visit. She was the head cheerleader of our rival high school, El Modena. I noticed that she was cute, funny, and looked an awful lot like her father. I always had to have a girl by my side, and she fit the bill.

It caused a stir when I asked Paula out. My teammates thought I was insane to get involved with the coach's daughter. There were plenty of pretty girls in my own school, and I can see now that I was using her subconsciously to get closer to my coach.

Paula was a cautious daddy's girl, and I pressured her to fool around before she was ready. She stood firm, so I did what any self-respecting teenage boy would do: I kept right on cajoling. Late one night senior year, we were in my '69 Volkswagen in the hills just above the Meiss family home in Orange. We were making out, and before long I'd stripped down to my underwear.

The Cars' "My Best Friend's Girlfriend" was blasting on the stereo. The windows had fogged up, and we were lost in full lip-lock. *Enrique Espinosa, eat your heart out,* I thought.

Then a loud knock on the driver's side interrupted our bliss. I rolled down the window to find a policeman staring at us. Paula turned down the music as I fumbled with my jeans.

"Get the hell out of here and get her home," the cop ordered.

We drove home in silence. Shortly before we arrived back at her place, we looked at each other and cracked up. What could have been a nightmare had turned out to be a hilarious moment.

Coach Meiss was a football legend in the area as well as a born-again Christian who frowned on premarital sex. We'd narrowly averted disaster. Even though we dated the entire year, we never made that mistake again. When I realized I would be going away to college, I lost interest in dating and stopped seeing Paula. A few weeks later, before I left town, I stopped by the house to say good-bye.

Mrs. Meiss jumped all over me right there in the front yard.

"Billy, you really disappointed me," she said. "How could you be so insensitive to Paula. All she does is cry about how you treated her."

What could I say? She was right.

~

GIRLS TOOK A backseat to sports. Home became a place to eat, sleep, zip through my schoolwork, and then race out the door to the next practice or game. Buoyed by a great performance, I would announce to Mom that I was going to lead the football team to the championship or make it to the major leagues "when I grow up."

"That's nice, dear," she would say.

She thought these were the empty boasts of a precocious child, and she underestimated just how rapidly I was developing. She loved me for who I was, and she would have supported me whether I wanted to be a cop or a quarterback, though I have a feeling she would have preferred the former. Her indifference made me more determined to show her I could do it.

Her new husband, Ed, a six-foot-three mountain of a man and a former high school football player, took my enthusiasm far more seriously. He came up with what soon became my mantra of competition:

"Just remember, young man," he'd say solemnly to me. "It's you against him, and you're better."

It felt great to have his backing. After I got over my initial jealousy, Ed and I bonded. I think my negative feelings toward him had more to do with departures than arrivals. If he arrived, it meant he would leave. That had always been the pattern, after all.

When practice ended, I would shower and head home, looking forward to more competition. As soon as I walked in the front door and kissed Mom as she was cooking dinner, I was challenging Ed to a game of H-O-R-S-E or a free-throw shooting contest in the driveway. We used the metal hoop Ed had secured to a plywood board over the garage.

The loser drew dinner washup duty. At first Ed won most of the time, and with eight people in the house, I was up to my elbows in greasy plates. But after a while, I improved. I learned to let the laces of the ball spin softly off my index finger exactly the same way every time, increasing my accuracy. Before long, Ed was complaining good-naturedly about spending more time in the kitchen than his wife.

Those hours in the driveway paid off when my basketball coach entered the team in the California Interscholastic Federation National Free Throw Competition. At first, we moaned and groaned about having to participate. Arriving at the Santa Ana College gym one Saturday morning, I waited for my name to be called. There were dozens of players from around the city, and I figured I would shoot my 25 free throws and go home. I didn't even get a chance to warm up. After burying my first shot, I went on a roll, making 23 of 25. About 30 minutes later, I was informed I'd won. I was to show up at a junior college the next Saturday for the second round.

Sniffing victory, I practiced all week. I sunk 24 of 25 that day, and I lugged home another trophy. Next up was the qualifying round for the state title at Cal Poly Pomona College. A crowd of family and friends gathered to watch me shoot it out against six other guys. Since I'd had the highest percentage so far, I was slated to go last. One puny kid made 22 of 25.

Worried I had to be perfect, I missed 3 out of my first 10. For a tie, I needed 15 in a row. I made the first 10 without blinking, but then started to get shaky. I managed to down the next 5, even though I caught a piece of the rim a couple of times.

Now we were to stage a 5-shot shootout. We flipped a coin, and the other boy went first. He made his first 4 in a row.

As he readied himself for the decisive shot, cries of "MISS, MISS, MISS" rose from far up in the stands. It was my brother Jason, only three years old, screaming. The crowd laughed at his youthful squeals. But the kid, distracted, rimmed out his fifth shot.

I took a couple of deep breaths and tried to visualize the hoop in our driveway. "One at a time," Ed would say to me when I became anxious. So I did, swishing the fifth one to become a state champion. Jason got the assist.

Winning the state title meant that Mom, Ed, and I got a free trip to San Francisco, where we stayed at the elegant Sir Francis Drake Hotel. It became clear there was more to the world than Santa Ana.

We jumped in a cab for a celebratory tour of the city. I couldn't believe how many buildings they could fit on a street. I had no idea that cities could be built on hills. It was my first taxi ride, and soon we were heading down a wide, bar-lined street called Polk, right in the heart of the city.

As I peered out the windows through the fog, I spotted two young men sitting at a bus stop. I froze. Were they holding hands? My inclination was to ask Mom and Ed, "What's going on with those guys?"

Then I stopped myself. I just gazed at the couple until they were out of sight. I sat silently in the car until we returned to the hotel.

"Is anything wrong, Billy?" Mom asked.

"Everything's okay, Mom. When do we get to come back to San Francisco?"

~

GOING INTO MY senior year, the baseball team wasn't supposed to do much at all. But we ended up taking the California Interscholastic Federation 3-A title at Dodger Stadium. I was an all-state first team selection and the MVP of the Orange County all-star game.

Despite my passion for baseball, it was the gridiron that served as the ultimate proving ground, the test of my mettle. After starting out as a 103-pound tailback in my freshman year and then a 130-pound defensive back who took a pounding every game, by senior year I had grown six inches and put on thirty-five pounds, to a height of six feet and a weight of 165. I finally owned the body I needed to match my expectations.

I still had my eye on the coveted starting-quarterback job. I'd spent the summer before senior year, when I wasn't playing baseball, working on my passing. Ed set up a tire in the backyard, and I would fire the ball through it, often on the run from imaginary defenders.

Coach Meiss sent a receiver, Rod Harmon, and me to a passing and receiving camp for high school standouts. Rod, as lithe as his name suggested, was the defending league sprint champion in the 100 and 200 meters. I'd float a pass down the field, and Rod would run under it.

Beating out Yale and several more experienced players, I landed the prized starting-quarterback job. Early in 1981, we faced Edison High School, the number-one-ranked high school football team in the nation. This was the ultimate challenge. It was all anyone spoke about all week, and our pep rally turned the gym into a thunder dome.

When we arrived at Orange Coast College Stadium, the stands were overflowing with 10,000 fans. The cheerleaders who lined the field couldn't even hear one another. The stadium featured a long walk from the locker rooms high above the field down a winding ramp to the field.

We were champing at the bit. When the Edison Chargers strutted down for warm-ups in a single file, they seemed to be nothing special. But then we realized they weren't even wearing shoulder pads—this team could have been the USC Trojans.

It was David vs. Goliath. I needed to do something to pump up the team. Early in the game, a linebacker hit me late, after I was out of bounds. I jumped up and slugged him across the helmet. Before long there were ten players in a pile, fists flying.

In the second half, an Edison player dove onto the right knee of our best offensive tackle, Matt Vest, whose athletic career ended on that play. Enraged, we mounted a comeback. I hooked up with Rod Harmon on a couple of long touchdown passes, but we fell short, 42-28. Goliath had won, but like the biblical monstrosity, they were ugly. We consoled ourselves with the notion that it was a moral victory, but everything paled compared to Matt's injury.

I lay on my pillow that night nursing the bruises that dotted my body and replaying the game in my head. As usual, I fixated on my mistakes. If only I'd seen Sal "Sugar" Falcon, my longtime buddy and studly slot back, open down the sidelines. That would have given us another score. If only I'd been there to lead the interference when that bully jumped on Matt.

I still saw myself as the "little guy" who had to fight for everything. Being a late bloomer kept me hungry and disciplined when a lot of guys would have relaxed and enjoyed the status. I simply didn't allow myself to feel the pressure, to fuck up, fall down, clang the ball off the rim, or strike out. Sports were my ticket out of Santa Ana. Although I lacked insight into why I wanted to escape that sunny enclave, the only home I'd ever known, athletics focused my energy at an age when most kids are simply looking to have a good time.

Even I couldn't deny that I'd played well in front of all those people, surpassing everyone's expectations. It dawned on me that perhaps one day I might actually be capable of accomplishing something special under the bright lights of a far bigger playing field.

~

OFF THE FIELD, I hung out with a close group of buddies—Yale, Brad, Tim, Kenny, Jonny, and Jeff. We spent a lot of time lounging around the shimmering blue pool at the home of another buddy, Jon Ostberg. These guys were like brothers.

Love and romance were mysteries. I had always pursued sex with girls, because that's what boys did, or at least that's what they said they did. Other than sports, sex was the main topic of conversation. Since I always had a girl by my side, the guys egged me on.

"Go for it, Billy," they would say, living vicariously through the one they assumed got all the girls.

But then one clear night my pal Steve Bradley and I spent a night out drinking. We ended up at Ostberg's house, and as we were getting ready to go home, Steve and I sat in his car in front of the house. He and I had always trusted each other, and on this night we really opened up. We must have talked until four o'clock in the morning.

Steve didn't play competitive sports, so it felt great to be able to leave the tough-guy banter on the sidewalk. I told him all about my fear of screwing up on the field, and my doubts about my athletic future.

"It feels great to be able to tell you how I really feel about stuff, Stevie," I said. "I feel like we could be brothers or something."

"You're the only guy on the football team who doesn't care that I'm not on it," he said. "It's cool you don't give a shit about that stuff. You're not stuck-up like the others."

It wasn't exactly your everyday verbal interaction between high school boys. After a while, a kind of calm descended over us. The windows fogged. I sensed that I was becoming nervous and my heart was racing, as though we were boy and girl on the verge of a first kiss.

Suddenly, spotlights flooded the dark car. Police ordered us out. To our shock, the cops actually pushed us against the car and slapped cuffs on us. *Had they read my mind? How could two boys just sitting in a car together be a crime?*

It turned out they only thought we were preparing to rob a house. Steve had been flipping the car lights on and off when another car would happen by so they wouldn't accidentally ram into us. One of the Ostbergs' neighbors had seen the blinking lights and dialed 911. I pleaded with the officers to knock on Jon's door so that his parents could vouch for us, and they finally relented. We got a stern warning. Thank God we didn't have any alcohol in the car. For weeks afterwards, whenever I saw Steve I wondered where our conversation might have led, only to stifle the thought. I didn't want to know the answer. I told myself I'd just had way too much beer.

It would take years for me to figure out that athletic stardom doesn't make reality easier, only easier to ignore. The standards I set proved increasingly difficult to live up to, especially in my private life, where desire would find a way to intrude on the carefully tailored fantasies I'd created.

Superman couldn't go 0-for-4. Batman couldn't throw interceptions. The pressure was so great that sometimes a great game no longer made me happy, only relieved. *Well, at least I didn't let my family and friends down*, I would tell myself. *At least my self-image is intact for one more day.*

I grew up as Billy Bean the ballplayer, Billy Bean the athletic wonder kid. Even though I wasn't from a baseball family, stardom had been my dream since the age of eight. I believed that if I was a good player, then I was a good person, and everything else would fall into place. For a straight-A student, the good-looking quarterback of the football team, the heavily recruited outfielder with the sweet swing, what could possibly go wrong?

3 *Layanaland*

During my senior year in 1982, the letters started showing up in the mail, bearing the emblems of USC, UCLA, and Cal State Fullerton, to name just a few sports powerhouses. The schools were offering full-ride, four-year scholarships. Since I was still considered undersized to play football, it was the baseball programs that were expressing interest.

These opportunities were what I'd dreamed about. It had been hard to believe this could actually happen, and I can't say I was prepared. I'd never imagined it could be this easy. It was only later that people told me that the combination of my 3.8 grade point average and my collection of varsity letters made me an ideal college recruit.

No one in my family had attended college. To the extent she thought about it, Mom probably assumed I'd become a cop like my stepfather. It was a secure job, with a steady income, benefits, and a chance to help others. Fearing that coaches might change their minds about the scholarships, they pushed me to accept the first offer. Today athletes spend more time weighing their options with a battalion of paid advisors, coaches, and family members. They negotiate terms with schools, laying the ground-work for a lucrative professional career. But we quickly settled on Loyola Marymount University, a strict Jesuit school in L.A., an hour's drive up the highway from home.

Marv Wood, a heavyset man who spoke in complete sentences, did not fit the image of a head baseball coach at a major university. He contacted me after the Orange County high school all-star game, where I went 2-for-2 with three runs batted in and pitched the South team to victory. The next day he called and invited us for a visit.

Mom, Ed, and I were impressed with the campus. Acres of well-tended lawns fanned out from a turn-of-the-century chapel, and the spring sun made it all glow. My parents were sold. They felt comfort-able with the school's religious underpinning and academic emphasis. Ed said it was better to be a "a big fish in a little pond" than risk get-ting lost at a large program like USC or UCLA.

Deep down, they still didn't think my future was on the diamond. I wasn't so sure. I had to admit there was much to like about Loyola. For one thing, I was fascinated by the pretty young women I saw sauntering around the campus in shorts and tank tops, books slung casually under their arms. I was even more turned on by the 3,000-seat baseball sta-dium under construction, a development that went a long way toward allaying my concern about the school's underachieving sports program.

Wood appealed directly to my healthy ego, saying that I could be the cornerstone of a team he was determined to transform into a NCAA Division I contender. He seconded Ed's point that young players can get lost in the shuffle of big programs. He assured me I would start in center field as a freshman.

"Billy," he said, "you could take us to the top."

~

UPPER-MIDDLE-CLASS KIDS from private Catholic high schools, mostly in Southern California, dominated the student body. They wore designer brands, drove brand-new cars, and had pretty much anything they wanted. Then there was a bunch of scruffy athletes admitted only because they'd won scholarships. My rickety '69 Volkswagen stood out in the sea of BMWs and Saabs that crowded the parking lot.

When I walked into my room in the freshman dorm, a friendly giant greeted me. Tim Layana was a strapping right-hander who'd been drafted by the Chicago White Sox out of Loyola High. He had followed the advice of his uncle, former major leaguer Jim McAnany. Despite having gone to the World Series with the Sox in 1959, Jim counseled his talented nephew to get a college education before thinking about the pros.

At first, I found it difficult to relate to Tim. He was your typical athlete, seemingly without a care in the world, while I was already serious about too many things. I had barely unpacked when Tim and another ballplayer, Damien Bonenfant, were giving me a hard time.

"Loosen up, Bean," they would say in unison. "It won't kill you to have a few beers."

A few beers had a way of turning into a six-pack and then two. Then anything could happen. They wanted to party every night. I couldn't decide whether to succumb or isolate myself from the temptations.

Half-Spanish and half-Irish, Tim came from a large, outgoing Catholic family. His mother, Carol, was a saint. We affectionately called their home, just ten minutes from campus, "Layanaland" because it was a popular stop for many wayward youths. Even I lived there one off-season.

Tim was a man among boys. He had dark hair, brown eyes, and a five-o'clock shadow even after shaving. He wore a baseball hat even in his sleep, and he always had a tobacco chew between his cheek and gums, staining his teeth yellow. He was a total slob, never wore clean clothes, and had the manners of a farting, belching teenager.

We became the Felix and Oscar of college ball. But underneath the jocular exterior, I soon discovered a sweet and even vulnerable guy, and it wasn't long before we were inseparable. He had a preternatural calm about him, the perfect makeup for a pitcher and friend. Treating school like a pit stop to the majors, he slept through classes and never worried when he inevitably fell behind.

For a worrywart like me, it was a relief to go through life next to a guy like this. I never stopped cracking up around him, and when I was stressed out about a test score or a slump, his very presence put everything in perspective. While Tim was the class clown and team cutup, I became "Mother Bean," as he liked to call me. I tried to keep him out of harm's way as best I could.

~

WE BEGAN PREPARING for spring season about two weeks into the fall. Though I missed the variety of high school sports, it was a luxury to be able to focus on one. I expected to battle for playing time. Instead, it immediately became clear that Marv had simply anointed Bean and Layana as the program's saviors. The returning team had heard quite a bit about us, and they were understandably resentful. After all, we hadn't even stepped on the field yet, and guys we'd barely met were hearing about our prowess.

I'd often assumed that my only obstacles were on the field, the "me against the other guy" philosophy. But the further along I got, the more I realized that was only half of it. The mental and social aspects of the game ruled. The attitude of your teammates is as crucial to your performance as the way you swing the bat or throw the ball. I would have to earn my teammates' respect, and it wasn't going to be as easy as getting a bunch of hits.

By the time I'd filled out in high school, it had been too late to contemplate the big-league draft. My underdog image as an undersized, working-class kid who happened to become a ballplayer made it difficult for me to imagine making the big leagues, despite my youthful boasts to Mom. At Loyola, that attitude was starting to crumble. Tim, who had the quiet self-assurance of all great athletes, encouraged me to think big.

Since he'd already been drafted and had a major-league family background, he didn't see pro ball as out of his reach. He felt we were destined for the bigs, even before we'd ever achieved anything. He would state that he was going to throw a shutout and strike out ten batters, and then go out and do it. His energy rubbed off, and soon we were setting some lofty goals.

I started thinking through how I might make it happen. Thanks to the coaching I'd received at the lower levels, I had sound fundamentals on which to build. George C. Page Stadium featured a high left-field wall that was a collegiate version of Fenway Park's Green Monster. But the wall was far shorter than in right, my natural power field. I hoped to send a few more shots the other way over that wall, as well as into the giant eucalyptus trees that towered just beyond the center- and right-field fence. I was never going to be a slugger like Chris Donnels, who would become my roommate in the fall of 1984. At nineteen, he already had huge shoulders and forearms. He effortlessly stroked twenty-one homers, mostly the opposite way over the monster, a school record.

Knowing that college pitchers would probably add five miles per hour to average fastballs and several inches of break to curves, I spent countless hours in the batting cage fine-tuning my swing, long after everyone else had gone home.

Watching Donnels' raw power and Layana's rocket arm taught me a lesson. While I may well have been the better all-around player, I lacked a "tool," the single shining skill—power stroke, blinding speed, rocket arm—that I could ride to the majors. Layana's fastball, which he maintained no matter how many beers he'd downed or how many women he'd chased the night before, was a gift from God I'd been denied.

I'd have to keep developing every aspect of my game if I were to make the ultimate leap. My best bet was to pattern myself after a guy like George Brett, then tearing it up for the Kansas City Royals. Brett was a solid third baseman. He had a little pop, but most of all he was one of the best line-drive hitters around, one of those guys who could hit .300 in his sleep. I'd seen Fred Lynn play as a Little Leaguer. Like Brett, he could scorch the ball to all fields and batter the fences when he got hot, carrying his teammates along for the ride. If I could hit anywhere near .300 in the bigs, I had a feeling I'd be well on my way toward a long—not to mention lucrative—career.

~

I MAY HAVE been at a Jesuit school, where the priests taught abstinence until marriage, but the good fathers would have been shocked at what was going on in the dorms just across the lawn from the chapel. I marveled at the Catholic kids who'd get stoned on Sunday afternoon and then meander to the chapel for six-o'clock mass.

Students scoffed at the proscription of premarital sex, and the athletes I bunked with were getting laid pretty regularly. Religious notions about sex were a big joke, and we chased "it" with the zeal of linebackers rushing a quarterback, even though AIDS appeared on the horizon my freshman year. I don't remember anyone mentioning it, *ever.*

Layana was determined to lead me down the primrose path. He didn't have to pull very hard. I felt ready to explore what I'd sublimated to sports. We spent a lot of time hanging out at the local tavern or just drinking with Damien and as many girls as we could squeeze into our room. After I'd been cajoled into going out, we would spend a few hours "gathering the babes" and bring them back to our room. My first sexual experience at Loyola was a shared one with Tim and a gorgeous freshman co-ed. We laughed and high-fived each other all the way back to our own dormitory room.

The next morning, I worried about "the girl."

"But she wanted it just as bad as we did," Tim retorted with a big grin.

Girls gravitated to me, even though Tim worked harder at it. So in a reprise of my grade-school efforts to win approval, I'd lure them back to our room with funny stories or a chance to "just hang," and then, at the last moment, I'd defer to Tim and sneak out of the room.

When it came to women, my teammates loved to exaggerate their exploits. I found myself curiously detached from this behavior, and I always felt like an intruder into their erotic world. I wanted to remain close to them, and playing along seemed the best way to do that. Our escapades built us a reputation before we'd even played a game that counted.

~

DESPITE THE PARTYING, I came into my own in my junior year. Catching everything hit my way in right field, swiping bases, and hitting over .400, I was selected for the Division I All-America Team. I'd finally caught the attention of big-league scouts. There was talk I could go as high as the first two or three rounds of the draft. The team was gelling, too. For the first time in years, we finished with a winning record. We were one recruiting class away from becoming a national contender.

Near the end of the season, I was standing on third base when Dave Snow, our new head coach, called for a suicide squeeze. I broke for the plate just as the batter missed the bunt attempt. When I reversed course, my cleats stuck in the dirt infield, tearing my right quadriceps muscle. It felt like someone had stuck a knife in my thigh, and I lay in the baseline writhing in agony as the third baseman put the tag on. With one play, we had lost more than the game.

In a sport where a tenth of a second in the sixty-yard-dash can make or break a career, the injury dropped my stock. The Yankees, who had once considered taking me early in the draft, waited till the middle rounds. But after haggling all summer, they offered a $60,000 signing bonus plus performance incentives. Even though it was moderate by baseball standards, this windfall would've been a lot of money for a kid whose mother had supported him on a modest salary.

The Yankees were hardly the same franchise they had been or would become. Their owner, George Steinbrenner, was not long removed from feuding with his star, Dave Winfield, and the manager's office had a revolving door. The place was a circus. Even so, it was sorely tempting to sign with the storied organization of Ruth, Gehrig, DiMaggio, and Mantle and wear the pinstripes.

The Mets drafted Tim in the fifth round. Coach Snow was adamant we return. He argued that we shouldn't pass up an opportunity to finish our studies, get a degree, and play for a College World Series contender. He said senior year wouldn't be worth passing up for a million bucks, let alone a fraction of that amount. If I had an injury-free senior year, he reasoned, my draft stock would only rise.

I did look forward to making a run at a national title. Sure, I foresaw a major-league career. But even at my cockiest, I knew I needed a backup plan, something a college degree (in business administration) could help provide. Mom and Ed thought I should accept the Yankees' offer, fearing I might never have another chance at fulfilling my dream and cushioning my financial future. Tim's decision to return made my decision easier—after all, he was making the bigger sacrifice. Pitchers are always one throw away from a career-ending arm injury, and the consensus is that they should always take the money and run.

Loyola's gain turned out to be Tim's loss. I believe he left his best stuff on the Loyola mound. He pitched 170 innings his senior year, compiling an astonishing 17-2 record. The team took advantage of his tremendous output, but his arm never really recovered from his four years as our workhorse.

~

TO GIVE US a taste of minor-league competition and prepare us for the senior season, Coach Snow sent me, Tim, and Tim's first cousin Jim McAnany to play summer ball for the Fairbanks Goldpanners of the Alaska league. Chris Donnels went to the archrival North Pole Nicks, a team loaded with future big leaguers Todd Zeile, Mark Grace, Billy

Hasselman, Andy Stankiewicz, and Torey Lovullo. Jim Bruske, who would attend Loyola the next year, played for the Matsu Minors.

Getting off the plane, I was greeted by a hand-painted sign that read "BILLY BEAN'S ALASKAN PARENTS." It didn't take me long to warm to Bob and Sharon Clark. This down-to-earth couple lived in a modest home about ten minutes from the stadium in Fairbanks. They showed me to a small but comfortable guest room on the main floor.

Bob was a fisherman and hunter who cooked what he caught. He would take off for three days, returning with enough fish for the winter. He prepared three-inch-thick king salmon steaks on the grill, wrapped in bacon and served sizzling hot. Before long, the couple was feeding the team. Tim and Jim McAnany lived with a *Deliverance*-style family in the woods, where what they called a "mystery fish chowder" simmered on the stove every day. It was scary, smelly stuff, so they were always over at "my" house for meals.

My leg injury healed long before the sting of falling in the draft order. But the challenge of new competition lifted my spirits. High summer in Alaska was cold enough to be winter anywhere else, and it felt like my hands would shatter like an icicle when my bat didn't make solid contact with the ball. Our ballpark was located in downtown Fairbanks, but most of our competitors' fields loomed up in the middle of nowhere, set in a swath of forest where the trees had been logged to make room for a park. The summer light, which never went away, was ideal for baseball.

The mosquitoes were so big that they threatened to pick you up and carry you away when they latched onto your skin. The smoking coils erected everywhere to keep them at bay were ineffective, and it was common to see a pack of the buzzing bloodsuckers hard at work on someone's face. I wore two long-sleeve shirts, not only to stay warm on the field but also to keep the little buggers from biting me during games. Repellent served as my aftershave. It was hilarious to watch locals stand stoically as the ballplayers jumped around, swatting air.

Every year, thousands of men came north for logging jobs and to maintain and repair the oil pipeline that ran through the city, bringing energy to the "lower 48," as the locals affectionately called the rest of us. This created demand for diversions, from strip clubs to bars. Like the oilmen, we were a bunch of overgrown kids in a foreign land with little responsibility except to show up at the park at 3 P.M. each day. The social and sexual antics up in Alaska made the Loyola dorm look like a church nursery. Being thrown together with all these guys from other schools seemed to up the partying ante several notches.

On one of our first nights there, Tim, Jimmy Mac, and I went out to a club called Jezebel's. It was early, and the action was pretty slow. We sat at a table and ordered beer. Before long, Tim was chatting up a chick. We always made fun of Tim because he had a thing for girls who would never qualify as Victoria's Secret models. This one, however, was quite impressive.

"Hey, guys, this babe digs me," he finally announced to us. "Beaner, give me some money so I can buy her some drinks."

We knew he'd find some way of screwing it up, but I handed him a ten spot anyway. A few minutes later, another young woman walked onto the bar—wearing nothing but a G-string and boots—and started dancing to Madonna. We looked around to see the girl Tim had been scamming dressed in nothing but bikini briefs, her uncovered breasts wriggling in our teammate's face. It was a classic Layana moment.

"I knew all along she was a dancer," he said sheepishly after his lap-dance.

The local girls competed to snag the biggest stars, most of whom hailed from major colleges around the country. With condoms an afterthought, several of the guys came down with chlamydia, a sexually transmitted disease I'd never heard of. The guys complained about "the burn" every time they relieved themselves.

I'll never forget one of the first of many eight-hour bus trips from Fairbanks to Anchorage along a road bumpy from permafrost. Everyone stocked up on food and drinks because there was only one stop en route. About halfway there, a player named Vince had "to go" so badly that he urinated into a cup he had been drinking from. I watched with amusement as he tried not to spill while the bus lurched and rocked under him.

Sitting behind Vince was one of the most committed born-again Christians I had ever met. Steve was also one of the fastest runners from home to first. He avoided most of the partying, worked hard, and seemed serious about everything. When Vince finished filling the cup, he tried to open the bus window with one hand while holding on to the cup with the other. Watching this drunken juggling act, I had a sense something bad was about to happen. He opened the window about six inches, and stupidly tried to throw the whole cup through it. Sure enough, the cup ricocheted off the glass, drenching Steve.

Steve screamed, leapt from his seat, and jumped on Vince, fists swinging wildly. A melee broke out right there in the bus as it hurled down a two-lane highway at seventy-five miles per hour. It took about ten guys and fifteen minutes to pull them off each other. The driver forged into the eerie night sun as if nothing was happening behind him. There were bloody noses, cuts, and scrapes. Luggage was strewn everywhere. My heart went out to Steve, who made the rest of the trip in damp clothing stinking of ammonia.

As usual, I played along as best I could. But watching my teammates carry on like a bunch of adolescents began to make me feel like a babysitter. Since childhood, I'd always been controlled, even fastidious. Mom called me her little "neat-freak" and "kid with an old soul," descriptions I doubt would have been applied to any of the other guys. I was gradually becoming more observer than participant, a feeling that intensified as the summer wore on. I started to look forward to graduation, when I could at least have my own apartment. Didn't big leaguers get their own suites on the road?

I tried not to let my alienation from my teammates get in the way of my play. After getting off to a slow start and shaking off the lingering effects of my muscle tear, I came on as strong as the Alaskan weather. My batting average dipped under .400 only on the last day of the season, when I went 0-for-4. I was named the team's player of the year. I also came in second in the voting to Mike Scanlon for Alaska League MVP.

~

I ENTERED SENIOR YEAR brimming with confidence. I'd had a stellar junior year that culminated in being drafted by the Yankees. I'd excelled up north. Now the college athletic department was hyping me as a superstar. Dodger manager Tommy Lasorda spoke at our annual Hot Stove banquet to kick off the season, where he sang my praises as a ballplayer. Neither of us could have guessed how our paths would cross again, just down the freeway at Dodger Stadium.

The cover of the Loyola media guide featured a full-length photo of me doing my best slugger imitation, glowering at the camera and wielding a big aluminum bat under the headline "BIG MAN WITH THE BAT." It was a ridiculously potent shot, and I chuckled at how far I'd come from "little Billy Bean" in the locker room back in junior high.

Dave Snow was not about to let any of his returning "big men" rest on their laurels. A master motivator, he knew instinctively that my ego could get in the way of the team welfare and my own play. The minute a guy thinks he's got the game figured out, he knew, is the minute he falls flat on his ass.

He ordered us to meet for mandatory aerobics at 6:30 A.M. three days a week. Showing up late meant running with him the next day from 5:30 A.M. until class started, then completing the aerobics as well. The team resisted this weird idea of fitness training, contending that "aerobics is for girls." We already were getting our butts kicked running drills on the diamond later each day. The first victim of this brutal regimen was our carousing, which made getting up early impossible. Mother Bean managed to get everyone out of bed and out the door.

Tim and Chris loathed the workouts. But even they had to admit there was a method to Snow's madness. It forced us into tip-top shape, and helped us become more limber and better balanced. It also created an even playing field. Coach wanted to show the rest of the players that he would not coddle Donnels, Layana, and Bean. We would sacrifice like everyone else.

When the season started, I got off to a sluggish start. Fearing my reputation, teams pitched around me, preferring to take their chances with Donnels, who hit in the fourth spot, right behind me. Worried the scouts would notice my lack of production, I grew frustrated at my inability to pile up big numbers. I watched Donnels clean up while I was leading the country in bases on balls. In my eagerness to hit, I flailed at balls out of the strike zone.

Despite my struggles, we won our first twelve games. Layana and Bruske were a potent one-two punch. Our catcher, Jimmy Mac, called a solid game and hit, too. Donnels was crushing the ball. We were starting to believe in ourselves. But my frustration was showing. During a game at Santa Clara University, we were up by a dozen runs late in the game. Ahead of the count 2-0, I chased an outside pitch and popped up to short.

When I arrived back at the dugout, Snow called the entire team together. Our mood was upbeat because we were way ahead, our perfect record intact. So it shocked everyone when Snow walked right up to me, turned his hat around backward, and started screaming.

"Bean, you selfish son of a bitch," he said, spitting every word in my face. "If you ever do that in a game again, you'll be watching the rest of it from the bullpen. This isn't about you. *It's about the team.* You've got to let the game come to you."

I was embarrassed, but, taking my medicine like a man, I nodded as he yelled expletives. As I walked out to center field in the bottom half of the inning, I could still feel the intensity of his dressing down. I also realized that Coach was right. I *was* being selfish. It was one of the hardest but best lessons a coach had ever imparted to me.

Snow was sending another message as well—no one was exempt from his rage.

"Wow," I heard the younger guys saying, "Did you hear what Coach said to Beaner? This guy is fucking crazy."

Taking me aside later, Snow took a kinder approach. "Give the scouts some credit," he told me. "They know what's going on. They will be impressed that teams don't want to give you anything in the strike zone."

Remembering what had gotten me to this point, I stopped worrying about statistics and played hard. I regained my patience at the plate, breaking the school record for walks with eighty-five in sixty games. When I did get a good pitch, I usually hit it hard.

Before long, we were ranked number one in the nation, winning twenty-six of twenty-seven games. In the western regional playoffs, we defeated UC Santa Barbara, UCLA twice, and then knocked off Hawaii to earn a trip to the College World Series in Omaha.

ESPN televised the first game against Louisiana State, which featured right fielder Albert Belle and pitching standouts and future big leaguers Ben McDonald and Mark Guthrie. With the game knotted 3-3 in the ninth, Louisiana brought in the lefty Guthrie to match up against the two lefties, Donnels and me. The strategy backfired when I led off with a double. Chris drove me in with another sharp double, giving us a 4-3 win.

Next up was national powerhouse Oklahoma State. With Layana hurling a masterpiece, we were up 7-1 when it began to pour. After an hour, the umpires sent us back out onto the field. Out of rhythm, Tim walked the first hitter and allowed a bloop single. He whiffed the next batter for the first out. The following hitter tapped a weak ground ball to Donnels at third. Slippery from the rain, the ball squirted out of his usually reliable hands for an error.

It should have been an inning-ending double play. Now the bases were loaded with one out. Tim gave up a double down the left field line, and suddenly the score was 7-4. The rain resumed, and play was suspended until the next afternoon. Tim had thrown well over 100 pitches, and would be unavailable.

Play started with two runners on, one out, and the score 7-4. Oklahoma beat up on a succession of pitchers, and we lost 9-7. Deflated by blowing a big lead with our best pitcher on the mound, we started to press, losing the next game to eventual champion Arizona, 4-3. Boasting future big leaguers Trevor Hoffman and J. T. Snow, Arizona was the better team.

Stupidly, the major-league draft is held during the College World Series, placing even more pressure on guys who are ready to turn pro. It was bittersweet when Tim and I were both drafted by storied franchises. The Yanks, who'd gone another direction after my injury, drafted Tim in the second round while I was the third player chosen by the Detroit Tigers, two spots ahead of Bo Jackson.

~

ON A SUNNY FALL DAY my senior year, I spotted a young woman skateboarding across campus. My eyes followed her as she sped past, reminding me of an old RC Cola commercial in which a girl is riding a skateboard down the sidewalk while singing a silly jingle.

A *wild bird,* I thought.

Catching my eye, she flashed a big grin.

I had seen this pretty girl on campus from time to time, but I didn't even know her name. As I returned to my room after dinner one night, there she was sitting on my bed, studying with my roommate, Bruske. It turned out he had a class with her.

With her million-dollar smile, Anna Maria Amato was my image of the classic beach girl. I loved her carefree attitude and flirtatiousness, which seemed a relief from my own relentless, overachieving perfectionism. Her indifference enflamed my desire, and suddenly I was the one pushing for more.

Anna surfed, could dash off a ten-mile run like a walk in the park, and starred at varsity soccer for Loyola. I remember watching her kick a goal against a great USC team, then get into a fight with the defender she'd already beaten. I was impressed, but I still wasn't sure whether going out with Anna was what I thought I should do or what I truly wanted.

I'd decided that a baseball star should have a certain kind of girlfriend, and she fit the image I created. Whatever my motive, I fell hard. For the first time, a romantic attachment did not distract me on the field. It was nice to finally find inspiration outside myself, a role Anna was happy to fill. Yet even as we developed an intense sexual bond, it dawned on me that I didn't share my teammates' intense attraction to the opposite sex. There was always something missing, and I felt a restlessness I couldn't quite define or shake. At the same time, I couldn't fathom the alternative.

It wasn't long before I got a major clue. As the team was looking forward to the series that spring, I began suffering hamstring problems in my right leg, an injury that would become chronic over the years. After one road game in Northern California, I worried I might pull or even tear it, as I had in my junior year. I wasn't going to let this spoil my shot at the pros again, so as a precaution I went to speak to one of the opposing team's trainers.

The relationship between trainers and athletes is extraordinarily intimate. They are forever bandaging scrapes, massaging tight muscles, taping ankles, and flushing dust from eyeballs. Athletes think nothing of running around naked. There is a very fine line separating the "professional" work of a trainer or coach and "personal" space that can be easily violated. The physical proximity and dependence on medical judgment make trust absolute.

After a hot shower, I lay face down on the trainer's table with a towel around my waist while he wrapped a bag of ice around my leg. He was carrying on a conversation with someone else on one of the many other training tables, which had barriers between them. Music was blaring, TVs were showing sports, and there was the usual commotion of a Division I training facility.

As he massaged the kinks in my hamstring, I felt his hands inch toward my inner thigh. He was treating me, all right, but in a way that's not usually considered therapeutic. Closing my eyes, I pretended nothing was happening. But the furtiveness of this spontaneous act was intoxicating. The hidden, physical evidence of my excitement made it clear I wasn't objecting.

I walked back to the locker room in a daze. *Had I really just allowed a strange man to touch me, in public no less?* I reminded myself that I hadn't reciprocated. I vowed never to let it happen again. I blamed *him* and went running back to Anna. I made love to her with special vigor the next time we were together, then fell into a postcoital slumber, reassured of my normalcy.

Part Two

First Pitches

4 *The Bushes*

Nice job, Hobbs ~ *Maricón* ~ Bigger is better ~
Sweating bullets ~ Pride parade ~ Pretty redhead ~
Cup of coffee ~ The white boy can dance

EVERYONE WAS PRETTY leery of me the day I walked through the clubhouse door of the Glens Falls Tigers in June 1986. I had been drafted in the fourth round by the Detroit Tigers—no big deal. My $20,000 up-front money hardly qualified me as a bonus baby, even in those relatively modest times. But the Tigers had enough confidence in my ability and maturity to send me directly from college to double-A ball, skipping rookie league and single-A, a highly unusual move.

Nowadays, with the plethora of teams and the huge expense of paying veterans, it's much more common to see major-league rosters filled with relatively inexperienced players, some of whom have not paid their dues either in college or the minors. This trend shows up in the lack of fundamental play. Back then, franchises invested more money and time grooming players in the minors.

A lot of the men on the team knew all about the all-American outfielder from Southern California. Shortly before I arrived, they'd seen me play on TV in the College World Series in Omaha. I fretted that my star billing would breed resentment and make it harder to win my

49

teammates' confidence and acceptance. To succeed, it's crucial to find a safe place where you can concentrate on the game and forget about everything else. The last thing I needed was to worry about hostility, especially since I was about to face some of the best players I'd ever seen.

My first professional game took place in Pittsfield, Massachusetts. I was batting third; the first pitch was a ball. The second pitch plunked me square in the back. *Welcome to the pros, kid.* I was determined to even the score. My next time at bat, I belted the second pitch I saw, a fastball, over the 400-foot sign in right-center field. I stepped on the plate, and made my way to the dugout, expecting an enthusiastic welcome from my teammates. But no one said a word. I quietly went to the end of the bench, sat down, and stared straight out at the field.

I was unfamiliar with the baseball tradition of ignoring a rookie's first home run—a way of saying, "One day doesn't make a career." A few minutes later, all the other guys walked over, slapped me on the back, and congratulated me. Message delivered.

"Nice job, Hobbs," said one of the guys, referring to Roy Hobbs, the sweet-swinging left fielder of *The Natural.*

I even wore the same number as Hobbs, 9, and played the same position. My career certainly clicked at the start. In addition to the homer, I hit safely in the first seven games, staking my claim to the number-three spot in the batting order and as one of the organization's top prospects. I saw a lot of good fastballs and sharp breaking balls, and the pitchers seemed less likely to throw the same pitch twice in a row. In college, I'd learned the art of patience at the plate, and that was one reason I was able to jump right into the battle and compete.

But like the fictional character, I was in for some off-field surprises, not all of them pleasant.

~

MINOR-LEAGUE LIFE wasn't all it was cracked up to be. The romance wears off pretty quickly during the long bus rides and lonely nights at fleabag hotels in small towns. After a while, the mere sight of another greasy pizza or hamburger joint nauseated me. The ballparks were small and the locker rooms overcrowded. The facilities did not measure up to those at many colleges. I'd heard big leaguers complain about playing in Pittsburgh, but Pitts*burgh* seems like Paris compared to Pitts*field*. And I was one of the lucky ones. I had a $20,000 bonus (though it was dwindling quickly) to supplement my salary of $700 a month. A lot of guys were supporting wives and kids.

Even though I was playing well, there were no guarantees. I realized that I could be out of a job as fast as you can say "batting slump." After four years of being taken care of at Loyola, playing professionally was a lesson in humility. I discovered more competition among teammates than against the opposition. In fact, the desire to earn a promotion was so great that, if you looked closely enough, you'd see guys rooting against teammates on the verge of breaking through, making it impossible to look to them for support. A guy would trip you rounding third to get a shot at the big time. There was no patience for your on-field struggles or personal problems. So everyone learned to put on a charade of invincibility. Only after the uniform came off and everyone went home did the inevitable insecurities surface.

Anna was my lifeline. On the phone with her each night to L.A., where she was still attending Loyola, I poured my heart out. These conversations, along with the occasional chat with my parents, were my only consolation.

"I feel like we're all just meat for this organization," I said. "The competition to make it to the big leagues is just awesome. Guys like me are a dime a dozen."

"I know, Billy," she said. "But don't forget how much better prepared you are than most of the players. Remember what your father always said about your ability and determination."

Our connection meant everything. But in the back of my mind, I had a nagging suspicion that we were not right for each other. There was no question that I loved her. Yet there was something missing, something

I still couldn't quite define. It had only been about four months since the "massage" with the male trainer, and I couldn't quite get it out of my mind. But living in the hermetically sealed world of baseball, girlfriend, and family, I couldn't figure out how to test the hypothesis I was starting to form.

By pure coincidence, reality intruded. One year later, during my 1987 season with the triple-A Toledo Mud Hens, we traveled to Rhode Island to square off against the Pawtucket Red Sox. We were staying in a hotel nearby in Providence. A pride parade was scheduled for the weekend, and the place was overflowing with gay people.

My teammates freaked out. Their remarks ranged from bathroom humor to outright hostility. If anyone felt sympathy, they weren't about to show it. I certainly wasn't.

"Can you believe all the fucking homos around here?" one player said. "I'm going to make sure I lock my room tonight."

I, however, found myself—well—intrigued. I had no idea there was such a thing as a pride march. I secretly hoped to find a way to glimpse the goings-on, a dangerous idea with my teammates around. I was disappointed when I learned that the parade conflicted with a game. I made a mental note to do more "research."

Maybe my teammates are right. How could I be more interested in a bunch of homosexuals than the great game I was getting paid to play? In my naïveté, it would take me some time to put two and two together.

~

MY TEAMMATES ALSO had things on their minds besides baseball. I'm convinced that, more than anything else, idle time brings out the devil in ballplayers. When we weren't traveling, practicing, or playing, we had too much free time, especially on the road, with little companionship. Minor leaguers could make frat boys look angelic.

During a Glens Falls Tigers' trip to Burlington, Vermont, I returned to my hotel after dinner. As I walked through the hallway of the single-story lodge, one of the guys hollered at me to join them in their room. I figured we'd have a brew and watch TV. Opening the door, I saw four of my teammates having sex—with what looked for all the world like a fourteen-year-old girl. My jaw dropped. I quickly turned to leave when they invited me to join them.

"Come on, Beaner," they said. "She's into it. Grab a beer and have some fun."

It didn't look like fun to me. The term *statutory rape* came to mind, and I high-tailed it out of there. The next day, the guys immediately started giving me a hard time.

"Dude, are you a fag or something?" one said. "How could you pass on a hot girl like that?"

I thought of reminding him that *he* was the one having sex in front of three other naked guys, but I bit my lip.

I whipped a trusty photo of Anna out of my wallet and lamely defended myself against their "charge," using the pretext of being faithful to my hometown girl. I carried the picture around just for such occasions—it shut them up every time.

"If I had a girl like that, I wouldn't fool around either," he said. "She's quite the babe."

I doubted there was any woman on earth who could make them stop chasing "it," at least at that point in our lives. For my teammates, fooling around was about much more than sex. It wasn't enough to be a stud first baseman or slugger. You had to be a badass off the field as well, screw the most women, show off the biggest dick, and drink the most beer. Bigger was always better, a reaction to the unrelenting pressure to be the best on the field.

I was always shocked at how brazenly guys who professed to hate "homos" strutted around the locker room, showing off their well-toned muscles and flopping cocks. They were always bragging about the "abuse" their "baby" took screwing a chick the night before. It was hard to tell how much of the talk was nothing more than bravado, but that glimpse inside the hotel room told me there was something to it.

Rafael Garcia was a reliever and team clown. He'd been laboring in the minors, waiting for his shot, for nearly a decade. An extrtemely well-endowed man, he loved to put on a show by placing his "package" out of sight between his legs. Every time he'd record a save or win, this hyper-masculine guy would prance around the locker room mimicking the stereotype of an effeminate homosexual, earning the nickname "Marty," shorthand for *maricón* or "fag."

"*Ay papí, que rico!*" he'd say with a pronounced lisp. ("Hey big boy, you look mighty fine.")

Everyone howled. After one victory, the guys began to line up for the shower in the cramped clubhouse, which had only six heads in a small, open stall. The drain clogged, and brackish water backed up to the point where it was ankle-deep. Standing in the middle of this lake, Rafael took a piss as five other guys showered. His bladder must have been as large as the rest of his plumbing because urine flowed like water over Niagara Falls.

Most of those in the stall didn't notice until they heard everyone else cracking up. The water never did recede, and Rafael ended up having the shower all to himself. He stood there, a big grin on his face, soaping up under the hot water. It was clear the rest of us would be showering at home that night. About five minutes later, everyone had forgotten about it, just another day of chaos in double-A.

These hijinks made me miss my college teammates. They might've been crazy, too, but at least they were closer to my kind of crazy. I tried to keep in touch, but spending time on the road made it a challenge.

The previous summer in Fairbanks I'd dated a pretty redhead named Shelley. I'd met her at the stadium, and it was obvious she had a thing for ballplayers. Apparently, she had developed a crush on me. One night in Glens Falls, I heard her voice on the other end of the phone line.

"Billy, I've something to tell you," she said. "I'm pregnant."

"What? . . . We always used protection?"

"I'd like to get on the next flight to New York so we can raise our child together."

I sweated bullets until I heard laughter in the background. It was Donnels and McAnany. They had returned to play for the Goldpanners, and had run into Shelley. Jimmy got on the phone and started screaming. He and Chris had set the whole thing up.

"Beaner, we nailed you. We scared the shit out of you."

"You guys are fucking idiots," I lectured. "Don't you have anything better to do? I'm going to kill you both."

It was a cruel practical joke, no doubt, but after we talked for half an hour and caught up with one another, I realized it was their fumbling attempt to stay close. These guys missed me, and they wanted to remind me that no matter how our lives might change and where we would end up, we'd be brothers forever.

~

IT WASN'T LONG before I warmed up to my Glens Falls teammates. The team was divided into three camps. There were half a dozen black and Latino players, a few college guys like me, and the rest were "country" boys, straight off the farm, many of whom had been in the minors for nearly a decade. I had no idea where I fit in.

I was assigned to a room with Rey Palacios, a burly catcher born in Puerto Rico and raised in Red Hook, Brooklyn, a tough neighborhood known for its drug traffic and gang violence. A lot of the white players couldn't stand him, and most of the black players would roll their eyes when he launched into his withering commentary on their athletic shortcomings. Rey was just one of those guys who called things as he saw them. If you busted your butt, he'd give you the shirt off his back. But if you were weak, selfish, or played like a coward, he'd let you know it in no uncertain terms.

I took a liking to Rey right away. He walked the talk, playing his ass off every night. At first he sent a flury of barbs my way, but my hustling play earned his respect. Being around a freewheeling, sensual guy like Rey felt somehow liberating. He told me about all the crime he'd witnessed in Red Hook. Baseball, he said proudly, was going to be his way out.

Before long, I connected with the half-dozen or so black players on the Tigers. Palacios told me I played ball like a "brother," one of the best compliments I'd ever received. My style came from growing up in a public-school district in which white kids were the minority. I spent much of my childhood on the playing fields and basketball courts of the inner city. We made no distinctions along racial and ethnic lines, only on whether a guy could play ball. How strong is his arm? Can he hit for power? Does he work hard?

On road trips, Ricky Barlow and Morris Madden would invite me to their hotel room for a few brews and a game of cards while we watched major-league games on TV. The Tigers' first-round draft pick right out of a Texas high school, Ricky was known as "Watercan" because of his ability to suck down beer like water. He never lived up to his "can't-miss" prospect status, reaching the majors in 1987 for only a brief stay.

Morris "A. J." Madden was a terrific singer who happened to be a left-handed pitcher with a nasty hook. He could be erratic on the mound, which explained why it would take a guy with great stuff ten years to make it to the majors. When you play that long in the minors, front-office execs don't give you much of a chance to fail at the next level.

The three of us became inseparable, sealing our friendship the way guys do: with pickup basketball at the Glens Falls YMCA. It helped that I could go to the hoop.

~

AFTER A JULY NIGHT GAME in Waterbury, A. J. and Watercan invited me along to a nightclub. In their own way, they were saying that I'd become one of them.

We wound up at Ike's, a huge club right in the heart of the city's black neighborhood. Looking around, I saw that I was the only white person there. When I say "only," I mean it. It took me some time, and a little bit of alcohol coursing through my blood, to get over the feeling I didn't belong. Watercan and A. J. didn't leave my side all night.

The girls thought I was the bomb. At one point, a good-looking young woman sidled up to me.

"Boy, you're crazy," she declared.

"Why?"

She responded with a giggle.

The guys were not so welcoming. They shot me suspicious glares.

"What's with the white boy?" one asked A. J. and Watercan. "Where did you find him?"

"He's one of us," I remember them responding. "It's cool."

After quite a few beers, I must have forgotten my race. I grooved to Kool and the Gang, Cameo, and Milli Vanilli thumping over the sound system. The three of us camped out in the middle of the dance floor, surrounded by young women, dancing the night away. I didn't get back to my room until about 3 A.M., exhausted but happy.

The next afternoon, I arrived at the park a little hungover, but ready to begin my pre-game routine. As we stretched on the field a couple of hours before the game, Watercan and A. J. regaled my teammates with stories of our previous night's adventure.

"Beaner parties like a brother," A. J. announced with a huge grin. "He's got the moves. The white boy can dance."

The rest of the guys were giving me a hard time. The stories contained more than a few exaggerations. But there was an undercurrent of respect and generosity to their description, so I kept my mouth shut. The night had brought us together as a team, and I wasn't going to do anything to jeopardize this rare moment of unity.

5 *The Long, Slow Walk*

GETTING CALLED UP ~ SECOND BASEMAN WALE-
WANDER ~ ADRENALINE PUMPING ~ WHAT IT TAKES ~ GET
THE FUCK OUT OF THE WAY ~ BEANED ~ THE LEGENDARY
SPARKY ANDERSON ~ THE RIDE IS JUST BEGINNING ~ THIS
GODFORSAKEN GAME ~ AT EACH OTHER'S THROATS ~
NOVEMBER 1963

AT MY FIRST spring training, in Lakeland, Florida, the Tigers had me running back and forth between minor- and major-league camps under the watchful eye of manager Sparky Anderson.

He was impressed enough to assign me to the organization's triple-A affiliate, the Toledo Mud Hens, a rarity for a first professional season. I hit home runs in the first three games of the season, and was leading the team in RBIs after one week. Once again the guys were calling me "Hobbs," showing respect while mocking my boyish ambition, which I'd developed even before I'd had a chance to fail.

At the end of April, manager Leon Roberts, a hulking former big-league slugger, called me into his office.

"The Tigers are calling you up for tomorrow's game," he said. Roberts was a sweet guy and an accomplished prankster.

"I'm not falling for that one," I said.

"Billy, it's the truth," he said. "I got the call from Sparky myself. You'd better get ready."

Between shock, nerves, and packing, I got about three hours of sleep that night. When I awoke, I realized I had no idea how to get to Detroit from Toledo. My good buddy, second baseman Jim Walewander, saved the day by giving me a lift the entire way.

We were rookies on the road, too, and before long we were hopelessly lost. When we finally arrived at Tiger Stadium, I looked at my watch—11:15 A.M.—at least an hour after I should have arrived for a 1 P.M. start.

I sweated like a dog. For good reason, the guard didn't believe I was actually a player, and he grilled us at the gate.

I had not seen the fabled Tiger Stadium before, and when we finally made it inside it actually looked like one of those old grainy black-and-white photos from the early days of the game, as though it were suspended in time.

~

ON APRIL 25, 1987, at the age of twenty-two, I had arrived. I walked toward the seats and peeked out at the field. Looking across the expanse of green where the great Al Kaline once roamed, I admired the famous overhang of the second deck in right field, which had caught many a home-run ball before it could fall into an expectant right fielder's mitt. I tried and failed to absorb the magnitude of the day. There was simply too much at stake.

I turned around and tried to find the players' clubhouse. When I informed the uniformed guard at the door that my name was Billy Bean, he gave me a big smile and said, "Welcome to the big leagues, boy. I hope you make the Hall of Fame." I could have sworn I heard him chuckle as I walked down the hall.

There is nothing more beautiful than a major-league clubhouse. Plush blue carpet fanned out from cavernous lockers, each featuring the name of a player stenciled above. Big-screen TVs flickered in every corner.

Four teenage boys polished shoes, organized gear, and arranged uniforms in lockers.

The middle of the room looked like a 7-Eleven. There was a refrigerator stocked with ice cream, racks of candy bars, and a tray loaded with doughnuts grazed by a herd of portly reporters. Music blared from the nightclub-quality sound system. The room was full of people, but not a single ballplayer. They were already on the field stretching.

I'd wandered around looking for this place so long that the gym bag on my shoulder was getting heavy. A tall guy in a white shirt—Jim Schmakel, the clubhouse manager—grabbed it and led me to my locker. Then he pointed to a cement column in the middle of the room, winked, and departed. I walked over to find the lineup card. I was batting leadoff and playing left field! I pretended to be calm.

Feeling shy and self-conscious, as though I were some kind of interloper, I donned the traditional white Tiger uniform with the famous Old English *D* on the chest, and headed out to the field. The uniform fit me perfectly, and though I was earning the major-league minimum, I felt like a million bucks. The team was in the midst of batting practice. Despite having gotten to know some of the players during spring training, I didn't know where to go or what the hell to do.

The dugout in Tiger Stadium was so small you had to crouch as you walked along its wood planks. I shyly dropped my bats into the rack and tried to figure out my next move. The echo of wood striking crisp new baseballs in that old stadium was like music. I shook hands with the superb pitcher Frank Tanana and one of the funniest baseball men I'd ever met, coach Billy Consolo, Sparky's sidekick.

Consolo's reputation preceded him. When games got tight, he was famous for swigging a bottle of milk of magnesia he kept in his back pocket. In the ninth inning of close games, he would stoop down and clean the sunflower seed shells and bubble gum wrappers off the dugout steps, avoiding the field until the play was over.

I saw both members of the famous double-play combination, Alan

Trammell and Sweet Lou Whitaker, taking grounders. I watched big Larry Herndon swat line drives over the fence. There was Matt Nokes, the power-hitting catcher, huddling with the pitchers, and the speedy outfielder Chet Lemon, shagging flies in the outfield. Almost everyone was friendly and encouraging, if a little distant, from the newcomer.

I ran out to left field to shag some flies only to be called in to take batting practice with the first group of five in the starting lineup. First-base coach Dick Tracewski patted me on the back.

"Welcome to the show, Bean," he said.

I jumped in the cage, trying not to think about the other four guys in my group—Alan Trammell, Lou Whitaker, Darrell Evans, and Kirk Gibson—major-league all-stars already boasting Hall of Fame credentials.

My mouth was so dry I couldn't swallow. I was on their turf now, and I knew it was time to put up or shut up. Fearing I might swing and miss the 75-mile-per-hour batting-practice fastballs, I told myself to *just hit the ball.*

With adrenaline pumping through my body, I took huge cuts and sent the first two pitches soaring into the upper deck in right field. This didn't impress anyone, so I concentrated on going the other way, to keep from getting over-eager during the game.

The moment I stroked a line drive to left field, coach Alex Grammas yelled, "That's better, kid. Don't get too excited."

From Little League on, I'd been fortunate to play for the best managers. Now I had one of the legends, Sparky Anderson, who I'd gotten to know during my first spring training. I knew he liked my mop-and-bucket brand of play because he kept looking for a spot for me on the big club. I still hadn't seen him yet, and it was almost game time.

After I finished batting practice, he beckoned me over.

"You're up first, kiddo," he barked and then turned away.

I wanted to ask, "Are you sure?" Instead I just gulped. "Yes, sir," I said as gamely as I could.

The Tigers' right fielder, Kirk Gibson—whom Sparky had famously compared to Mickey Mantle when Gibson was drafted in 1978—approached me. I assumed he was going to welcome me with a pat on the back. Ordinarily I'd be playing next to him in the outfield, but he'd recently been placed on the disabled list. He hadn't said a word to me during batting practice. He might not be playing, but he still hit with the starting lineup. I stuck out my hand and he ignored it.

"Hey Bean," he said gruffly. "When I'm out there, and I call for the ball, remember to get the fuck out of the way."

I wasn't sure whether he was kidding. There was no chuckle to punctuate the arrogance of that statement, so I held my breath and watched him walk away. After being around him for a few days, I realized he was serious. He didn't have many friends on that club. The guys would have loved to be tight with him, but he just seemed to demand distance, lost in his ferocious concentration on the game. He was one of the most intimidating players I'd ever seen, which made his occasional lapses into kindness all the sweeter.

During the playing of the national anthem, I looked down at my arms and actually saw goosebumps. I couldn't help measuring myself against these physically imposing veterans, some a decade my senior. If that wasn't enough, I looked across the field and spotted Bo Jackson and George Brett getting ready to bat.

As I'd progressed through the ranks and closed in on my goal, I found myself confronted with doubts I couldn't quite shake. Since I'd never had any inkling of uncertainty on the field, always brimming with the confidence of youth, I was now at a loss.

Is little Billy Bean tough enough to hang with these men? I wondered. *Do I have what it takes?* Then I stopped myself. *Do I even know what it takes?* For the first time Ed's adage—"It's you against him, and you're better"—didn't quite hold up.

I reminded myself that these were nothing more than the typical jitters of a rookie. Even these grizzled veterans were once nervous kids praying the ball wouldn't rocket their way. At least I hoped they had felt that way. They weren't about to tell me.

~

"Billy B-e-a-nnnnn," the loudspeakers boomed, drawing out the syllables. There was a smattering of applause. Only the most die-hard of the 20,000 fans had heard of me. They looked quizzically at each other and checked their programs. "Who is this rook leading off?" "I've never heard of the guy."

Placing one foot carefully in front of the other, I walked to the plate. Digging in, I tried to do what I'd always done in key moments: slow everything down. The first pitch from Mark Gubicza, a tough six-foot-five right-hander with an exploding fastball, caught the outside corner. There was no slowing down that 95-mile-per-hour heater. I barely caught a glimpse of it as it sped by. The umpire raised his fist. Strike one.

Taking a deep breath, I stepped back in. I'd gauged the speed of the first pitch, and by comparison the second pitch looked like it was boring down on me in slow motion. I took a step forward while keeping my hands back before exploding at the ball. I connected on the sweet part of the bat, sending a soaring drive toward the right-field wall. Watching the ball smack off the fence and bounce back into the field as I ran down the first-base line was one of the most exquisite experiences of my life. I churned toward second base, sliding in head-first. As the scoreboard flashed FIRST MAJOR LEAGUE HIT, I tried to look as composed as anyone could while hyperventilating.

I ended up 4-for-6 on the day, tying a major-league record for most hits in a debut. After I knocked my final hit, a single to right, the crowd rewarded me with a standing ovation. BEANED, BEANED, the scoreboard flashed in bright white lights. The Tigers prevailed, 13-3.

After the game, Sparky handed me the lineup card. Jack Morris, the Tigers' ace, who had started and allowed just two runs on four hits in seven innings, patted me on the back. I may have meant nothing to this veteran warrior, but this nothing had just helped him notch another victory, and he couldn't help but be grateful.

One by one, the guys stopped by my locker. They knew it was a special day I'd never forget. Darrell Evans and Mike Heath brought me a beer and hung out for a while after the reporters had left.

"Are you sure you're old enough to drink, kid?" Evans asked with a smile.

Before long, the clubhouse was almost empty again, and I realized that tomorrow's game would be here quickly.

The greatest compliment came in the morning, when I picked up the newspaper in the lobby of the Ponchartrain Hotel near the stadium. "Talk about too good to be true," the game report began. "Baseball lore is filled with great rookie debuts, and now Billy Bean's will rank right up there with the best of them."

But the accolades meant a lot less to me than Sparky's quote. "What's the best thing Bean did?" Sparky asked. "I'll tell you. He backed up third base on a throw from right field. You haven't seen a left fielder on this team do that in five years. Five years, I'm telling you!"

Wow. Of course I needed to hit. But I knew it was my smart, hustling, fundamental style of play that would give me the best shot of hanging around, especially after Gibby returned from the injured list.

The next day, I went 2-for-4 against the Royals' Bret Saberhagen, a Cy Young award–winner, *lowering* my average from .667 to .600.

~

BASEBALL IS THE most languid of team sports. There's endless strategizing, constant chatter, practicing, stretching, standing around—and simply waiting for the next pitch. You get enough time to know the character of your teammates. Which may be why you find so many memorable personalities.

Sparky was one of the most original. He'd won two World Series titles with Cincinnati's Big Red Machine before coming to the Tigers in 1979, then captured another series in '84, three years before my arrival. At the top of his game, he commanded respect.

Sparky sported an incredible shock of platinum white hair, and he was always running his hand nervously through it. Then he would pull on his ear as if expecting a strategy to fall out of it. He scurried around, hunched over, his eyes focused on the floor.

I was surprised by how relatively young he actually was. That famous face, prematurely aged by forty years of exposure in sun-drenched ballparks, made him look older. The deep creases in his leathery skin seemed to map every tough managerial decision he'd ever made, every ballplayer he'd delivered bad news to. He chewed tobacco leaf mixed with pink bubble gum, and he blew huge drooling bubbles that spewed brown spittle when they burst.

Sparky may have hailed from Southern California, but he was decidedly old-school. He still called every pitch of every game, whether we were up 10-1 or deadlocked in the ninth. I never heard him swear, not even once, in a sport where expletives are the primary form of communication. After a home game, I'd spot him sitting in his office smoking a pipe in his long underwear, glasses resting near the tip of his nose, chewing the fat with the beat reporters.

It became clear to me that ordinary ballplayers like Sparky often made the best managers. Compensating for a lack of natural ability, they gained a "feel" and mastery of the game's many intangibles in order to find a place in it. Less talented players must learn patience, a requirement for managers, and the key to winning over the eight-month season.

On my first road trip with the Tigers, in April 1987, we were staying in Seattle at the most luxurious hotel I'd ever been inside. I dressed for the trip to the ballpark in my off-field uniform—jeans, polo shirt, and white tennis shoes. Since I had just been called up two days earlier, the traveling secretary had not figured on my coming along on the trip.

As a result, I got a room all to myself. This was uncommon in the '80s, a luxury usually reserved for veterans. I was unsure of the ropes, but I figured if I kept quiet and arrived early for everything, I'd slip by unnoticed. I watched the clock nervously until 1 P.M., before departing for the park.

I entered the elevator and began my descent to the lobby. A couple of floors later, the doors opened and there was Sparky, clad smartly in a suit and tie. He glared at me.

"Young man, go upstairs and change your clothes," he declared. "You're in the big leagues now."

I had a tendency to react to every criticism from managers I respected as an affront rather than an exhortation to do better. Everything they said to me—good, bad, or indifferent—took on an exaggerated importance, the critical words of a disappointed father. Mortified, I apologized, stepped out of the elevator, and raced up the stairs to my room. Rummaging through my suitcase, I managed to find my trusty old tweed coat from JC Penney and the tacky striped tie I had worn on the charter flight, much to the delight of my wealthy and fashionable teammates.

A headline in the *Detroit Free Press* described me as "Green Bean." It was true. I was so naive I didn't even know there was such a thing as a dress code. Nobody had told me, which is pretty much the way things go for a rookie. Imagine a gay man, even a closeted gay man in denial, taking fashion tips from Sparky Anderson, and you'll know how green I really was back then.

After taking two out of three games in Seattle, we headed down the coast for a series against my hometown heroes, the California Angels. I paid a visit to my parents, who'd gathered the whole family to greet me. After only a couple of weeks in the bigs, I was being treated as a conquering hero, and as much as I enjoyed their attention, I felt uncomfortable. With all the pressure on me, I wanted to be just little Billy again, not some object of their fantasies.

As I was running out to left field at the start of the game, banners unfurled reading "BEANTOWN" and "NORTHEAST SANTA ANA LITTLE LEAGUE WELCOMES HOME OUR HERO—BILLY BEAN." The lower boxes were filled with friends and family. It was a proud moment, but I couldn't fully absorb it. It seemed to be happening to someone else, and I was just along for the ride. I didn't disappoint; in my second at-bat, I hit a line-drive single up the middle off the Hall of Famer Don Sutton that just about knocked his head off.

"Hey kid," Sutton said to me during batting practice the next day. "Take it easy on the old guys."

~

SKIPPER'S FASHION LESSON, was about far more than a dress code: don't disrespect the game and the opportunity it presents. It was part of a rough education in learning my place in the game. Until this point, I'd been pretty close to the best player on every team I'd been a member of. For the first time in my life, that wasn't remotely possible.

Despite my sizzling start, I struggled to hold on to my spot on the roster. As my playing time dwindled, I cooled down at the plate. Big-league pitching was a revelation. While minor leaguers had good stuff, they couldn't always locate or command it. These guys made you swing at *their* pitch, and you had to be patient enough to find the one hittable pitch in every sequence.

The Tigers' hitting coach, Vada Pinson, told me that after my hot start against Kansas City, the word was out that Bean could turn on a fastball. All teams have advance scouts to report on the tendencies of the opposition. They'd watched the Kansas City pitchers challenge me with fastballs, thinking they could sneak them by an unprepared rookie, and I'd stroked them all over the park.

I was blessed with bat speed. Now the league was going to test me with off-speed stuff to find out whether I possessed the balance and patience that hitters need at the big-league level.

I believed I could make the adjustment, but I didn't get the chance to prove it. Gibby returned from the disabled list, and while I was playing well enough for another player to be optioned instead, I became the fourth outfielder, pinch hitter, and runner. Every day I felt more comfortable in the bigs, but learning to sit on the bench was another thing altogether. I wasn't progressing. How could I hit big-league pitching if I wasn't facing it every day?

After a few months with the club, I figured I was there to stay. I was confident enough to invite my mother to a home game in Detroit. I picked her up at the airport, and we chatted excitedly about Tiger Stadium and my role on the team.

"Mom, I think I'm going to make it here," I told her. "With what they're paying me, maybe I can even get a little house."

Just after I arrived in the clubhouse, Sparky called me into his office. "Son, we're farming you out to Toledo," he said.

In the days before ESPN's *SportsCenter* kept everyone informed about every detail of the game, I wasn't sure what that meant. I actually worried it was the end of my major-league career. My throat constricted.

"But Skip," I offered lamely. "Was there something I wasn't doing?"

"You need to play every day. I can't get you enough at-bats up here."

At the time I thought of Sparky's words as cruel. They didn't seem to offer consolation, any hope for my future as a ballplayer. Later I came to understand them as hard instruction in mental toughness. He was telling me I'd have to earn my way back, and that it wasn't going to be easy. There were no guarantees.

I hastily packed my stuff as the other players tried to avoid eye contact with the humiliated loser being sent down. It was a sickening feeling to go from a hailed newcomer to outsider who didn't even deserve a spot at the end of the bench. Adding insult to injury, I had to go retrieve my mother, who had already found her seat in the stands.

When she saw me coming toward her in street clothes in the stands, her eyes teared up. On the way back to the hotel, I tried to explain to her what had happened without choking up myself. *Welcome to the cruel world of professional sports, kid. The ride is just beginning.*

~

At the age of twenty-two, athletic success was the only way I knew to rate my worth as a human being. Since I'd experienced few setbacks, I'd yet to develop a coping mechanism to fight through slumps. My meteoric rise through the minors now came back to haunt me. Most of the guys I had been drafted with the previous year were still in rookie or A ball. I had breezed through my first stops as a pro, but now I faced my first extended period of adversity.

Doubts crept into my head. Since baseball was the sum total of my life, I lacked the maturity and balance to keep in perspective what is, after all, only a game. I felt like a has-been at the age of twenty-three. My youthfulness and boyish appearance were no longer an advantage, a source of the pride of precocity. I was no longer the overachieving boy wonder of high school and college, headed for certain stardom. Now I was a kid among real men—men years older and far more physically imposing.

Sparky tried to impart wisdom to me in ways I didn't fully appreciate. Feeling sorry for myself and caught up in my own drama, I might have missed some of his nuances. Instead of looking at the big picture—I reached the major leagues at twenty-two—I feared the future and the prospect of failure. I couldn't tell yet whether I had the cutthroat nature that scoffs at obstacles.

Observing Gibby, Morris, Lynn, and the other vets up close had been an education. The guys who rise to the top have no fear; they stop at nothing to achieve their goal. These veterans developed a scary, single-minded devotion to winning. They were almost inhuman in refusing to allow ordinary niceties and considerations to interfere with their pursuit of superb ballplaying.

Gibby was a gruff and determined ballplayer, and I never once saw him let up in an at-bat. He led by example, but he would get in your face in the middle of a game for almost any reason. He screamed at coaches, players, and fans alike. He struggled to live up to that unfair comparison to Mickey Mantle, even after he won an MVP award as a Dodger in 1988. His dramatic pinch-hit home run in the

1988 World Series was voted one of the ten greatest moments in baseball history.

Experts will tell you that he didn't live up to his ability. Gibby had a strong arm, could hit the ball as far as any man alive, and put fear with a capital F into middle infielders when he was on first base. But he never took pleasure in being on the baseball field. I remember him taking batting practice before every game at Tiger Stadium hours before everyone else. "Fuck" and "shit" echoed across the empty stands. He was never content with his swing. Sparky seemed to walk on eggshells around Kirk. He was a time bomb waiting to go off.

Playing behind Jack Morris was no walk in the park, either. There was a lot of pressure in defending the outfield for the highest-paid pitcher in the game. He made no bones about his displeasure if somebody messed up behind him. I was among the most fundamentally sound outfielders on the team, so he never complained about my defense. He knew I would dive through a brick wall for an out.

In 1988 the Tigers rushed a close friend of mine, Rob Ritchie, to the majors to play right field. He had been a second-round draft pick the previous year, and the organization had him pegged as a future all-star. Hearing superlatives from Sparky probably didn't help him make the jump any easier. Jack was on the mound for Rob's first major-league start. Players often have huge financial incentives built into their contracts based on arbitrary numbers of wins and innings pitched. This makes for a very uncomfortable environment at the end of the season, even if the team is no longer in contention.

Jack had a ton of money at stake in this game. Midway through the game, a long fly ball soared to right. It wasn't a particularly difficult play, but in his nervousness and unfamiliarity with the lights at Tiger Stadium, Rob misjudged it. The ball hit him in the chest. The miscue cost Morris the game.

Jack paced the dugout, cussing. Rob's locker had been placed next to Jack's earlier that day, and he ordered the clubhouse attendant to move Rob's things to another locker on the other side of the room before the game ended.

It was a humiliating experience for a rookie. As a veteran with that much success, a long-term contract, and a World Series ring, Jack called the shots. In my mind, no amount of money could justify his behavior. But nobody, me included, had the guts to call him on it.

The incident scarred Rob. He retired from the game after that season, at the age of twenty-three. He was extremely religious, and he told me that he felt that money had taken the "fun out of baseball in the big leagues." The last time I heard from him, he had moved back to Toledo and was working as a counselor at a boy's club. I respected him for his principles. He is one of the few players I've ever known who chose quality of life over quantity of money.

~

MAKING THE TIGERS at a young age allowed me to play alongside my boyhood idol Fred Lynn, who had been traded to the Tigers from the woeful Baltimore Orioles in 1988. I couldn't believe how cool it was when he joined the team. It wasn't all that long ago that my Little League coach had taken me to watch him play center field in Anaheim. He laughed when I told him that I'd spent years mimicking his mannerisms.

"Just don't blame me when you fuck up," he said.

Fred was actually a really nice guy, but like a lot of veterans without a lot left to prove, he wasn't exactly the toughest character around. During the first week of the 1989 season, we were playing a day game in Detroit against Minnesota in freezing weather. The windchill pushed the temperature below freezing. In the ninth inning, we were down by ten runs, and Fred was due to lead off.

The Twins had brought in a left-handed reliever known for his wildness, Gary Wayne. As the catcher made his throw to second to start the last inning, I watched Fred walk over to Sparky. They huddled for a minute before Sparky yelled out my name, ordering me to grab a bat and hit for Fred.

After three hours of sitting in a cramped dugout, wrapped in a thick parka, sweats, and gloves, I was in no position to hit, especially without the chance to warm up. But when the multi-million-dollar center fielder decides he doesn't want to face a young lefty, what choice do you have? Begging out of a game for no good reason is taboo in baseball, or in any competitive sport. But even basic rules have celebrity exceptions, and the stars were indulged all the time.

It took me so long to get my outerwear off that I didn't even get to take any practice swings. The ump yelled at me to stand in so that "we can end this Godforsaken game!"

My hands felt like they were frozen to the bat. I struck out on three nasty pitches, and as I returned seething to the bench, Fred turned away. He couldn't even look at me. My humiliation had been obvious, penetrating even his armor of stardom, and he probably realized he was wrong to have done to me what he wouldn't have thought of imposing on another veteran. Sparky knew that I got screwed, but he had to protect his superstars; that's what managers do. He knew that in a few days it would all be forgotten, except by me. My hero became a goat.

Tension was always boiling beneath the surface. After the Tigers ran away with the World Series title in 1984, the expected dynasty never materialized. In 1987 the team was loaded with talent and high-priced veterans. We were expected to win, but were languishing well down in the standings.

A young third baseman, Darnell Coles, was coming off a solid rookie year. Going through the usual sophomore slump, he struggled mightily. After striking out to end an inning against Texas, between plays in the next inning he received a toss from shortstop Alan Trammell, turned around and heaved it deep into the stands.

The veterans did not take kindly to this outburst. They jawed at Darnell for the rest of the game. In the clubhouse after the loss, I could feel the tension mounting. The music was turned off, and everyone was whispering as if we were attending a wake. Guys stripped off their uniforms and headed toward the showers or stood around in their underwear, icing sore shoulders and knees, waiting for the inevitable. A few others helped themselves to the buffet laid out on a table.

From across the room, I heard Darrell Evans make a comment on Darnell's behavior. Darnell shouted an obscenity back. In an instant, they were at each other's throats, guys swinging and yelling and throwing stuff. Food and furniture went flying. I had only been on the team a couple of weeks, so I knew this wasn't my fight. I stayed back and let the vets handle the situation. After it was over, you could just feel the pressure release. It wasn't long after that the team mounted one of the most stirring comebacks in baseball history, coming from twelve games back with just over a month to play to take the American League East.

People forget that athletes are as emotionally fragile as anybody else. The relentless pressure to perform gets to you after a while, and the riches involved simply up the ante. There was little of the camaraderie that I had experienced in college; this was a game, but it was also a business, and a brutal one at that.

~

SITTING AROUND THE dinner table with Mom and Dad, it's easy to think you're on your way to big things, but you soon discover that the diamond is filled with humbling moments. The way in which a hitter handles failure—the long, slow walk back to the dugout after going down on strikes—is perhaps the most critical part of the game. For the trained eye, it tells you all you need to know about that player's mental strength, his patience, and how he learns from his mistakes.

The boos—or worse yet, the cheers from the opposing fans—ring in your ears. Your awkward, flailing attempt to hit a pitch in the dirt, frozen in your mind, feels like the summation of a pathetic season. The called third strike is worse yet, because it means you've been defeated without a fight.

If you swing and miss, at least you tried, but going down on called strikes is crushing. Bat resting on shoulder, you've just watched a fastball whiz past you like a bullet in the night. The home-plate umpire, always thrilled with the chance to show up a rookie, is calling you out with his most histrionic body language. It's not exactly the ideal circumstance for contemplation.

Even the best hitters fail six or seven times out of ten. As for pitchers, on any given day Cy Young candidates get shelled, reduced to the worthless mound of dirt from which they must deliver their pitches. For a prospect like me, lacking a single overwhelming talent, failure at the plate could be even more demoralizing. An 0-for-4 night would send me to the bench or, worse yet, on a one-way ticket back to Toledo.

Rather than beating yourself up, you must learn to lay off the curve in the dirt. The next time up, you're more likely to get good wood on the ball. Watching Nolan Ryan throw a baseball or Bo Jackson round third base flying toward the catcher was absorbing. No amount of hard work could gain me these extraordinary skills. I knew I'd have to draw on other, more subtle talents to survive. And I couldn't allow my focus to waver, not even for a second.

~

AT THE AGE OF TWENTY-FIVE, during my last year with the Tigers, I learned a secret that shook me to the core. In my parents' home, we were rummaging through some old photo albums when I stumbled on Mom's wedding book for my dad, Bill Bean. The date read, "November 1963," the month of JFK's assassination. I was born May 1964, seven months later. I did the math, and in front of several family members I realized that I'd been a mistake. I began to understand why my biological parents hadn't made more of an effort to stay together after their hastily arranged marriage.

The revelation hit me like a sucker punch to the gut. But after pondering it for a while, the news came as a relief. Maybe it wasn't my fault that they had broken up after all. No wonder the marriage had been tempestuous. Perhaps, I thought, I could let go of the disappointment by understanding that it was out of my control.

As a kid, I had tried not to let on how much my father's abandonment hurt. I'd spent years blaming myself. Now I could take some tentative steps to rein in my desire to please everyone. Maybe I could just be myself.

6 *Babyface Bean*

CLUELESS GRINGO ~ NAVIGATING THE OCEANS ~
SHRIVELED FROM ESTROGEN ~ TWO-HEADED SNAKE ~
BROTHERS ALOU ~ THE DEVIL'S ALTERNATIVE ~ PULVER-
IZING THE POOR BASTARD ~ DRENCHED IN BLOOD ~ A
DEEP SLEEP ~ BALL TO PLAY

TALK ABOUT STARING down the barrel of a gun. As I disembarked from the plane at the Caracas airport in Venezuela in October 1987, boys as young as fourteen or fifteen patrolled the terminal in green military uniforms and black berets, toting AK-47s as large as their bodies. They stared into space or winked at the clueless gringo.

At twenty-three, I was only a few years their senior. The sight did not exactly ease my nerves. Lugging several large suitcases, I searched in vain for the welcoming party I'd been told would greet me at the gate.

After being sent down by the Tigers, I'd spent the rest of the 1987 season back in Toledo. I began the off-season in the Instructional League in St. Petersburg. Toward the end of the seven-week training period, the team shipped me to Venezuela to play for the Valencia Navigantes de Magallanes. Though I had no idea what I was getting into, I leapt at the opportunity to play for Felipe Alou, one of the best baseball minds and teachers, who would go on to become a major-league manager.

The best translation of Valencia's team nickname may be "globe-trotters," in honor of Magellan's sailors, who navigated the oceans under incredible hardship. In Latin America, the name stands for a kind of fierce determination. Granted, it's a bit of a stretch to compare playing ball to the sailors' ordeal. Yet the owners were on to something, because ballplayers in Venezuela competed with a ferocity I hadn't experienced before, and the dream of a better life that drove them was the mirror of my own quest to follow the game wherever it took me. I'd come a long way from St. Pete.

So there I sat on the curb on a broiling October day, exhausted and stressed from the ten-month grind. For three hours, I paced back and forth, wondering what to do next. I had no idea where Valencia was, let alone how to get there. I couldn't locate the currency exchange, and I didn't have a single bolivar, the Venezuelan dollar. I had nothing but clothing, my baseball gear, an American passport, and a vague dream of leading the famed Venezuelan league in hitting.

I was lonely. My Toledo teammate Scott Lusader had been assigned to play winter ball as well. But at the last minute he'd backed out, leaving me hanging. Anna was in Los Angeles, still in college at Loyola.

I was on the verge of charging a ticket back to Miami when I noticed a fat guy running through the airport. As he approached, he held up a cardboard sign with what looked like "B-E-A-N" scribbled across it. Apologizing profusely, he explained in Spanish that he'd had car trouble and had to return home for another vehicle.

I stared out the window in a trance as we made the long drive in an old Chevy rattletrap. The roadside was one endless slum. Tiny clap-board shacks lined the streets and up into the steep hillsides above. Clotheslines extended between makeshift fences. Boys and girls in little more than rags dodged cars to play in the unpaved streets.

My poorest immigrant neighbors in Santa Ana were rich compared to the people I watched going about their daily lives with so little. No wonder the dream of hitting the big time in North America took hold in so many boys here, at the earliest glimmer of a strong arm or a quick bat.

~

BASEBALL IS A truly international sport. At some point in their careers, most major leaguers will do at least one tour of duty in Mexico, South America, Canada, or Japan. To survive in a place like Venezuela, you learn to respect the people who serve you, pay your salary, and turn out for your games. You seek out the chance to experience the unfamiliar, in everything from food to music, and to appreciate the colorful diversity of the local culture. That's one reason why racial prejudice has diminished in the game today.

Black Latinos of African and Spanish descent tend to ignore the racial divisions that so paralyze the United States. Interracial marriage is no big deal, and a sizable percentage of the population is biracial. Living in this environment frees American ballplayers from the lingering racism and stereotypes they struggle with in the States. For black and white American players in South America, the only pressure is to perform and stay healthy.

Learning they could bring down $3,500 a month in cash, American minor leaguers, mostly in their early twenties and earning only $1,000 to $1,500 monthly back home, suddenly decided they "needed" to play winter ball. The jobs, however, were scarce. Only six Americans were allowed to play for each of the eight teams, so you had to be a stud to get a chance, and then produce when you did. Even at that young age, a lot of guys had kids to support back home. So they busted their butts. "Do well or get sent home" quickly became our battle cry.

~

VALENCIA TURNED OUT to be a *very* small town. The driver proudly dropped me off at a shiny new hotel. It was one of a half-dozen or so buildings in a ragged commercial strip. After the airport ordeal and going without sleep for almost two days, I was looking forward to a shower and shut-eye.

Setting one of my bags on the bathroom sink, I watched as the entire bathroom counter tipped heavily onto the floor. As the wall behind ripped open, the plumbing connections broke. Water gushed out of the pipes. Grabbing my stuff, I pulled the first maid I could find in the hall into the room to show her the problem. Seeing water cascading into the floor below, she let out a bloodcurdling scream. For a moment, amid the chaos, I feared I'd be accused of attacking her. It would've been the appropriate ending to my day.

I rose early the next morning and headed to the ballpark. The bigs have a way of spoiling even a working-class ballplayer. You get accustomed to the plush facilities, VIP travel arrangements, highlight reels, huge direct deposits of salary, and scores of adoring fans.

The stadium in Valencia, which seated about 15,000, wasn't much better than the hotel. It featured an expanse of green bleachers beyond the outfield wall, which was festooned with plywood signs advertising everything from soap to tires. I made a mental note not to crash into the cement fence while chasing balls hit over my head. The grass outfield was brown and uneven, the dugouts a shambles, the locker room small and grimy. The showers reeked of urine. The trainer's "room" was a bench in the corner.

We traversed the country in an old bus that belched noxious fumes and broke down in the middle of the road. The highways were full of potholes. Because the buses lacked air conditioning, I was always drenched in the sticky sweat created by 100-degree humidity mixed with smog so thick you could smell it.

In North America, it's easy for spoiled ballplayers to forget their roots. In Latin America, it's impossible to keep your head in the sand. I saw some crazy things over there. Returning from road games in Caracas, Venezuela's capital, the driver always found a way to take us through a neighborhood frequented by transvestite prostitutes and their johns. As the bus passed, the "Latinas" showed off their breasts and lifted their skirts to reveal tiny penises, shriveled from estrogen and God knows what other drugs. The native players stuck their heads out of the bus windows and whistled to get the "girls" to put on a bigger show.

"*¡Mama los Huevos! Chupa la pinga!,*" they'd shout, invoking the Spanish street commands for oral sex. "*¡Maricón!*"

Every road trip was an adventure. When we arrived in a town for a game, we were shown to filthy hotel rooms with musty sheets and, often, floors crawling with cockroaches. The meals, which consisted mainly of rotisserie chicken, rice, beans, and Coke, gave me constant diarrhea. Swarms of flies served as condiments. The American guys had a competition to see who would become "regular" first. I lost. I fed most of my meals to the stray dogs begging at all the food stops along the road and learned to survive on dried fruit and fresh bread.

The old stadiums were so poorly lit it was sometimes hard to track the ball through the night sky. And when I did locate the ball, I dodged swarms of moths as thick as the humidity to snare it. Batting was downright dangerous, and pitchers exploited the poor visibility by playing on hitters' fears of getting nailed. The outfield was so spacious that even power hitters didn't have more than four or five dingers the entire season.

The native players' lack of conditioning made their athleticism all the more impressive. Everyone smoked and drank. They paid no attention to diet and nutrition. They scoffed at weight lifting, mostly because they just didn't have the time. These guys were on the field six hours a day, twelve months a year, for their entire careers, some of them holding down jobs on the side.

By the end of the day, they were simply too tired to train. At the time, few Latin players were making the millions they bring in now, so even those lucky enough to have a big-league contract couldn't afford to sit out winter ball. In a poverty-stricken country, the demands on the money could outstrip the supply. Vast networks of dependents had designs on small salaries, and family members came to expect financial support.

The teams didn't help. When a player got injured, the trainer shot him up with cortisone and sent him right back into action. The clubhouse was filled with syringes for B-12 shots and a variety of painkillers. I remember the trainer showing off a two-headed snake in a jar of rubbing alcohol. He would rub this "formula" on a sore shoulder or muscle and boast of its healing power.

Management hated it when "soft" Americans begged out of a game. The Navigantes featured the standout pitcher Les Straker. He was coming off a stellar rookie year with the Twins, including a start in a World Series game, making him a sensation in Valencia, his hometown. His arm was dead from pitching so many innings in the States, but the local fans wouldn't hear of giving him a rest.

At first, he pitched up to expectations. But he developed a blister on the middle finger of his pitching hand. In an attempt to relieve the pressure, the trainer pulled out a razor blade and sliced open the blister right down the middle of his fingertip. The blister was gone, but the deep cut put Les out of action for the rest of the winter. The fans were so pissed I was afraid they would shoot the trainer.

~

OUR MANAGER, Felipe Alou, amassed 2,000 hits and 200 home runs in his big-league career. At one point, three of the five Alou brothers—Matty, Jesus, and Felipe—roamed the Candlestick Park outfield together. Felipe's son, Moises, went on to become a standout major leaguer. Baseball had been very good to the family, but it required a lot of sacrifice. "When I played, they wouldn't give us permission to go home to be with our wives," Felipe once said. "When my wife had Moises, by the time I got home he was walking."

I could have predicted he would become one of the top managers in the game. He always seemed to be several steps ahead of the other team's strategy. We would sit in the dugout and marvel at how he anticipated nine outs in the future. But he also had the intangibles that make a leader. A native of the Dominican Republic, he had an easy way about him, and not just with Latin players.

He had another important quality in a manager: he adored me. He broke into a huge grin when I greeted him in his native tongue. Spanish ballplayers, who become bilingual to play in the States, always appreciate it when Americans, who can be provincial, take the time to learn their language.

Felipe let me know I would play center field and bat third every game. "Unless you are on your deathbed," he added with a wink.

I grew close to my American teammates—Tom Prince, Tommy Gregg, Rick Raether, and Gary Wayne, all of whom had, or went on to have, major-league careers. It felt like we lost a family member when Prince was sent home. He could catch and throw with the best of them, but in South America they don't pay Americans to play defense. You have to hit, and he struggled at the plate. Tom got the last laugh, however, enjoying a long, lucrative major-league career as a backup catcher.

We lived in an old stucco house, rented for us by the team, ten minutes from the stadium. Our housekeeper, María, became our adopted *madre,* cooking, cleaning, and generally looking after us. Every day, there would be a chocolate or coconut cake cooling in a tray for us to devour when we arrived home from a game, famished.

After night games, we played cards, drank beer, listened to music, and bullshitted our way through the season. In the morning, we walked one block to the Intercontinental Hotel and its Olympic-sized pool. Tourists mingled with oil executives, sunbathing in Speedos and bikinis around the perimeter. While striving for a tan that rivaled the rich olive tones of the natives, I made my way through Frederick Forsyth's thrillers *The Day of the Jackal* and *The Devil's Alternative;* the latter contained a scene describing a debonair Russian military officer who happened to be gay. I was surprised at my desire to read that passage, over and over again until I'd memorized it.

~

LATIN FANS HAVE an unrivaled passion for baseball. They love it so much that they sometimes become unruly. Alcohol flowed like water in the stands. Bottles of Polar Beer cost a quarter, so anyone could get drunk for a dollar.

Not long into games, male fans would strip their leather belts from their pant loops, wrap them around their fists, and go after one another.

There was a concerted effort to maintain order. Barbed wire circled the field, which was patrolled by cops armed with shiny metal swords hooked to their belts and fierce German shepherds at their side. During one game early in the season, a drunk Caracan fan found a way through security and jumped into our dugout. He insisted on taking on the team. Two of our players took turns pulverizing this poor bastard before the rest of us could pull away. The fan broke the glass water-cooler bottle and used a shard to defend himself.

Finally, the cops leapt into the dugout, and after smacking the fan with the blunt ends of the swords, they dragged him off to jail, a trail of blood flowing in his wake. As I sat trembling in the dugout trying to assimilate what I'd just witnessed, the other guys just shrugged and laughed as if it were an everyday occurrence.

We spent as much time watching the fans as they did us. We howled about all the drunken fans until we realized, after one road game, that our bus driver was just as wasted as they were.

The intensity of the atmosphere was contagious, and I played every inning of every game as if it were my last. Freed from worries about my role, I pounded the cover off the ball, hitting .321 over the four months I was there. I finished second in the league in hitting to future Tiger Cecil Fielder, a massive slugger on the brink of celebrity, who hit near .330.

The combination of my batting average and youth caught everyone's attention. I became the toast of Valencia. The fans affectionately nicknamed me *cara de niños* ("babyface"), and by the end of the season they were chanting *"niño—niño—niño"* when I came to bat. It was like being a high school hero all over again.

We may have lacked big-league stars, but we developed the hard-nosed, fundamental style of play favored by Felipe, and it helped that we all got along. We qualified for the playoffs, squaring off against our archrival Leones de Caracas (Caracas Lions) in a five-game series. The Leones were considered the Yankees of Venezuela, so we were the underdogs. Security was even tighter than usual.

This was the native players' World Series. The fans would go ballistic if a player made an error or failed at the plate in the clutch. They were a little more forgiving of the Americans. Anna had flown in for the playoffs, adding to the excitement. I told myself to just relax and let the game come to me.

We lost the first game in Valencia. I had three hits, but we really missed our ace, Les Straker, who watched from the dugout with a bandage around his finger. We fared better the second night, and I rapped two more hits. Now we had to play two in enemy territory. After the game, a bunch of us went out looking for a bar where we could celebrate. Happening across a watering hole named "Billy's," we decided it was our fated destination. The pulsating Latin music fired us up.

In the middle of the bar was a mechanical bull operated by a bar employee. We watched a procession of locals get thrown to the floor. After a few beers, some of us were cocky enough to try to tame the robotic bull. Anna went first. She looked great in her tight jeans, tank top, and long curly brown hair. The crowd roared drunkenly as she bucked slowly up and down. Never one to back down from a physical challenge and eager to share in the moment, I took my turn on the saddle. The operator was not nearly so generous toward me, and the bull started jerking back and forth maniacally. Suddenly I was flying through the air, but this time I lacked my Superman outfit. I was so smashed I didn't feel the impact of the wooden rail.

The next morning I dragged myself out of bed and into the bathroom to relieve myself after the night of drinking. I watched with horror as the toilet water slowly turned a rusty brown color. Then I noticed a bruise the size of a baseball on my right side.

"Anna," I yelled dramatically. "I'm bleeding."

I headed to the park anyway. The stakes were so high I was afraid to tell anyone other than Anna about my condition. I was hitting third. We'd skipped batting practice that day. But I could tell during stretching that every swing would feel like a dagger in my lower back. About thirty minutes before the game started, I asked one of my teammates for a "boost," otherwise known as ephedrine. My first time up, I doubled sharply to the right-center gap. Trying to conserve energy, I was efficient at the plate. I just missed a home run my second time up, getting underneath the ball a fraction of an inch. My third time up I nailed a sharp single to left. The little white pill worked.

It was a seesaw battle. Every time Caracas scored, the public address system played a booming recording of a deafening lion's roar, and the crowd went wild. Even we had to admit it was pretty cool, though less so when you were playing for the opposing team.

Our lanky reliever Rich Raether, a member of the Texas Rangers' system, was holding a two-run lead in the eighth. The lion was ready to roar again, and fights were breaking out everywhere. Rick held the lead. In the ninth inning I drove in a run, giving me a perfect day at the plate, and we took a 6-3 lead. Raether gave up a run in the bottom of the ninth, but we hung on for a 6-4 victory. We were one win away from knocking off our foes. We had to take one more game in Caracas, but the momentum had shifted in our direction.

The locker room was jubilant. But pulling off my uniform, I froze. My jockstrap was drenched in blood. Panicked, I showed it to Felipe, who ordered me to the hospital just down the road. As I lay in a bed in a dreary room, the exhaustion of the long season and panic of the injury sank in. It was a relief to have Anna by my side.

I spent the night sedated in the hospital as the doctors poked and prodded. It turned out that my fall had bruised a kidney, and I was bleeding internally. The doctors seemed to think that bed rest alone would take care of the problem, and they suggested I return to the States immediately so I could rest comfortably at home.

Coming on strong with the bat at the end of the year, I'd hoped to lead the team to a championship. But the doctors deemed it too risky. The Magallanes' GM encouraged me to "play through the injury," implying I was letting the team down. He was more concerned about my ability to roam center field than my health.

I'd gone from being the team's best hitter to a "problem," feeling like nothing so much as a prized bull. The Lions came back and won the next two games to take the series. When the plane to Los Angeles took off from the Caracas airport, where I'd started out four months earlier, I leaned back in my seat and fell into a deep sleep.

~

I ARRIVED HOME exhausted but happy. I needed to put back on the fifteen pounds I'd lost playing winter ball—and fast. I devoured everything Mom put in front of me, then ordered milk shakes to top it off. I spent a lot of time on the couch in front of the television set, soaking up all the American culture I'd missed while resting a weary twenty-three-year-old body that suddenly felt old.

It didn't take me long to recuperate. I hoped to take the confidence of winter ball into the regular season, and two weeks later I was on my way to 1988 spring training in Lakeland. In the clubhouse, each player sized up what his competitors for a starting position or a spot on the roster had done to prepare for the season. Amid the bustle, Sparky Anderson greeted me with a pat on the back.

"Did you enjoy your time off this winter?" he asked.

I was crushed. I assumed that excelling in Venezuela would have some major-league payoff. But my manager hadn't even noticed. The only thing that mattered was how I performed at the big-league level. If you stunk up the joint in winter ball, everybody back home was sure to hear about it. If you tore it up, it was dismissed as a big leaguer taking advantage of sub-par competition.

I felt sorry for myself until I remembered how much fun I'd had, the experience I'd gained. Now I was faced with proving myself all over again. After I sheepishly summarized my winter ball play, Sparky flipped me a ball.

"Get back out there, kiddo," he said. "We've got work to do."

It was time to turn the page. There was ball to play.

7 *Playing to the Home Crowd*

ROAMING CENTER FIELD LIKE RICK MONDAY ~
LARGER-THAN-LIFE WARRIOR ~ DEADLIEST STUFF ~
STRAIGHT OUT OF MAYBERRY ~ BIGGER CONTESTS

THE SUMMER I got my driver's license, I'd jump in my VW Bug, pick up my friends, and cruise to Dodger Stadium in Chavez Ravine, about an hour away on Highway 101. We would spend entire weekends in the sun-filled bleachers, back in the days when seats were five bucks apiece and we were still under the legal drinking age.

To wide-eyed teenagers, the stadium, built on a foothill overlooking downtown L.A., seemed big enough to be a city unto itself. We were accustomed to the vast open spaces of Southern California, and it was incredible to see so many people packed into one place, underlining the stakes of the game.

The players were my new superheroes. As we took in the games, I imagined roaming center field like the great Rick Monday, though I was too shy to admit my goal to my buddies, who might've considered it grandiose. Back at home, I strutted around imitating the batting stances of slugging Steve Garvey and speedy Davey Lopes.

I lived and died with the fortunes of the men in blue. It was a good time to be a Dodger fan. The hiring of Tommy Lasorda, only the team's second manager, in 1976, when I was twelve, ushered in another golden era. In 1981, my senior year in high school, the team took the World Series.

"I'm going to play for that man someday," I told Mom. "You just wait and see."

~

IN JULY 1989, after spending the two years after Venezuela shuttling between Detroit and Toledo, I was living with Jim and Louise McVicker, two die-hard Mud Hens fans who took a liking to the lonely young ballplayer in need of a roof over his head. They said my hustling style of play assured them I was "a young man of good character." I wasn't so sure of that, but at lunch one day at their spacious Toledo home, with a pool and tennis court in the backyard, they offered, rent-free, a basement room with a private bath, no small inducement to someone on a minor-league salary. They were kind, generous, and I wanted to make them proud.

It was a decent existence, a small-town minor-league life with a doting couple, at a comfortable distance from Anna and the problems I wasn't ready to confront. It may not have been exactly the fantasy life of a player with relentless big-league aspirations, but it wasn't too far off, either. In Toledo I was able to hone my game without the pressure of sell-out crowds, grizzled veterans looking over my shoulder, and unforgiving highlight reels on the nightly news. I played solid ball, hung out with my teammates, and waited for another call-up from the Tigers, which got closer every day as my average climbed to the .325 mark.

About half-way through the season, I got a call from my agent, Dennis Gilbert. I expected to hear the details of the recall, but instead I was told something very different.

"Billy, you're coming home," he said. "The Dodgers shipped two prospects to the Tigers for your contract. This is your shot. The Dodgers believe you are going to be a big-time player."

I was in shock. Just a decade earlier I had fallen asleep every night dreaming about playing for the home team. Now, at the age of twenty-five, I would actually be donning Dodger blues.

Sometimes the worst thing about your dreams is that they come true. As I talked about the trade over dinner that evening with my Toledo teammate and friend Torey Lovullo, I fought back tears. I was going to miss him and all the other Mud Hens.

"Dude," he said. "What's up with you? One of the best organizations in baseball just traded for you. You're gonna play for Tommy friggin' Lasorda."

~

I COULDN'T SEE parking my Honda among the Dodger millionaires' luxury autos. So I borrowed Anna's white Porsche, took it through a car wash, and made my first drive to the stadium as a player. When I approached the parking lot this time, I didn't even have to shell out. Smiling, they waved me through to the player's lot.

In the past, I'd waited in long lines to get through the turnstiles. Now I could walk through the tunnel underneath the stadium, passing the bullpen and indoor batting cage until I reached the clubhouse. It was divided into spaces for weights, trainers' quarters, locker room, huge bathroom with showers, and a lounge stocked with every kind of food you could imagine. At the far end sat the manager's office and a fully equipped video room. Even with twenty-four other players around, you could get a sense of space and even privacy.

When I arrived, reporters, coaches, and front-office staff buzzed around the players. As a kid, I'd paid good money for a jersey from a sta-dium vendor. Now the jersey was not only free but the real thing, with my name neatly stitched, in big bold capital letters, on the back. It was hard to absorb the idea of wearing the same uniform as Steve Garvey, Ron Cey, Davey Lopes, and Fernando Valenzuela.

Dodger Stadium was a long way from the cozy confines of Tiger Stadium, where players could practically reach out and touch fans from their positions along the chalk. In this stadium, you could get lost in foul territory. Hollywood celebrities like Jack Nicholson and Don Rickles hung out on the field, chatting with players, and watching batting practice in the sun. Even the coaches—former big leaguers—were rich and famous. There were television crews everywhere.

Dennis was right. This really was the big time. The Dodgers were the defending world champs, and even though I was now fully grown, I felt as small as I had as a Little Leaguer attending my first game here. I checked out the big, bright orange Union 76 ball in center field that I'd admired as a kid.

As it had been with the Tigers, my teammates expressed little interest in the new acquisition. The tone was survival of the fittest, and almost no one other than coaches said more than "hey kid" to me that first day. Finally, third baseman Mickey Hatcher greeted me and told me to make sure I got something to eat before the game. But I wondered whether I'd be able to keep anything down.

On the surface, my arrival seemed like a perfect marriage between local boy and storied franchise. But on the inside, it felt cold and impersonal, and I wanted to run away, all the way back to Toledo.

~

BALLPLAYERS DREAM OF playing before the home crowd. The lure is so strong that some will make a financial sacrifice just for the chance. There are many advantages, from spending more time with family to the possibility of becoming hometown hero. But there are pitfalls, too.

"Playing in front of your home fans will be the hardest thing you'll ever have to cope with," Kirk Gibson, in a moment of reflective candor, told me when I joined the team. Gibby was one to know. The former

Michigan football star had played in front of his home crowd for eleven years with the Tigers. He'd joined the Dodgers the year before I arrived.

I became fixated on the possibility of failure and exposure. I'd become accustomed to seeing superstars run across the diamond at Chavez Ravine. Why would the Dodgers want a regular guy like Billy Bean in a town ruled by studs like Steve Garvey and my other boyhood idols?

From the Dodgers' perspective, I could understand the logic behind the trade. Fans adore homegrown boys, and they turn out in droves to watch them play. General manager Fred Claire figured I hadn't had an adequate chance to blossom in Detroit, where the franchise had demoted me to Toledo. General managers love getting credit for uncovering diamonds in the rough.

While the players didn't exactly embrace me, the city laid out the red carpet. When Vin Scully learned I spoke Spanish and had played in Venezuela, the legendary Dodger broadcaster dubbed me "Guillermo Frijoles" on the air, an honor in the heavily Latino city. The *Los Angeles Times* ran a flattering profile under the headline, "Local Boy Billy Bean Comes Home and Makes Good."

I met Dodger figures such as Don Drysdale, also an announcer, and Sandy Koufax, who served as a special pitching instructor exclusively for top prospects. I got the nerve to introduce myself to Garvey, who'd recently retired. When I confided that as a child I had been too shy to ask for his autograph, he shook my hand with the strong right hand and forearm that had electrified his bat. The guy could rake with the best of them. As a kid I'd looked up to him. Now I was literally looking down at him, as I was several inches *taller* than the man I'd worshipped as a larger-than-life warrior.

Other members of the team whispered about Garvey's reputation when he wasn't in front of the cameras. Apparently, they'd pegged him as a selfish ballplayer and teammate. I'd no idea how much of this was just envy of his prodigious numbers, and in any case I found him engaging and always ready with good advice and encouragement.

Even the greats are human beings with critics and failings. I'd always striven to be great so I would be liked. Now I realized there was a difference between the person and the player. My game would have to speak for itself.

~

PRO SPORTS ARE exacting. If you're not performing up to your own expectations—or those others have created for you—things can turn ugly. You can't get too comfortable in your surroundings. The minute you do, they are sure to be yanked out from under you. A guy can go from "Hometown Hero" to "Local Boy Fizzles" in the space of about four at-bats.

Determined to show my teammates and management I belonged, I heaped pressure on myself. On the road, where I could relax, I hit the ball pretty hard and nearly at a .300 clip. But at home, with family and friends watching from the box seats, my confidence vanished. The more I worried, the more I struggled. My paralyzing fear of failure, which had plagued me since I was drafted, returned with a vengeance.

Since I wasn't hitting a lick, I'd go for days without stepping on the field during a game. When I finally did, I felt lost. The National League was known for its fastball pitchers, and they exploited my weakness for high heat. When I earned a rare start, Tommy Lasorda would pinch hit for me the moment there was a chance to drive in a run in a close game.

My best moment came on the field, about two weeks after the trade, in front of a packed house at Chavez Ravine. Tim Belcher was pitching a shutout against our rivals, the despised San Francisco Giants. In the ninth inning, the Giants put runners on second and third with two outs. Will Clark, the Giants' best hitter, strode to the plate. Tim was pitching masterfully, and he got in on Clark with a nasty cut fastball. Clark hit a duck fart down the left-field line. I got a great jump, dove, and managed to come up with the ball as I slid across the foul line. I leapt to my feet, holding the ball aloft so the umpire could see I'd made the catch, which had saved not just the game but Tim's shutout. Belcher practically picked me off the floor with a huge bear hug as I ran in from left field. It was a stark reminder that the best way to prove myself to my teammates was to help out on the field. No one wanted a shaky young teammate; they wanted someone who could produce.

But then it was back on the bench for days. My teammates had no way of knowing what kind of a play I was capable of, and this drove me to distraction. For the first time, the scrapbook Mom kept stopped growing. Rather than show off my box scores, I wanted to bury them in the backyard. The compliments that major leaguers invariably get—whether they're playing well or not—sounded like put-downs because I believed I wasn't living up to them.

I dreaded the humiliation of getting sent down again in front of friends and family. I did everything I could outside the chalk to please the organization. I made myself available for every charity function, hospital visit, and media appearance. I was especially eager to visit disadvantaged kids, whose gratitude always cheered me up and took me out of my own woes. They reminded me of a time in my life when players were gods and playing was not just another pressure-filled job. My parents cherished a letter they received from the father of a shy little girl whom I'd befriended.

I went out of my way to spend time with fans, even though I certainly wasn't much in demand. I never could understand how the stars could just blow people off—the same people who were paying their salaries. I was so eager and friendly that *they* were blowing *me* off. *Hey, Bean, can you get us Gibson's autograph?*

Ordinarily I loved it when friends and family wanted to enjoy the big-league experience along with me. Even average ballplayers receive enormous goodwill for simply doing their job, and in the past I'd always worked hard to deserve this privilege. But now I felt overwhelmed by phone calls. They demanded everything from tickets to Dodger gossip. Even the sportswriters, usually the last people to get inside your head, could tell I was off my game. Bean "felt he was carrying not only his dreams, but the hopes of hundreds of others," wrote Bill Plaschke of the *Los Angeles Times*.

It was true. Dreams are meaningless without a shot at fulfilling them. I'd always been good at blocking out distractions and concentrating on the next pitch. Now I could sense everyone watching me, scrutinizing my every mistake. My high school chums wondered aloud why I was struggling. My old coaches asked where my fundamentals had gone. My complexion turned pale, and the pounds started dropping off. I couldn't sleep. Everyone wanted to know whether I was ill.

My only consolation was negative: a lot of us played like minor leaguers that year. The Dodgers had upset the Oakland A's in the previous year's World Series. Kirk Gibson's pinch-hit home run off Dennis Eckersley in the ninth inning of game one had set the tone. The feat was all the more remarkable because Gibson was hobbled by a leg injury and Eck had the deadliest stuff in baseball. He flew at you, arms and legs flailing, and then the ball would dart at the last second. He had pinpoint control. I'll never know how Gibby pulled that one off.

"I don't . . . believe . . . what I . . . just . . . saw," play-by-play man Jack Buck had shouted as Gibson limped around the bases.

By the time I arrived, the Dodgers were well off the pace, the beginning of a decade-long slide. Two of our stars, Gibby and Mike Marshall, were in open revolt, and most of the veterans were on the downside of their careers. Orel Hershiser, the staff ace, had just signed the largest contract in baseball history, $8.7 million over three years. He was a good guy, and he had such perfect command of his stuff that I always thought he must have had a magic wand hidden up his shirtsleeve. His "aw-shucks" looks of an overgrown Opie, straight out of Mayberry, were misleading. Inside, where it counted, he fit the description of his nickname, Bulldog. I prayed that some of his confidence and determination would rub off on me, but it just wasn't happening.

~

IN BETTER TIMES, I fought my way out of slumps, but now I needed help. In the majors, there's surprisingly little coaching. In fact, the higher a ballplayer ascends, the less tutoring. Major-league coaches, assuming you've been taught in the minors, don't provide much more than technical advice. Lasorda didn't bother to explain why I was sitting at the end of the bench, chewing the fat with the batboys. He didn't need to. If you don't produce, you don't play. It was understood.

In college and the minors, coaches go out of their way to create the conditions for your success. In the bigs, they want to see the stuff a young guy is made of right away. If you're not up to the challenge, the front office wants to know as soon as possible so the organization—and the fans it must draw—doesn't waste time on a kid with no future.

Third-base coach Joey Amalfitano exemplified the old-school mentality. When he noticed my name in the lineup, he'd declare, "I want to see a couple of hits out of you today Bean, or you'll be back on the bench with splinters up your ass." Another example of the "Dodger family."

Manny Mota and Ben Hines, our hitting instructors that year, were much more helpful. Manny, one of the best pinch hitters of all time, wanted me to choke up on the handle and use a heavier, thirty-three-ounce bat. Ben counseled me to hold my bat up higher and let go with one hand on my follow-through, a style popularized by George Brett. He felt it would help me lay off high fastballs and hit fewer pop flies.

I tried hard to please both coaches, taking batting practice until my hands bled. But I only became more confused and lost at the plate. Again, my need-to-please personality was leading me astray. I was more worried about accommodating my coaches, who would have little bearing on my career, and couldn't be asked to take any responsibility for the results of my experimentation. The best advice I'd ever received came back in my rookie year. "Just keep it simple," Sparky Anderson used to say.

I'd made the same mistake many of us did that year: forgetting what had gotten me there in the first place. And bigger contests were already starting to play out in my head and my heart.

8 *Dodger Blues*

HEART OF WEST HOLLYWOOD ~ ALMOST GETTING
CAUGHT ~ THE DEFINITION OF HOMOEROTICISM ~
LONELIEST VIEW ~ YOU'RE A LUCKY MAN, BILLY BEAN

I FELT LIKE A pitcher in a ninth-inning tie, the bases loaded, no outs, and a ball-three count. Everything was happening at once, and there was no margin of error. All I could do was fire a fastball right down the middle and pray the batter would hit it right at an infielder.

During the first Dodger home stand after the trade, I checked into the Sheraton Grande in downtown Los Angeles. It was odd to be staying in a hotel so close to where I'd grown up, but I had nowhere else to go. We had a game the next day, so there wasn't time to run around and look for an apartment. It's not uncommon for a player to spend an entire season in a hotel when he arrives. You never know when you might get sent down or shipped out to yet another team.

I paid a visit to my agent Dennis Gilbert at his opulent office on the top floor of a Beverly Hills high-rise. Every secretary in the office wore a mini-skirt and a blouse that showed off ample cleavage—it must've been a job requirement. Dennis wore perfectly tailored suits, drove a Bentley, and draped his beautiful blonde wife, Cindy, on his arm in public.

He had gone into the sports business after a short minor-league playing career, and he ended up making more money than a lot of players. On his roster of all-stars, I stuck out like a sore thumb. But I was proud to be on his list, and I appreciated that he stuck by me through the ups and downs of a journeyman. I wasn't pulling in the kind of money his other clients did, but he made me feel welcome anyway. A couple of times, he even put me up at his estate in the valley, where I whipped him at tennis on his private court and hung out by the pool.

After we discussed the trade and my contract, I told him I needed a place to live. He suggested I move into "that apartment building you own."

"What're you talking about?"

Just the year before, Dennis explained, he'd invested some of my cash in a building with a bunch of his other clients, including Jose Canseco, Bobby Bonilla, and Bret Saberhagen. The plan was to convert it to condominiums and sell it at a profit. For the time being, he said, I should move in. It was a fifteen-minute drive from the stadium, practically walking distance in Los Angeles.

The next day, I took a drive to check it out.

I pulled up in front of white stucco building on Curson Road—located right in the heart of West Hollywood, the gayest neighborhood in L.A.

~

Anna gave up her apartment in Manhattan Beach and moved in with me at my new West Hollywood pad. Anna's parents made it clear they disapproved of our living together out of wedlock. it seemed like the right thing to do, and I knew it would make everyone happy, so I proposed to Anna. We decided to get married after the season.

Not long after we settled in together, Anna signed us both up for a gym just a few blocks from the apartment. A few days later, we headed off for a workout at The Sports Connection, on Santa Monica Boulevard.

By the age of twenty-five, I'd spent plenty of time inside gyms. But as we checked this one out, I barely suppressed a gasp. Unbeknownst to either of us, the club had been dubbed The Sports Erection, and I could see why. It was impossible not to notice the glances I was getting from other men, mostly because I was new there. What bothered me was that these stares *didn't* bother me.

This gym really wasn't all that different from the ones in which I'd spent much of my youth, except that guys in this place wore more stylish workout gear, were friendlier than I was used to, and were a little likelier to check each other out.

I pretended I wasn't participating in these flirtatious games, rationalizing that I was just a "straight" guy who just happened to be working out in a predominantly gay gym. As long as I didn't touch anyone else, I assured myself, I was still hetero. The situation reminded me of a time in Toledo. Out of a combination of curiosity, desire, and loneliness, I'd bashfully rented a gay adult video starring some guy named Al Parker, only to return it for fear that watching it would mean I was gay. I imagined that while I was viewing it in the McVickers' basement apartment, where I was living at the time, Louise McVicker would choose that inopportune moment to bring me a fresh batch of her amazing chocolate-chip cookies.

The weight-room vibes were nothing compared to the locker-room energy. It took me quite some time to get the nerve up to check out the steam room, where I learned the definition of "homoeroticism." I'd never seen men together before, and I received a classical education in getting around the bases.

I made sure to keep to myself in such close quarters, rarely exchanging more than a curt "hey" with anyone. I was pretty sure no one would dare break through my gruff demeanor. As time passed, I found myself spending more and more time at this gym, often without Anna.

A year or so later, I was toweling off in the locker room after a long workout when a good-looking man walked up to me and stuck out his hand.

"Hi. I'm Alex," he said, looking me up and down. "I've been noticing you for a long time in here. And it seems you have changed yourself from a boy to a man."

He asked me to have a "cup of coffee" with him. For some reason, I didn't mind this blatant come-on. In fact, it was kinda nice. He seemed like a good person, and I really needed someone to talk to. *What was the harm in spending a little time with him?* Surely it was possible that some of my teammates and coaches had gay friends—or at least their wives did.

Alex and I quickly struck up a friendship. Deep down, I suspected that Alex had ulterior motives. He wanted to hook up while I only wanted a friend to help sort out the confusion. The tension between our conflicting needs made for a rocky relationship, and we would go weeks without talking. Then I would miss his counsel and support, and seek him out all over again.

We'd usually hang out at his place. But one day the phone rang while I was at home, just getting out of the shower. It was Alex. He asked to stop by for a visit because he was "right around the corner."

Anna had left for school downtown, so I thought it might be cool. The doorbell rang only a few minutes after I hung up the phone, and I greeted him in my bathrobe.

"That was quick," I said.

"I really wanted to see you."

Alex looked around the place approvingly, but he obviously had other things on his mind. The next thing I knew, we were sitting on the bed. After some uncomfortable small talk, I pretended not to notice that he'd moved closer than a conversation required. He leaned over as if to kiss me when I heard a key turn in the front door and the familiar sound of the hinges swinging open.

It was Anna letting herself into the apartment. She hadn't felt well at school and had decided to skip her last two classes. Panicked, I pushed Alex into the bathroom and told him to stay put until the coast was clear. There was only one way out—through the front. I rushed to the front door, blocking Anna's path. I searched my mind for a reason to turn her around. Then, out of the blue, I remembered that her Porsche had been making a rattling sound.

"Anna, show me where the loud noise is coming from," I said, practically yanking her out the door and down the stairs toward the garage below. "I want to take care of it NOW."

Fortunately, it wasn't out of character for me to be more than a little manic. She shrugged and followed. As I leaned down in mock examination of the problem, I glanced toward the street. Alex was walking away. I felt as if I'd been in a car crash. I deserved to get caught, and it might've been for the best, but Anna never said a word about the episode. I couldn't believe how stupid I'd been. I dressed and drove the car to the shop, my heart racing and my hands trembling on the steering wheel.

~

MY CONFUSION WAS hard to shake, even at the ballpark, which always had been my sanctuary. I would stand in center field, my every move scrutinized by 40,000 screaming fans, worrying about my parents' reaction to the inevitable tabloid headlines about the queer ballplayer when I should've been focusing on the location of the next pitch or on getting the best possible jump on a hit my way.

Striding to the plate, I'd catch myself wondering about how my otherwise sturdy, dependable body could possibly harbor such desires. Players often point toward the heavens after making a play or blasting a home run. For the thoughts I was having about members of my own sex, I was convinced God was going to strike me down right there in the outfield.

Watch the ball, you fucking idiot. You're taking the biggest chance of your life and flushing it down the toilet.

Overcompensating for my sense of shame and lack of focus, I played with the abandon of a stunt man, diving for balls and sliding head-first into base, ready to crash through Wrigley Field's ivy-covered brick wall to prove my worth. I'd lost the subtlety and smarts so important to a scrappy, overachieving ballplayer. Instead of playing savvy, I regressed to the stage of a rookie who tries to overpower the game. I'd forgotten that finesse is the secret to success.

After one of my rare good performances, Don Drysdale asked at the end of an interview whether I would like to say hello to anyone.

"Well, I'd like to say hi to my fiancée, Anna, who's out there watching," I stammered. "We're engaged, so this is a very special time."

~

ON NOVEMBER 11, 1989, Anna and I were married. The setting couldn't have been more idyllic. The Loyola chapel, with its priceless stained-glass windows and mahogany pews, was decked out with fresh-cut white roses. Perched on the bluffs of Marina Del Rey, the setting offered one of the most spectacular views I'd ever seen. It was also one of the loneliest, despite being surrounded by friends and family.

Jim and Louise McVicker had flown in all the way from Ohio. Most of my teammates from over the years were there. Our families mingled politely together, putting aside differences for our sake. I wore a black tux with a white bow tie and a red rose fastened to my lapel.

Every one of the dozens of guests that day believed I had it all, yet I was desperate for reassurance. *You're a lucky man, Billy Bean,* I repeated to myself. At the reception afterwards, champagne glass in hand, I sought out words of wisdom. All I heard were platitudes like "You're going to be a great husband and father" and "Anna's lucky to have you."

A few months earlier, my Loyola teammate Jim Bruske, who'd married Anna's college roommate Amy, had been the only one to tell me what I needed to hear. He made a strong case that I wasn't ready for marriage. He said he could sense that something was up with me, but couldn't quite put his finger on it. I should have listened to my good friend. The more worried I became about my true nature, the more desperate I became for marriage to "fix" the "problem."

During the pre-wedding photograph session on the lawn next to the chapel, I unwittingly stepped in some dog poop. Brad Turner, my best man, noticed my gaffe. Always the comedian and thinking it would be funny to see what would happen next, he pretended not to see what I'd done.

The next thing I knew we were at the altar, and there was a foul odor in the air. Everyone in the wedding party, including the priest, sniffed around to see who might've been the culprit. When Anna and I kneeled down to take communion, the mystery was revealed. The stuff was still smeared over the soles of my shoes, and I'd managed to get it all over the train of Anna's white dress. It was a catastrophe. At first she was furious, but after a few drinks at the reception she was laughing at me. I laughed along.

Secretly, however, I worried that it was another bad omen for our future together.

9 *Lasorda's Lament*

SUCH A SISSY ~ THE BOY OF EVERY GIRL'S DREAM ~
TAKE ME TO THE CASTRO ~ BASEBALL'S EQUIVALENT OF
JOHN WAYNE ~ BILLY MARTIN, GLENN BURKE, AND
DUSTY BAKER ~ SPUNKY IS DEAD ~ JESUS CHRIST IS MY
BEST FRIEND

D ON'T RUN LIKE a faggot, boy." I'll never forget the first time I heard the word on an athletic field. *Faggot,* I remember repeating to myself. *Faggot.*

I was in fourth grade, playing quarterback for my Junior All-American team, the Wolf Pack. The angry command came from the coach, Jimmy Thompson. It wasn't directed at me—being the best player on the team generally left me above reproach.

Instead, it was aimed at Bobby Smith, who had just missed a tackle. Every kid on the field that day got the message, despite what I suspect was our collective ignorance. What, exactly, was a faggot? How did faggots run? Clearly, it wasn't a good thing. It was probably the worst thing imaginable. It equaled weakness and timidity, everything a budding, insecure jock wanted to avoid. We were only kids. How were we supposed to know the truth?

A six-foot-four military veteran, Coach Thompson was a lovable guy who taught me the right way to play the game and helped instill in me a drill sergeant's fire for competition. As former Marines, he and my stepfather, Ed, bonded.

An African American, Thompson wasn't the kind of guy associated with prejudice. He was married to a white woman, and they were raising a biracial child. Even in our integrated neighborhood, this family provided a positive model. Coach had hardly invented the put-downs—*fag, queer, girl,* and *pussy*—he threw around. At the time, in the early '70s, the word *faggot* wasn't considered bigotry any more than the word *nigger* had been thirty years earlier. My Latino teammates used the term *maricón,* so I figured that the insult was universal. By the time I reached the majors, I'd heard the terms from almost every coach I'd played for—and many I hadn't.

As motivational strategy, it was effective. Coaches invoked the terms again and again. Players responded, almost reflexively raising their intensity level, and I could already see how much more Bobby bore down after Coach singled him out. Even at that age, just a rag-tag band of skinny boys, we were required to prove our manhood to coaches, teammates, and dads who roamed the sidelines, keyed up by vicarious intensity.

It wasn't long before kids were berating one another with similar epithets, especially when we did anything out of the jock norm. Crying or even whining was sure to bring a rebuke. It was common for a kid to cry if he dropped a pass, but we learned quickly that this was a huge mistake. Getting mad was far more acceptable. Copying the coaches, we would go on the attack.

"Damn, Bobby, hold onto the fucking ball," we were saying to each other before long. "You're such a *sissy.*"

Nearly twenty years later, those words still haunted me.

~

SOMETIMES THE HARDER a pitcher tries to throw a strike, the less likely he is to get the ball over the plate. That's how I felt about my burgeoning attraction to men. The harder I fought to deny it, the more it took hold of my erotic imagination, and I eventually let down my guard and explored a little. On a short trip to San Francisco to play the Giants during my 1989 season with the Dodgers, I walked a few blocks from the team hotel to hail a cab out of sight of my teammates.

"Take me to the Castro," I ordered.

I'd no idea exactly where or even what the Castro was, only that it was supposed to be some kind of haven for homosexuals. As the driver navigated the steep streets of the Victorian neighborhood, I slumped in the backseat and watched young men stroll along the wide sidewalks. I was amazed to find a place where men walked hand in hand. I was even more amazed no one else was batting an eyelash.

I wanted to get out and walk among these guys, perhaps step into one of the bars that lined Castro Street. But I feared that if the taxi stopped, even for a moment, I'd be spotted. It didn't dawn on me until much later that this teammate would have had some explaining of his own to do.

On our next trip to San Francisco, my fears were confirmed. The team was staying at a luxury hotel on Nob Hill, but I couldn't have been less interested in its amenities. Imagining the possibilities of the city as I lay in bed after a night game, I couldn't fall asleep. I still hadn't realized any of the delirious visions dancing in my head. Since we didn't play until the following evening, I got up, dressed, and headed out into the night. I found my way to an adult bookstore I'd noticed from the team bus on the drive up the hill. I did my best to appear interested in the hetero selection, while keeping my eyes trained on the homo section in the back. Just as I'd gotten the nerve to check it out, one of my best friends on the team walked in the front door.

Ducking into one of the video booths and watching him from behind the crack in the door, I might as well have been an escaped con. My heart was beating so fast it threatened to jump out of my chest. My fellow Dodger wandered among the shelves, picking up videos, examining the covers, and then replacing them. Noting that he stayed away from the gay section, I wondered if he'd ever leave.

In the dark recesses of the dingy joint, I promised myself that I'd NEVER go near another place like this. Finally, he bought a couple of magazines and walked out. I waited until the coast was clear before making my way back to the hotel. As I look back, it was laughable to feel so guilty about being in the video store. It was even sillier that I waited thirty minutes in a tiny video booth like a kid playing hide-and-seek.

But at the time, it wasn't funny. I was wracked with shame. I hadn't the slightest idea how to reconcile my desires with my life inside or outside the game. My emotional turmoil was obviously contributing to my inability to concentrate on the field. My self-confidence, the foundation of any player, was shot. Soon one of the game's greatest figures would underscore the depths of my dilemma.

~

TOMMY LASORDA IS the baseball equivalent of John Wayne. He wasn't just a manager; he was a legend. It was an honor to play for one of the all-time great baseball field generals. Lasorda had been so faithful to the Dodger organization, which put such a premium on loyalty, that people said he bled Dodger blue.

So it was with a lump in my throat that I knocked on his office door inside the clubhouse in Pittsburgh after the big trade in '89. I'd flown the red-eye from Albuquerque, where I'd been working out with the team's triple-A affiliate for a few days. I reached Three Rivers Stadium just in time for batting practice before the Dodgers took on the Pirates. In blue jeans and a T-shirt, duffel bag slung over my shoulder, I must have looked about fifteen.

"Hello, Mr. Lasorda. I'm Billy Bean," I declared with all the authority I could muster.

Tommy may have achieved the status of movie star, but he sure didn't look the part. A white-haired Italian, he was as bow-legged as an old cowboy. He'd been pitching Slim-Fast on TV. He actually did slim down, but it didn't help his appearance. His image almost demanded the famous belly.

"How ya doin,' kid?"

"Thrilled to be here, sir. I feel great."

He smiled warmly and told me to take some batting practice.

The clubhouse director, Dave Wright, a sweet, mild-mannered guy, was the spitting image of Friar Tuck. He had the presence of a mouse, but it was clear he was the man in charge. Handing me a uniform, he showed me to a locker. Despite my doubts and nerves, I allowed myself a moment of satisfaction at joining this storied organization. Most players would have given anything to step into my shiny new blue cleats.

I dressed and was ready to go. So it came as a shock that when I walked past Tommy's office again he barked, "What the hell are you doing in a uniform?"

I was confused. Only three years before he'd been singing my praises as the keynote speaker at a Loyola banquet. Had there been some terrible mix-up? Was I in the wrong place?

"Well, uh, I'm Billy Bean, and the Dodgers just acquired me from the Tigers."

"*You're* Billy Bean?" Tommy bellowed. "Why didn't you say so? I thought you were some high school kid they brought in here for a workout."

"I *did* introduce myself."

"Son of a bitch," he said with a shrug.

Once he figured out who I was, Tommy displayed an almost paternal fondness. Like the McVickers—and a lot of the adults who knew me in my youth—he saw me as a dedicated, all-American kid who wanted nothing more than to please his coaches and teammates. He loved my grasp of fundamentals and my hustle.

Tommy had an odd way of showing his affection. A few weeks later, I heard him yelling for me from across the locker room. He was in the bathroom. The stall was wide open, and he was sitting on the toilet with his pants around his ankles. Here was a side of John Wayne I wasn't ready for.

"How ya holdin' up, son?" he said and then grunted in an attempt to relieve his perpetually upset stomach. (Probably too much Slim-Fast!)

I didn't realize it until later, but he was putting me through one of his hazing rituals, trying to see what I was made of. Maybe he was also attempting to shatter any remaining illusions I had about my famed manager.

I know that Gibby and Hershiser would not have put up with such an indignity. It was bizarre to be standing there in the middle of the bathroom, talking to this living legend in the most vulnerable position possible, while he acted like nothing was going on. It was all I could do to keep from laughing. I began to wonder if there was a video camera trained on me, waiting to "roast" me down the road. A couple of other players were around the corner, muffling their laughter, knowing I could do nothing but wait until Skipper finished his business.

~

DURING MY EARLY DAYS with the Dodgers, I realized I wasn't the only one having an off year. Lasorda had spent the winter racing around the country making speeches, filming commercials, and generally enjoying the accolades that came the way of a World Series champ. Success allowed him to take for granted what had brought him to the top of the game.

He'd quietly handed the day-to-day operation of the team to Bill Russell, a longtime Dodger shortstop and thirty-year member of the organization. This freed Tommy to play the role of a movie producer, riding around Dodger stadium in a golf cart, giving orders, cracking obscene jokes, and directing traffic while leaving the details in Russell's capable hands. When the cameras rolled, Tommy would materialize out of thin air.

Fans tend to equate managing with strategy: when to bring in a reliever, when to bunt a runner over, when to play the infield in. All that is important, of course. But any reasonably intelligent triple-A manager can handle it. What separates the great managers from the also-rans is far less tangible. Tommy exuded charisma. He was right up there with Sparky Anderson in his ability to command the respect of athletes.

By the time I reached the team, Tommy had been at the helm for almost twenty years, an unheard-of tenure in a sport where managers have the job security of politicians during a recession. In addition to three World Series rings, he boasted the highest winning percentage of any active manager.

Tommy liked my style of play. But he thought he saw something else in me, too. Whenever he found himself in shouting distance, he would announce, for all to hear, "Billy Bean, Billy Bean, the boy of every girl's dream."

At first, I'd just laugh. It was odd to be praised as a lady killer. There were plenty of other young guys around, but he never talked about them that way. Why was I being singled out for the very thing I couldn't be? From the first time I'd stepped onto a playing field, I'd been the one above reproach, one of the few guys spared the inevitable fag jokes. It didn't make any sense. Why was my true self so at odds with everyone's view of me?

Once again, I found myself alternately bowing to and fighting the expectations that a respected, influential person in my life had unwittingly palced on me. If Tommy Lasorda thought I was straight, maybe I really was.

Or maybe not. A few weeks after my arrival on the team, I was standing near Tommy in the dugout before a game when I overheard him tell a joke that sent shivers down my spine.

"Why is it that if you hit one home run it don't make you a home-run hitter, but if you suck one cock, it makes you a cocksucker?" he said to a group of players hanging out in the dugout.

The guys roared with laughter, even though I found out later he'd used that same dumb line a thousand times. My private reaction couldn't have been any more different from my teammates'. The joke was a stake through the heart of my denial.

Turning away, I ran to the outfield to shag flies—I just wanted to get as far away as I could. It hit way too close to home. He could bill me the "boy of every girl's dream," but it wasn't girls I was dreaming of in the midst of those feverish nights in anonymous hotel rooms across America.

The ridicule didn't end there. On the first day of 1990's spring training, the newest members of the forty-man roster were asked to stand up in the clubhouse. Dodger tradition calls for rookies to answer embarrassing questions about their high school days. Most are naive enough to fall for it.

This time Tommy asked a hulking pitching prospect to stand up. Zak Shinall was a surfer with a huge tattoo of a shark on his back in the days before they became fashionable. He was big and strong, with a rocket arm.

"Zak," Tommy said with a big grin. "If you woke up in the middle of the forest, all alone, completely naked with Vaseline spread all over your body, would you tell anyone?"

"No way, dude."

Tommy: "Hey, Zak, wanna go camping?"

The clubhouse erupted. Zak looked like he wanted to disappear into his locker. So did I.

~

I WASN'T THE ONLY one with a lot going on off the field in my Dodger years—though I wouldn't learn the full story for some time. Something else taking place in my manager's life might have been distracting him from his on-field duties. Tommy's only son, Tommy, Jr., was gravely ill.

Like his father, Junior had been brought up in minor-league towns and had developed into a pretty decent player. According to Peter Rich-

Above left: A Superhero Is Born! ~ My fourth birthday, May 11, 1968. *Above right: My Best Steve Young Imitation* ~ #4, Quarterback of the varsity football team, senior season, 1981.

Above: Our First Brady Bunch Photo ~ The whole Kovac-Bean-Briggs family together in 1979. *Left: The Three Musketeers from Loyola Marymount University on Our Alaskan Adventure in 1985* ~ Tim Layana, me, and Jim McAnany. Nice shorts!

The Majors Can Wait ~ Returning for my senior year at Loyola, 1986.

Top left: *Rituals* ~ Pre-game batting practice on the road with the Tigers, 1987. **Top right:** *Father Figure* ~ Talking with Hall of Fame manager Sparky Anderson. At the time I was playing for the Triple-A Toledo Mud Hens; soon thereafter, Sparky would call me up to play for the Tigers. **Left:** *Topps Rookie Card, Detroit Tigers, 1987* ~ A babyfaced big leaguer at the age of 22.

Left: *Kicking Back* ~ Me and my fiancée on a tiny island beach getaway in Venezuela during winter ball, 1987. **Above:** Me and Tim Layana at my wedding, November 11, 1989.

Above: *Locked In* ~ Zeroing in on a fastball for the Kintetsu Buffaloes in Japan in 1992. **Below left:** *Happy Times* ~ San Diego, 1993. **Below right:** *Beach Boys* ~ Surfing with my buddy, longtime L.A. Dodger Dave Hansen, during the off-season in Huntington Beach, Calif., 1990.

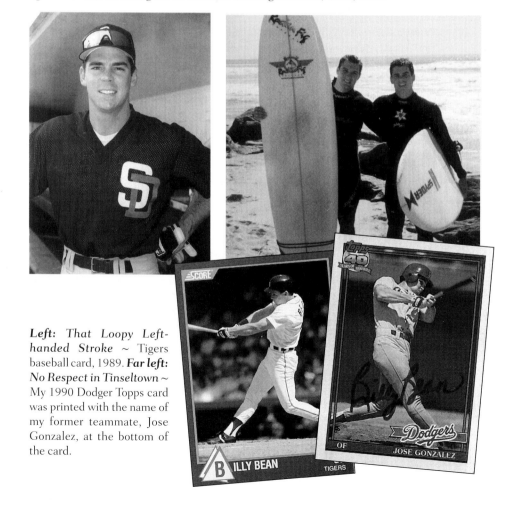

Left: *That Loopy Left-handed Stroke* ~ Tigers baseball card, 1989. **Far left:** *No Respect in Tinseltown* ~ My 1990 Dodger Topps card was printed with the name of my former teammate, Jose Gonzalez, at the bottom of the card.

Above: Going the Other Way ~ Stroking the ball to the opposite field for the Padres against our archrivals, the Dodgers. Mike Piazza is catching. 1993.

Above left: Fleer Padres baseball card, 1994. **Above right:** Topps Padres card, 1993. **Right:** *A Ballplayer's Best Friend* ~ A base hit during a night game at Jack Murphy Stadium, 1994.

My Best Barry Bonds Imitation ~ Watching one leave the park in 1993.

Left: *Hot Pursuit* ~ Chasing 'em down in the gaps during a day game at Jack Murphy stadium in 1993.

Right: *Just One of the Boys* ~ Together at Brad Ausmus' wedding to his wife Liz in Connecticut in 1995. *From left to right:* Archi Cianfrocco, me, J. T. Snow, Andy Ashby, Brad, Trevor Hoffman, and ESPN analyst Chris Fowler.

Left: *Rush Limbaugh I'm Not* ~ Sports radio co-host at WQAM in Miami, 1996.

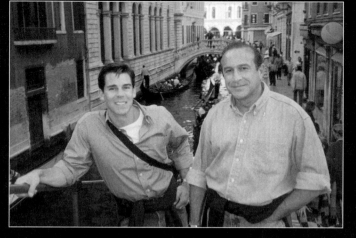

Left: *Life after the Game ~* Me and Efraín in Venice, 1997.

Right: *Brothers in Arms ~* Former NFL defensive lineman Esera Tuaolo and me having fun at xl in New York City after a bruising day of hoops at Basketball City, 2002.

Left: *Together Again, this Time for Keeps ~* With my mom on her first trip to New York City, December 2002.

mond in the October 1992 issue of *GQ*, some longtime Dodgers who saw them both play swear son was actually better than father, who had made his name as a pitcher.

When Spunky, as he was affectionately known, was a teenager in the '70s, more than a decade before I joined the Dodgers, he spent a lot of time hanging around the team, where he was befriended by Dodger center fielder Glenn Burke, who had been compared to a young Willie Mays.

Not long thereafter, Lasorda got rid of Burke. He believed that Burke, who made no bones about his homosexuality, was a bad influence on his son, according to Burke in his memoir *Out at Home*. The Dodgers denied the charge.

"When [I] refused to get married or cool down my friendship with Spunky, [I] was soon traded to the Oakland A's for aging outfielder Billy North," Burke wrote.

The trade didn't stop Spunky from living a gay life—he spent much of his youth in the bars and clubs of West Hollywood.

When the A's manager, Billy Martin, learned of Burke's sexual orientation, he called him *faggot* in front of his players. Martin cut Burke after he suffered a knee injury. After struggling with drugs and homelessness, in 1995 Burke died of AIDS-related complications. One of the few baseball people to visit him in the hospital was the Giants' then manager, Dusty Baker, who'd played with him in L.A.

The guys closest to Lasorda—Orel Hershiser, Bill Russell, and veteran catcher Mike Scioscia—may have been privy to what was going on in our very public manager's private life during my days with the team. Tommy Lasorda is said to have been an excellent father. In 1991, my last year in the Dodger organization, Spunky died of AIDS-related complications. His father was at his bedside.

Having spent most of his adult life in the world of gladiators, Tommy must have found it difficult to deal with the truth about his son. It must have been equally hard for Spunky, having spent his youth in this same world, to accept himself.

Even though the cause of death was printed on his death certificate, Tommy denied that his son had died of the disease—or even that he was gay. "My son wasn't gay," he told *GQ*. "No way. I read that in the paper. I also read in the paper that a lady gave birth to a fuckin' monkey. That's not the truth."

Glenn Burke wasn't traded because he was gay. Tommy Lasorda, Jr., didn't die of AIDS. Spunky was straight. Billy Bean was the boy of every girl's dream. It was all part of bleeding Dodger blue.

~

MEANWHILE, I WAS trying to bridge the gap with my own father.

During a 1990 stint with the Dukes, the Dodgers' triple-A affiliate in Albuquerque, my biological father, Bill Bean, reemerged in my life. He lived in Mesa, Arizona, not far from Phoenix, where we played many games. This would be my best chance to finally see what the man was really made of. I had a father now, Ed Kovac, who'd been there for me through thick and thin. I made sure Ed knew he'd always be my "real" father, no matter how well I got to know Bill.

Mom had never bad-mouthed him, even though he'd left us when I was only two. I went into our meetings with an open mind. I'd spent much of my childhood longing for this man's presence. Seeing him in the flesh, I discovered he was an ordinary person, a devout Mormon who managed drugstores. He'd remarried and had four children. As a kid, I'd been the spittin' image of the photos Mom showed me of him. Now he was a bearded, out-of-shape, middle-aged man. I felt closer to his wife, Joanne Bean.

If anything, *he* was the one who needed to reconnect. After taking in my minor-league games with my half-brother and -sisters, who looked up to me as though I were some kind of celebrity, Bill would take me out to dinner so we could talk, just the two of us. He was so proud to see his name on the back of my uniform. He'd never been a ballplayer, and he often said that he couldn't figure out where my ability had come from.

"It must have been your mother's doing," he said.

I didn't want to say it, but he was right. I soon found myself comforting *him*. My presence gave him permission to open up about his life. He felt that he hadn't lived up to his potential. He told me that he'd always loved Mom and me. When he'd left us, he explained, he was young and confused. (Now *that* was something I could understand.) His religion helped him through these hard times, and he spouted phrases like "Jesus Christ is my best friend."

Sometimes I felt uncomfortable listening to him, and I never knew exactly the right thing to say. I tried to tell him how lucky he was to have such a great wife and kids, but he just seemed sad. He wanted to say he was sorry about the past, but I told him to forget it. What was the point? There was nothing we could do about it now.

I was playing in Mazatlán the next winter when I got permission from the team to travel to Mesa for Jim Bruske's wedding. After a brutal day of bus rides and flights, I finally made it there in time for the nuptials. Anna and I stayed at Bill's house for the rest of the weekend. When it was time for me to return to Mexico, he drove me to the airport. For some reason, he'd made me a batch of cookies for the trip. As we were saying good-bye, he choked up.

"Billy, I'm so proud of you," he said again and again, always on the verge of tears. "You've made something of your life. No matter what happens, never give up on your goal."

The next day, Mom called from Dana Point to tell me that Bill had died from a massive heart attack at the age of forty-five, leaving behind five children and Joanne. I got right back on the plane to attend the memorial service. Our brief reunion had taken on a whole new meaning, and I was grateful that we'd had a chance to get to reconcile. He'd made it clear how much he cared for me. I'd grown up believing he'd left because he didn't love us. Now I knew he'd spent all those years wishing he'd never left.

At his viewing ceremony, I couldn't believe how young he looked, how short life is. I was unhappy with my game and my life. It was time to find out who I really was.

Part Three

Seventh-Inning Stretch

10 *Bedhop or Drop*

ENDUROMAN ~ HEADING EAST ~ 49ERS AND COWBOYS ~
BUD LITES ~ MICKEY MANTLE SYNDROME ~ PITCHERS
AND CATCHERS ~ LIKE A TACKY PORN FLICK ~ THE
PROSPECT OF LOVE ~ SUICIDE SQUEEZE

THE MOST BEAUTIFUL young women have an uncanny way of shadowing big-league clubs. The moment we walked through the front door of the team hotel, they'd be ensconced in the bar, hoping we'd wander in for a drink. On the road, they knew, players are easier targets than closer to home, where mothers, wives, and girl-friends stand guard.

In the clear light of day, guys would vow to stay in, order room service, watch a game or a movie, and get to bed early. But by evening, after a stressful game and a few drinks, inhibitions would be ready to crumble. I seemed to be popular among these female groupies. Most of the time I could duck out of sex—feigning exhaustion or the need to call home. But over the course of a season and a career, marriage was the best—and only—real excuse. And even that didn't always suffice. When two eager women get in the elevator with you and your roommate, you've run out of excuses.

"Hey, Beaner, you need to get laid," my teammates would chide.

"Man, I'm not really up for it."

"Come on, Beaner, you're struggling. You need to blow off some steam."

To be one of the boys, I played along. Later, in a hotel room, the lights would dim with our inhibitions thrown by the bedside. As my buddies and I caught one another's eyes across the room, we'd try not to laugh. When it was over, we'd send the girls away with the promise to call them back the next day, which of course never happened. The peer pressure to perform would have relented, and I could relax for a while.

I chuckled when I realized I'd earned a reputation as one of the biggest lover boys. Anna used to brag to her girlfriends that I had tremendous sexual stamina. Maybe my perfectionism spilled over into the bedroom, but in truth the reputation was based on the emotional gap I felt with the opposite sex. Word of my exploits got around, and soon my buddies were calling me "Enduroman."

I never got why some women, with so much going for them, would practically beg players to "hook up." After all, we were no better than other guys, and sometimes worse. It was a time when sleeping around was just part of the big-league mystique.

Ballplayers never spoke about other players' private lives, with any girl, no matter what. That was sacred. But I felt like a big brother to these women, and standing at the bar with them, I'd warn them by saying something along the lines of, "Protect yourself. It's so easy to get hurt because we're always on the road, and we'll be leaving soon." They were surprised to have a ballplayer treat them like human beings. They were young and carefree, and they were willing to risk their hearts. But watching them made me tell myself, despite my conflict about my sexuality, that Anna, with her indifference to big-league life, must be the right one for me.

~

IN THE WINTER of 1992, I'd come off a miserable nine-month stint in Japan after the Dodgers had sold my contract to the Kinetsu Buffaloes of the Pacific League for $100,000. It was weird to have my hometown team barter my rights away. But my future with the Dodgers was limited, and the deal gave me the freedom to pursue better opportunities.

Japanese ball was top-notch, and Dennis negotiated the best deal of my still-young career. A lot of big leaguers had played there, including Warren Cromartie. I received $195,000 plus $40,000 in incentives for the first year, with a mutual option for 1993 for $300,000. Not bad for less than a year of work. But as soon as I arrived, I felt lonely and isolated. Unlike South America, where I'd immediately felt at home, Japan held little interest for me. I spent most of my time playing ball, working out, reading, and watching videotapes of American TV that my family mailed to me. I hope I never see another rerun of "Cheers" for the rest of my life.

I saw Anna only twice during this season in the Far East. I promised to join her in the off-season at her parents' rambling home in Potomac, Maryland, just outside Washington, D.C. I figured it would give us the time we needed to get reacquainted. I'd never lived on the East Coast, and when we weren't checking out the nation's capital, I could spend the winter days working out. Declining my option with the Buffaloes, Dennis secured me a minor-league contract to play for the San Diego Padres. I knew it was my best, and perhaps last, chance to stick.

Things were finally starting to fall into place. I hoped that by making my marriage a priority, I could get beyond the "gay thing" I'd happened across in West Hollywood. I convinced myself that my uncertainty about marriage was nothing more than age-old male resistance to intimacy after taking the plunge.

~

ON A SNOWY SUNDAY afternoon in early January, I settled into the couch, protein shake in hand, to watch one of those classic playoff duels between the San Francisco 49ers and the Dallas

Cowboys, back when that rivalry mattered. I'd been looking forward to the game all week. But among the many things Anna and I didn't share was a passion for football. She decided we had to go shopping *right* then.

"Billy, I don't want to go out in the cold alone," she whined. "I want you to come along for the ride."

I wasn't in the mood to argue, so off we went to the fabric store. As I listened to the game on the radio as we drove, I noticed a Bally's gym that was much closer to our home than the one we had been going to. I suggested we start working out there. Knowing my near-obsession with getting in shape to prepare for the season, she agreed.

The next day, we headed to our new gym. As I changed into my workout gear in the locker room, minding my own business, out of the corner of my eye I noticed a striking man. The idea of homosexuality may still have been pretty new to me, but I'd managed to develop a type anyway. And there he was, incarnate, my fantasy come to life: black hair slicked back, loose blue jeans, perfectly defined chest. With his square jaw, chin dimple, and dark skin, he looked like he could be Mediterranean.

Our eyes locked. I tried and failed to imagine myself being as appealing to him as he was to me. Then I reminded myself of my renewed commitment to my marriage. Fortunately, I'd had plenty of practice suppressing my desires. Nine months in Japan had seen to that. I finished dressing, slammed my locker shut, and hurried out to meet Anna in the weight room upstairs, where we would begin our grueling routine together. And I kept trying to forget about that handsome stranger.

~

As I LAUNCHED into leg presses, my mind wandered back to my first true experience with a man, a little more than a year earlier, in 1991.

I was playing for the Dodgers' triple-A club in Albuquerque. With the way all the guys behaved that year, we might as well have been a triple-X club. After one summer day game, a group of players went out to a country-and-western bar. We were off the next day, so we were looking forward to a wild evening.

Like a character from *Urban Cowboy,* a bouncer hurled a drunk out the door just as we arrived. As we stepped over the body, Brian Traxler, our rotund first baseman, roared, "Men, this is the place!"

It was dominated by a giant, oval, two-step dance floor that looked like a racetrack. Garth Brooks, Travis Tritt, and Wynona Judd boomed out of the massive sound system. Even the women were decked out in cowboy hats and boots.

I stood at the bar and downed Bud Lite while my teammates hit on the prettiest girls. The crowd was having fun, but no matter how hard I tried and how much alcohol I consumed, I couldn't get into it. For the last decade I'd been hanging out in bars just like this, and I didn't know how much longer I could cope with stale beer, loud music, and bad pick-up lines. Before long, I'd polished off about eight drafts, and I was ready to head home. This was always the time when the pressure to flirt with girls escalated, the time when the ballplayers prove they can party all night and still perform on the field the next day. I thought up a term for the mind-set: the "Mickey Mantle syndrome." I was no Mantle, in more ways than one.

"Beaner, you haven't picked anyone up yet," Traxler said, leading me back to the bar and ordering me another beer. "Get out there and dance."

"Give me a break, Traxy, I'm married."

"If that chick knew what was good for her, she'd be here instead of jerking off in L.A.," he said.

I promised to hang out until I finished the beer. The only good thing about all the drinking and cruising was that by the next morning everyone tended to forget exactly what had transpired. Pretending to go to the bathroom, I made a dash for the door.

I made my getaway, but the night was still young. I had a buzz going, and I figured it was only fair that I have some fun of my own for a change. I grabbed a taxi and, as casually as I could, asked the cabbie if he knew of any gay bars in town. You can always count on cabbies in tough situations. They know everything about a town, and some nervous young guy looking for a gay bar is pretty tame compared to the stuff they've seen. After all, the driver had no idea I was a ballplayer. Laboring in minor-league obscurity, *I* wasn't even sure I was a ballplayer.

He reeled off about five or six options. Not sure there was any such thing, I asked him to take me to a "nice" bar. He dropped me off in front of The Ranch, a country-and-western club that was divided into video and leather bars.

Flipping him a $20, I thanked him for being so kind. I was so nervous I thought I was going to be sick right there on the sidewalk. As the door opened, I envisioned my parents sitting on bar stools, staring disapprovingly. I darted straight to the bathroom. Where was my Superman outfit when I really needed it? After a long motivational speech to myself in the stall and a splash of water on my face, I took a deep breath and walked into a whole new world. I found an empty seat in front of the bartender. Even ordering a drink became a challenge.

"I've never seen you in here before," the bartender said, breaking the ice. "Where you from?"

I told him I was on a business trip and asked for a beer.

"Welcome to Albuquerque," he said with a big grin. "This one's on the house."

Wow. A gay bar *and* I didn't even have to pay for beer! I took a big slug. I'd imagined this moment for some time. As I scanned the place, I was surprised by its ordinariness. Since most of my knowledge of gay life came from lurid movies and my teammates' expletives, I expected something a little kinkier. But here were all these regular guys, not unlike me. The only difference was that there were more guys than girls and the girls were only interested in each other.

I stared at the music videos. After what couldn't have been more than ten minutes, a nice-looking man, probably in his mid-forties, introduced himself. With his sandy hair, glasses, and polo shirt, Jim looked like a preppy college professor. Buying me another beer, he asked me if I wanted to see the other bar, which was separated from the main one by a swinging door.

This scene was a little less ordinary. Guys roamed around in leather. Four video monitors ran continuous porn loops. My eyes were popping out of my head, but I did my best to pretend I was used to all this. The subject of the videos inspired us to get right to the point. I wanted him so badly I was shaking like a rookie pitcher in Yankee Stadium, but I'd apparently swallowed my tongue. Jim took the lead and invited me home.

Gulp.

We made the five-minute walk in silence. A yard of cactus and sand led up to a small adobe house. Jim offered me another beer. I settled for water. He led me to the couch. Only an idiot believes it when someone says it's his first time, but it didn't take him long to figure out that in my case it really was.

After some awkward conversation, we headed to the bedroom. As I fumbled eagerly with his clothing, I'd no idea what went where and how. Like a veteran catcher working with a wild young pitcher, Jim managed to slow me down and put me at ease. Pretty soon we were moving together with the rhythm of experienced battery mates. It felt like the most natural thing on earth. Even though fireworks never went off, it was exactly what I was looking for. Afterwards, he kissed me and asked me to spend the night. I wanted to avoid hurting his feelings, but as my buzz faded, reality came crashing down. I was a married man.

As gently as possible, I told him that I had to go. He wrote down his number, stuffed it in my pocket and asked me to call him. As I left, I placed the card in his mailbox as I ran out to the cab he'd called for me. I was too secretive to see him again or thank him for his contribution to my life. But Jim had unwittingly helped me figure out who I really was.

It wasn't long before these bars became a sporadic part of my post-game ritual. To feel comfortable in these dusty joints, I made up an alternate identity. I usually went by the name "Bobby"—just some good ole boy on a business trip. No one caught on. The bad thing about being a benchwarmer is that you rarely get recognized. The good thing about being a benchwarmer is that you rarely get recognized in a gay bar when you are trying your best to keep your secret identity intact.

The occasional sex I had with the men I met was more intoxicating than the alcohol I swore off after every encounter. But I never allowed myself to form anything other than a brief attachment, knowing full well the likely effects of something more on my perfect marriage and my perfect career. The sex was hot but furtive and lacking in the warmth and intimacy I craved but didn't yet know how to handle. After a quick shower, I'd be heading back to my hotel room across town, berating myself for yet another "relapse," and trying to get my head ready for the next day's game.

~

AS I GAZED at the handsome stranger in the Bally's locker room, I realized just how deluded I'd been. This was clearly no phase or relapse. I steadied myself long enough to complete my workout with Anna, once again channeling my sexual energy into physical activity.

Back in the male bastion of the locker room, after my workout, there he was again, freshly showered, combing his hair in the mirror, towel wrapped around his narrow waist. I'd planned to meet Anna for a swim, but now I thought, *Maybe I am done working out for the day!*

If my teammates had ever suspected the easy sexual camaraderie of gay men, they would've laughed—or perhaps cringed. What developed was like a scene from some tacky porn flick. As I stripped off my T-shirt and shorts at my locker, I tried my best to look at him in a dignified way. My effort must have been pathetic. He could tell I was transfixed. As I passed by him on the way to the shower, I gently brushed against his body with my arm.

I closed my eyes and let the scalding water relax my body. When I opened my eyes, I was startled to see him, through the steam, showering all over again. The locker room was deserted, and I said a silent prayer for it to remain that way.

Then this stranger did the most startling thing. He walked directly into my shower stall, reached down and grabbed hold of me below the waist. Talk about taking matters into your own hands.

"When can we get together?" he whispered in my ear, stroking me.

I didn't know what to say. The boldness of this proposition made Jim's approach seem positively demure. Should I tell him the truth?

"My wife is waiting for me outside," I responded. "I can't see you now."

This revelation didn't discourage him. After all, he had all the evidence of my interest he needed right in his hand. He whispered his name—Sam—and phone number into my ear and departed. I repeated his number until it became permanently fixed in my brain. I felt my heart thumping in my throat. I turned off the hot water. I needed a cold shower before I could find Anna and head home.

~

THE NEXT DAY, I made up a cockamamie excuse about seeing a trainer about my cranky throwing shoulder. I ran down to the basement to find the privacy to call Sam so many times that Anna finally asked me what I was looking for. The first two times I dialed I hung up without leaving a message. There was only one phone line in the house, and I was afraid one of Anna's parents would pick up the extension and overhear me talking with a strange man. On the third try, I croaked out a time and place onto his answering machine.

I was thinking of Sam in the pornographic terms of our first encounter. After all, I'd never allowed myself to become romantically attached to any of the men I'd been with. This had the effect of intensifying the pleasure of the encounters—I knew they would be one-time deals. I couldn't even imagine what it would be like to be with a man romantically. Could two men develop anything more than a sexual relationship?

It was twenty degrees and snowing when I pulled up at the Bally's around lunchtime. There he was, sitting in the lobby of the gym. Wearing a black leather jacket, he looked as fidgety as I felt. Smiling, he told me to follow him in my car. A few minutes later, he pulled up in front of a big, modern town house.

I had only one thing on my mind. But it didn't take me long to realize that Sam had a very different agenda. He took my coat and showed me around the house, lingering over photos of family and friends. I asked him about his national origin. After hesitating, he told me his family was from Iran. It turned out later he feared I would reject him for his ethnic background, a common concern for Americans of Middle Eastern origin. He led me into the kitchen, where, over my protests, he began preparing lunch.

Before long, the place filled with exotic fragrances, as he whipped up a salad with lemon dressing, Persian rice with seasoned chicken, topped off by homemade baklava and rich Iranian tea. In less than an hour, he'd made me feel completely comfortable. He seemed to understand instinctively that asking me too many questions was a bad idea, so we chatted mostly about his life.

Sam Madani had a story that couldn't have been more different from my own. His family had been among the elite whose financial fortune was frozen and then seized during the Iranian revolution of 1979. He'd lived a life of luxury in Paris and New York City until it all vanished. Now he sold insurance for Prudential, but he was grateful to have found a home in the United States.

After lunch, we sat down on his long white couch. The closet teaches some weird notions about the rules of love and affection. I'd never willingly kissed a man before, reserving that for women and especially my wife. Women, I had told myself, were about love, commitment, and affection; men about sweaty, physical sex.

I surprised myself by reaching over, placing my hand on the flat stomach I'd admired at the gym, and gently touching my lips to Sam's. I tasted the warm, salty, tea flavor of his mouth with a kind of wonderment. My eyes closed, and I felt a warm feeling spread across my body. As my cheek brushed against Sam's, the sensation of stubble against skin captivated me. It made a noise almost like two sheets of sandpaper rubbing together.

This was different from my other experiences. There was no rush to disrobe. We felt content just being near each other, and it was a while before we headed downstairs to his bedroom. I had planned to be with Sam for an hour, max. By the time I finally showered and dressed, it was after 5 P.M. We'd spent the entire afternoon together.

I hurried out the door. *Anna's gonna kill me.*

~

As I DROVE, I choked up. I'd never felt so at peace with someone. *So this is what it's like. This is what I've been missing all these years.*

Then reality sunk in. I'd just thrown my resolution not to be with another man out the insulated window of the Amatos' house. Anna and I were headed for heartbreak right under her parents' roof. I wasn't only a cheat. According to my born-again teammates, I was going straight to hell. In my cycle of guilt, shame, and repentance, I started loathing myself all over again.

When I got back home, I could barely even look at my wife. I resorted to my most ridiculous rationalization yet. I told myself that being with a man wasn't really cheating. It didn't "count" in the way being with a woman would have. At the same time, I realized my excuses weren't helping either of us. In a matter of days, my life took on a frightening clarity. My marriage was a sham. I hatched a plan to separate from Anna before I left for spring training in a few weeks.

Could I really fall in love during a single afternoon? And with a man? I'd no idea where this was going, or if Sam was even interested in me, but for once I didn't care. I had to find out where it might lead. I even thought about inviting him to visit me in San Diego. The prospect of happiness, the sense of fulfillment this man seemed to offer, was impossible to deny any longer. I'd sacrificed everything for the game since I was a skinny, dirt-splattered kid racing around the diamond. Some people give everything up for love; I'd given it all up for the game—a glorious game to be sure, but one which, I was then beginning to realize, forced me to compromise my personal life for my livelihood.

I was ready to take the next step—trying to maintain my professional life while leading some semblance of the personal life I wanted. In the back of my mind, I knew I was squaring around for a suicide squeeze. I just had to focus on getting the bunt down and in fair territory.

11 *The Big Show*

ONLY IN AMERICA ~ THE PASSION OF FARSI ~ TRADE
YOU TO SAN FRANCISCO ~ BRAD AUSMUS AND MY FEAR OF
FAGGOT BOMBS ~ TONY GWYNN'S TEAM ~ A BOXER, NOT A
BASEBALL PLAYER ~ FIRST BIG-LEAGUE HOME RUN ~ THE
ROXY ~ SAD MANTRA OF MY DOUBLE LIFE

S AM WAS SUPPOSED to be a mere dalliance. But just one week
later, I found myself on the way to the San Diego airport to pick
him up. We had spoken on the phone twice since I had returned
to train with my new teammates that January.

He didn't even know my real name; I'd introduced myself as
"Bobby." I was so used to lying about my identity that in my hasty exit
on that snowy day, I'd forgotten to tell him the truth.

The reality of what I was doing hit me as I walked through the airport. I reminded myself that I should be in my hotel room, resting and
focusing on my training in hopes of making the big-league roster. But
here I was, complicating my life in ways I couldn't foresee.

I was patrolling the baggage-claim area when I felt him tap me on
the shoulder. I was so happy to see him that I dropped the cool
demeanor I'd practiced on my way there.

On the drive home, I owned up about the lie. It was the first time
I'd told another gay man the truth about my identity—Billy Bean. I

held back the ballplayer wrinkle. But once we got to my hotel room, he saw bats, gloves, cleats, and workout gear strewn everywhere. Even a sports innocent like Sam could figure out what I did for a living. He wasn't impressed.

"They pay you to run around the bases?" he laughed. "Only in America."

~

After spending the 1992 baseball season in the Far East playing for the Buffaloes, I'd signed a minor-league contract that winter with the Padres. From the moment of my arrival in San Diego, I was on a mission. This was my big chance to get back in the bigs, and I wasn't about to screw it up. At the age of twenty-nine, time was running out.

Maybe I couldn't control the bounces, the speed, or movement of the pitches or whether my name appeared on the lineup card. But I could control the shape my body was in. While being fit might not help me get around on a 95-mile-per-hour fastball, it certainly wouldn't hurt. If I lined a pitch toward right field, my athleticism and strength might help propel the ball into the gap, allow me to take an extra base, or even hit the ball out of the park. With my position on the cusp of the majors, I was going to give myself every conceivable advantage. I'd seen too many guys lose their edge by becoming content and lazy.

I got up at the crack of dawn each morning, consumed a breakfast of oatmeal, toast, and orange juice, and headed to Jack Murphy Stadium. I got to know a large group of players who lived in the area during the off-season, including Tony Gywnn, Trevor Hoffman, Brad Ausmus, Brady Anderson, Steve Finley, Andy Benes, and Jesse Orosco. The guys with guaranteed contracts tended to skip the endurance workouts organized by our team trainer, Larry Duensing, whom we affectionately called "Dirt."

When you're not playing winter ball, the only pressure during the off-season is to stay in shape. Free of the stress of competition, guys tend to cut up and just enjoy the camaraderie. The talk is about which player signed with what team, and for how much, who got released, and which guys went to seed as soon as the season ended. A lot of my new teammates were married or had steady girlfriends. For ballplayers, the off-season is known as "the wives' time." Guys worked out and then went home to their families, just like working men everywhere. So the fun stuff had to wait until spring training, when the endless travel began.

The morning workouts started off with six sprints up and down the four massive spiral ramps that are the stadium's signature. By the time I'd gone up and down the steep grade for the final time, my legs were on fire. It was a measure of how maniacal I was—or how resigned the guys were to letting me prove it—that I invariably finished first.

After running came half an hour of abdominal and lower-back exercises and then stretching as we cooled. It would've been easier to sleep in and rely on our natural talents. You really find out what your teammates are made of—and it wasn't all muscle, I can tell you—when they are on the verge of puking their guts out. There was major bonding going on. We were busting our butts, and our first game was not for another two months.

There were long lines to hit in the indoor batting cages, and a dozen or so players on the field, working on fielding drills. I'd spend the next two hours working on my stroke, with my simple formula: batting tee, hitting soft-tossed balls into a net, and then live batting practice in the indoor cage on the third floor of the stadium. After hitting, I'd spend half an hour long-tossing, ice my shoulder. Then I'd drive home, where I'd eat lunch, take a short break, and head right to the gym, this time for weight training.

Baseball is as much mental as physical, and you spend a lot more time thinking about your next play than you do actually making it. The game moves at a slow pace with quick bursts of activity followed by rest again, so I was always looking for more strenuous outlets. I wanted to run around and break a sweat the way basketball and football players do. I got a tremendous rush from flirting with the limits of exhaustion, and even though my teammates were always saying I was nuts, I think they admired me for my discipline. Still, I would have traded my conditioning for Tony Gwynn's swing any day. I found the baseball saying "you can't teach talent" is sadly true.

After every session, I couldn't wait to get back home to Sam. In my state of romantic bliss, it occurred to me that some of my on-field ambition had stemmed from the lack of love and joy in my personal life. Overnight, everything seemed less grim; I laughed out loud when I swung awkwardly in the cage or overthrew the cut-off man in a drill, and I actually felt like I was living in the moment. My usual calculated control was disappearing. I was falling in love, and there was nothing I could do about it.

"I love you more than my eyes," Sam told me in the language of his homeland.

Huh?

"The passion of Farsi does not translate well," he said with a gleam in his gaze. "It means I love you more than life itself."

He was adamant that we were right for each other.

"We do this 'thing' between us all the way, or it's over," he announced after our first week together in my cramped hotel room. "Long-distance relationships are too painful. I can't live without you."

As usual, my love was more complicated. I was a married ballplayer from California. I'd fallen for an Iranian exile living on the other side of the country. It was hard for me to wrap my simplistic emotional life around this radical new arrangement. Gay or straight—which way should I go?

Sam advised me to "listen to my heart." It wasn't about my sexuality, he said. By that point, after all, he had a pretty good idea of exactly what turned me on. "Do you want to live honestly, or live a lie? Do you really want to be happy?"

He was right. But given the unfriendly atmosphere of my job, living honestly with him meant I had to lie about everything else. Acting "straight" meant I only had to lie to myself. It always had been easier to be miserable. To be happy I would have to begin the longest, most arduous undertaking of my life. It would make getting around on Roger Clemens' fastball look easy.

The hardest thing was facing Anna. Deep down, I knew our marriage was over. Overcompensating for the guilt I felt, I soft-pedaled my desire to break up. Succumbing to her sadness and tears whenever I hinted at divorce, I told her I just "needed more time to figure out what I wanted from my life." I had placed my baseball career above her right to be aware of a change of heart that affected her future. By failing to be more decisive, I made her endure more pain than necessary. After much back-and-forth, we reached an agreement. We would separate and, after the season, decide whether to go through with a divorce. I was pretty sure I'd already made up my mind.

~

SPRING TRAINING CAME as an enormous relief. Shortly after putting Sam back on a plane to D.C., where he still had a job and a home, I was on my way to Yuma, Arizona, home to the Padres' training facility. There was nothing to do there but play ball, golf a little, and watch TV with my new buddies. I had plenty of time and space to sort out my feelings toward Anna and Sam. On the phone each night to Sam, it wasn't hard to figure out what I wanted.

While starting out in minor-league camp was no fun, I was confident that it wouldn't be long before I started turning heads. Playing every day in Japan, where I'd hit .330 over the previous summer, had locked me in at the plate. Sure enough, when the season rolled around, the Padres started me at their triple-A affiliate in Las Vegas, the Stars.

After batting .350 the first month of the season, I got the call up. For the first time in my career, I believed that I belonged. I wasn't overwhelmed or overmatched. My stomach had butterflies the size of baseballs, but in a strange way that's the best part of being a professional. The feeling reminded me I was back in a wonderful world where every day is a test of wills, where the gladiator mentality ruled. The Padres manager, Jim Riggleman, told me from the outset to be ready for anything, so I pretended I was going to be in the starting lineup every day, and let the chips fall where they may.

I didn't take long to settle down and feel at home.

The small-town atmosphere of San Diego was so much more relaxed and low-key than either Detroit or, especially, L.A. had been. Which may explain why it was not usually a contender. I knew a couple of the guys on the team from my Dodger days, and I had played in Detroit with outfielder Phil Clark, who was one of the Padres' best hitters. I roomed with Phil until the team acquired catcher Brad Ausmus, and then he and I ended up sharing a room. I barely knew the guy, but he practically stepped through the door giving me a friendly hard time.

"Hey, Beaner, this finally gonna be your year?" he said, slapping me on the back. "Or are you going to sit on the bench with splinters up your ass like you did with the Dodgers?"

"I get more hits off the bench than you do with 500 at-bats," I shot back. "They're gonna teach me to catch, and you'll spend the year backing *me* up."

Brad was the personification of a light-hitting catcher. But through hard work in the cage and one of the strongest arms around, he would go on to become an all-star. A Dartmouth grad, he was known for calling an intelligent game behind the plate. I envied his job security and his daily place in the lineup, which kept him sharp.

Brad and I talked about my looming divorce. With his rugged good looks and intellectual bent, he was in heavy demand with the women who seemed to follow him around. He was wise enough to realize it was probably *not* a good idea to settle down before he'd had a chance to play the field, and he saw my breakup with Anna in that context.

"You'll feel better once you start meeting chicks again," he told me one day over beers at the hotel bar, doing his best to reassure me.

"You're not so easy on the eyes, Beaner, but if I meet a chick I don't want, I'll send her your way."

Maybe if she had a brother. Despite his tough-guy banter and conservative politics, Brad was actually pretty sensitive. He was mature enough to handle my secret.

After three or four Buds, the truth threatened to trip off my tongue. But then the familiar dread of revelation swept back over me, and I imagined Brad dropping a faggot bomb on me in the clubhouse. *What would happen if we got into an argument? What would happen if he got pissed at me about some girl?*

I stepped back from the precipice. Guys were always squabbling about minor stuff, and it didn't take a lot to ruin your reputation. In this hyper-competitive world, you never knew when even a teammate would turn on you. I wasn't just being paranoid. I'd seen it happen. My teammate Bruce Hurst was a crafty veteran lefty who'd been very successful in Boston. He was very religious. He relentlessly rode one of our other pitchers for his fashionable dress. "If you don't stop wearing that stuff, we're going to trade you to San Francisco," he'd repeat.

Bruce thought he was being funny, but he wasn't. He was really questioning a fellow pitcher's manhood and heterosexuality because of the guy's concern for his appearance. I wasn't close to either guy, but the hazing was a reminder of how careful I needed to be. You didn't have to provide a lot of evidence to suddenly find yourself the victim of gay-baiting. Just an inkling of difference could set off some of the more homophobic players.

The Padres were a team in flux. Right from the start there was tension because Tom Werner, our owner, was threatening to dismantle the team to reduce the payroll, which was laughably low. High-price players like Gary Sheffield and Fred McGriff felt the pressure of a potential trade. It didn't take long for Werner to ship Sheffield to the Florida Marlins for Trevor Hoffman. Archi Cianfrocco arrived the same day as Trevor, and McGriff went next to Atlanta. Hurst and Greg Harris were packaged to Colorado. The shakeup left us with fewer stars and an even smaller payroll (though we weren't exactly going hungry), but we became a much more close-knit team. We were now the perennial batting champion Tony Gywnn's team. His calm presence, strong work ethic, and amazing ability made an impression on the young guys.

~

I WAS EAGER to put down roots. Between playing, working out, and traveling, there isn't much spare time during the season, so I'd get up early to go house hunting. I focused on Del Mar, a picturesque city on the ocean twenty miles north of the stadium. It was a comfortable distance from the rest of the guys, which would help protect my privacy— or so I hoped.

The three-level condo with ocean views that I chose was three blocks from the beach. I was earning close to $200,000, but I couldn't predict my income beyond the season. It was a financial stretch for a guy without a guaranteed contract. Flush with cash from my lucrative Asian stint, I took the plunge. I wanted a place nice enough to share with Sam, whom I'd been flying out to see me for long weekends every ten days or so. When I told him I'd found a house, he jumped on the next flight to San Diego to check it out.

It took us about five minutes to decide to live together. He quit his job, packed up his stuff, and moved in with me for good. I was stepping onto a whole new playing field. Except for short periods in the off-season with Anna, I'd never lived with anyone other than a slovenly, beer-guzzling teammate. Now I was shacking up with a male lover.

I devised an elaborate plan to keep our life together an ironclad secret. On the rare occasion when we were outside our home together, displays of affection were out of the question. Sam would avoid Jack Murphy Stadium and the public events associated with the team.

Then there was the little problem of my family. Mom and Ed lived just fifty miles north of me, in Dana Point. My siblings and their growing stable of kids lived nearby. The move had given me a chance to spend a lot more time with all of them. But how to explain Sam's presence? We came up with the excuse that he did a lot of business on the West Coast, and that I let him stay in one of my guest bedrooms. He and I joked about the kind of "business" he was actually doing.

Whatever questions my family may have had about Sam were deflected by the pleasure they took in spending time with him. They had never been close to a Middle Easterner before, and he was a charismatic ambassador to a wonderful culture. He mesmerized them with stories about his family and the Iranian revolution. One of four siblings raised by a nanny in a desert mansion with private drivers and chefs, at thirteen he'd been sent away to boarding school in Austria, where he learned four of the six languages he spoke. He regaled them with stories about his wealthy father, a top official in the shah's government, and the tragedy that befell the family.

Growing up in heavily Muslim Iran, Sam was no stranger to hiding. But he'd also lived a cosmopolitan life, and that helped give me perspective on baseball. My sacrifices paled in comparison to Sam's fleeing his homeland to escape religious and political oppression. Just by being comfortable in his own skin, he helped me overcome the stigma of homosexuality I carried around with me. Sam wasn't particularly religious. But he had a very simple moral framework that didn't allow room for the self-flagellation I practiced.

"We're all here for a reason," he'd say. "Everyone's life is important. Someday you'll understand what I'm saying."

~

THE HOUSE CAME together quickly. I gave Sam my credit card, and when I was on a road trip, he made use of the free time to pick out furniture and all the little things it takes to make a house a home. He set up the kitchen first, stocking it with Iranian spices and a peculiar pot for his beloved tea. Then he selected casually elegant furniture and contemporary art for the walls. He created a flower garden on the terrace.

Sam had impeccable taste. When it came to decorating the house, the benefits of my new "lifestyle" suddenly became clear. My wealthy teammates complained when their wives lavished money on their decorators, but I certainly didn't need to worry about that. I had one living with me.

The most wonderful addition to my home, however, was Sam himself.

"As long as I'm living in this house, you'll never have a bad meal again," he declared.

Boy, was he right. Every night was another adventure in Persian cuisine. Like a hurler working on a new pitch, he would spend hours perfecting a recipe before he even began to prepare the meal. I lacked the patience for that kind of stuff, but it isn't hard to respect the fine art of good food, especially when you're the beneficiary of it.

"Americans and their fast food," he joked. "You never rest. You've no idea how to enjoy life."

He did his best to teach me. After all these years in the desert of heterosexuality, Sam was an oasis. Our sex life had been robust from the first steamy moment in the gym showers. I'd known for a while I could enjoy sex with a man. But it was reassuring to discover that this was only the start of a solid relationship, not the relationship itself. We were just like any married couple. We had dinner together. We shopped. We argued about politics. We loved to rent three or four movies and hang out on the couch in the TV room and watch them.

Sam filled the house with music and lots of love. He seemed to wake up every morning in a good mood, and his natural cheerfulness soothed my competitive angst before I headed to the park. I remember wanting to freeze time right there, fretting that it couldn't possibly be this good forever.

"Oh, my Billy, you worry about worrying," he said to soothe my fears. "Everything is going to be all right."

I didn't believe him. When the clock struck one, and it was time for me to go to work, I could feel my body tensing up. I was living a double life, and I reminded myself to monitor my secret as closely as the

Russian embassy in the middle of Washington, D.C. One slip of the tongue, one unguarded moment, could cost me my career.

My new life still blew my mind. Could I actually pull this off? It wasn't like there was a hotline number I could call for advice. As far as I knew, I was the only one in the bigs living this way. Changing in and out of my uniform in the locker room, I would examine my body and remember our lovemaking from the night before. I still couldn't figure out how I'd ended up with desires so different from my teammates'. Or were they? Sam insisted we were all the same under the skin.

But neither of us understood the toll of this furtive way of life until we were already living it, and then it was far too late to turn back.

~

BY THE MIDDLE of my first summer with the Padres, Sam began following my games by radio and television. At first, he had a hard time wrapping his mind around baseball, and he wondered why players ran around the bases counterclockwise. But he caught on fast, and soon became our biggest booster. When I arrived home, he would question me about how I'd played—if I'd seen any action at all. He would erupt in mock rage if he felt someone wasn't hustling or flubbed a play.

I chuckled at his comments, trying to explain that players were no more perfect than cooks, and that errors were part of the game. Since I was basically a role player, I didn't get much chance to make mistakes. You can't throw to the wrong base from the bench. Sam was my biggest fan, and if you asked him, I should've started every game.

Sam began to appreciate baseball's beauty. He listened to me talk about the mental combat between pitcher and batter, and how every game is really just one battle in a grueling, season-long war of attrition. At first, it was hard for him to understand the day-to-day pressure of playing what is essentially a kids' game. I explained that every father wants his son to grow up to be a ballplayer, and that thousands of talented athletes competed for a few spots. He could see that, unlike some players, I respected the game and that I'd been groomed by the best coaches and managers to honor it every day I stepped on the field by playing as smart and as hard as I could.

After a game, he could see its effects on my body. He cleaned and bandaged my knees, skinned and bloodied from sliding and diving. He massaged the deep bruises I would get when I took a 95-mile-per-hour fastball in the ribs, hip, or forearm. He marveled at the calluses on my hands, hardened from swinging a bat hundreds of times every day for twenty years. He made fun of me each morning when I dragged my stiff joints and cranky back carefully out of bed, wincing. As I hobbled around the house or stood under the hot shower to wash the tension out of my muscles and joints, he would express his concern.

"Billy, you look like a boxer, not a baseball player."

Sam knew that the aches and pains were a small price to pay for living my dream. He also knew that our relationship posed great danger for my career, and he loved me for trying to make both work. His pride in what I did gave me a sense of strength, support, and belonging I'd never known.

After a workout at Jack Murphy Stadium one day, I invited Sam into the locker room. Waiting until everyone had left, I met him in the parking lot. As I led him through the corridor into the clubhouse, we traced the steps that I took each and every day on my way to work. He lit up on seeing my name printed in bold letters over my locker and my uniform hanging inside, and the pride he took in my accomplishment made it all worthwhile.

~

DURING A JULY 15, 1993, home game against the Philadelphia Phillies, I hit my first major-league home run, a towering shot against Larry Andersen, a tough right-hander. Sometimes sluggers stand at the plate for a few seconds longer than necessary to admire the ball as it disappears over the fence. My sprint around the bases, however, was the shortest trip

I'd ever taken. I made sure to touch all the bases, but it felt like my spikes never hit the ground. After the game, all I could think about was sharing it with Sam. I sped home, eschewing the usual clubhouse celebration.

Sam gave me a big hug when I walked in the front door. I had to leave soon after on a long road trip, so we planned a private celebratory dinner for when I got home a few weeks later. Sam pulled out all the stops in preparing a gourmet dinner to honor this milestone in my life. As we sat down to enjoy the candlelight meal, he asked me to relive the moment over and over so he could know how it felt. I was embarrassed because this homer was only the first of what I hoped would be many, but I took him through the at-bat anyway. Andersen, who may have lacked a good scouting report on me because I was new to the team, had tried to sneak a fastball by me low and inside. I got all of it.

I'd barely picked up my fork when I heard a knock on the door. I assumed it was a neighbor or a solicitor. Before opening the door, I peeked through the eyehole. Brad Ausmus and Trevor Hoffman, my best friends on the team, were standing there, each holding a six-pack. They were surprised I'd zipped out the clubhouse door on my big day, depriving them of a chance to celebrate with their buddy. They'd decided to surprise me. Somehow, the'd chosen the same night Sam had selected.

I couldn't pretend to be out. They could see my car in the garage and hear the music playing on the stereo.

"Guys, just a minute, I just got out of the shower," I yelled through the door. Since I'd just showered in the locker room after that day's game, the excuse didn't make much sense. But I didn't have enough time to figure out a more convincing lie.

My heart pounding, I rushed Sam out the back door and into the garage, making sure to close the door behind him. Then I raced back into the house and covered up the dinner with dishtowels, pushing the table and all the plates into the corner of the kitchen out of sight. By the time I got back to the front door to let my friends in, I was sweating. They probably assumed I had a girl in my bedroom.

"Hey, Babe Ruth, you can't get away that easily," Brad said, holding up the beer like a trophy. "That was probably your first and last home run, so we'd better enjoy it."

I counted the minutes as they sat there in the living room shooting the bull, drinking, and watching the game highlights on ESPN, and then another game on television, for almost three full hours. As they tried to create a party atmosphere, I kept glancing at my watch, always the sign of an unhappy host. As proper ballplayers, Trevor and Brad stayed until the last beer had been consumed before announcing it was time to go.

"I'll see you guys tomorrow," I said, practically slamming the door behind them.

I'm sure they must have been taken aback by my lack of enthusiasm, and maybe even a little puzzled. I loved these guys for their gesture, and I was dying to celebrate with them. But I couldn't bear the idea of doing it at Sam's expense.

When they finally drove away, I found Sam sitting quietly in the front seat of the car reading a book. As usual, he took my panic stoically, but I could see the hurt on his face when I "allowed" him back into his own home.

I hugged Sam tight, apologized profusely, and tried to reassure him of my devotion. But my proudest individual accomplishment on a baseball diamond had turned into an occasion of sadness and shame. That night was one of the few times I ever cried myself to sleep. I'd left Anna in part because I felt my emotional distance was causing her pain. Now my shame and secrecy had found a way to hurt Sam, too.

~

LATER THAT SUMMER, Riggleman told me I would start a night game against the Colorado Rockies. I decided to throw caution to the wind and make it up to Sam by getting him a ticket. This was his first trip to the park, and it promised to be a special night. Tony Gwynn's career hit total sat at 1,999. The stadium was packed in anticipation of his

2,000th. The sky was crystal-clear, and the San Diego fans were festive and uncharacteristically boisterous. ESPN televised the game to a national audience.

Warming up before the game, I located Sam in the stands and waved. He was sitting next to the parents of my teammate and good friend Phil Clark, and he flashed me a big grin. Beer in one hand, hot dog in the other, he was clearly enjoying himself. I was starting that day in center field, right next to Tony. He got his big hit, putting him well on his way to 3,000, where he would join an elite group of Hall of Fame hitters.

In the first inning, I came to the plate with runners on first and second base. The Rockies' pitcher, Willie Blair, missed with two consecutive curves. Enjoying a hitter's count, I sat on a fastball and got one right down the middle. I turned on the pitch as quickly as I could, belting it into the night air. It landed probably twenty rows above the right-field fence. It was one of those times when you know the ball's gone the moment it meets your bat.

As I rounded third base, I glanced toward Sam in the family section. He was standing in the aisle, giving me an ovation. It was as if I were back in Little League, hitting the winning home run in front of Mom. But this time I pumped my fist into the air and allowed myself, if only for a moment, to enjoy the reverie that Billy Bean, the gay baseball player, had just hit a three-run homer as his proud male lover cheered him on.

In the locker room the next day, Phil asked me, very casually, about my "friend Sam." Apparently, his parents had enjoyed spending the game with him. They simply wanted to know a little about him. They wanted to sit with him again in the future. It had been a completely innocent evening, like the hundreds of social interactions that take place among ballplayers and their friends and family every season. But I became convinced I was about to be exposed. When I got home that night, I told Sam it was the last game he could ever attend.

"That's okay, Billy," he said, looking away. "I like hearing the games on the radio, too."

As usual, Sam was a good sport. I only wish I could have said the same for myself. I was torn between two worlds, and both kept imploding.

~

I OWED IT to Sam to try to unify my life. After the 1993 season, with my teammates scattered across the country, we slowly but surely began to venture out in public as a couple. On a winter trip to New York City, we decided to check out one of the huge downtown gay discos, the Roxy.

On the way, we stopped at the apartment of an Iranian friend of Sam's. A bunch of guys were there warming up for a big night out with a few drinks, and I was introduced as Sam's boyfriend, Billy. This was the first time I'd been out socially with a group of gay men. There was a little buzz in the apartment about the "ballplayer." I played it down, describing myself as little more than a "role player." They looked puzzled at that term, but were really cool about it. Fortunately, Sam didn't know any journalists.

Inside the velvet rope, we were greeted by a blast of hot air. The Roxy looked like the inside of a gigantic gymnasium, except that flashing, multicolored lights darted every which way and the dance music of Madonna, Right Said Fred, and Black Box boomed from wall-sized speakers. Sam and I blended into the crowd. Before long we had taken off our shirts. The warmth of boys squeezed together like fish in a sardine can was a revelation. The music swept me away, and I dropped my guard for the time being.

Whatever stereotypes I had about gay men before that night were left at the coat check. I saw more muscles and young athletic guys than in all the major-league locker rooms I'd ever been in, combined.

Because the lights flickered hypnotically, there was little chance I could be recognized by even the most avid baseball fanatic. (Just to be safe, I kept a black cotton ski cap pulled down on my forehead.) It was one of the few times I *didn't* chafe at not leading the league in hitting and having my face on the Wheaties box.

Sam and I had so much fun that night that, a month or so later, we took a weekend trip to Las Vegas. We spent three days in a luxury suite at the Mirage, where we gambled and enjoyed some shows. Sam was an inveterate gambler, and I watched him play blackjack and baccarat. At night, alone in our suite, we'd fill the whirlpool bath and order a bottle of champagne. Looking at his handsome face, I thought I'd hit the jackpot.

Wandering through the casinos, where everyone is on display, we were likelier to run into another ballplayer than in a gay club in New York. When I found myself looking over my shoulder, Sam reminded me to relax. If I ran into someone from baseball, I could always come up with another story. "When in doubt, lie" became the sad mantra of my double life.

12 *High, Hard Ones*

Magic Johnson's heroism ~ Dangerous games ~
Facing Curt Schilling and Greg Maddux ~ Locked
out ~ Vials of blood ~ The scarlet letter ~ What
Sam knew

Watching Magic Johnson's 1991 television press conference announcing that he was HIV-positive, it was hard to imagine he would ever become ill. Magic looked like he could lead my beloved Lakers to another title, and I couldn't believe how composed he was. The savvy and strength he showed on the basketball court were nothing compared to how calmly he handled his ordeal at a time when AIDS was more deadly.

Johnson's revelation was a high, hard one aimed right at my temple. I'd spent years watching my favorite player slay dragons. He was invincible. How could this have happened? Like a lot of ballplayers, the sum total of my knowledge of HIV and AIDS came from that event, which rocked the sports world. A lot of guys talked about getting HIV tests, but I doubt many did. Many said a silent prayer for having avoided Magic's fate.

I remember devouring the November 18, 1991, edition of *Sports Illustrated* that came in the mail at my place on Curson Road in West

Hollywood while I was still with the Dodgers. One story described the "dangerous games" played by enormously promiscuous pro athletes. "You can get sex every night," Mets shortstop Kevin Elster was quoted as saying. "On the road. At home. It doesn't matter. We're next in line, I guess, after the gays and drug users. The Magic thing has put the fear into all of us."

"We're paid to use our bodies," said a basketball player. "So sex becomes the same thing after games. We become like dogs sometimes, and we all talk about the same women in every city."

The remarks dovetailed with my observations about many of my own teammates, from high school to the pros. Guys were having tons of sex, and few were taking precautions. The story went on to declare that "there is every reason to believe that free and easy sex on the road is just as available to the gay athlete as the straight one."

In fact, the articles appeared at the very time that I was beginning this kind of exploration. But for some reason, I didn't connect the caution to my own experience. At the time of Magic's revelation, I was playing winter ball in Mazatlán. My teammates labeled Magic *"Maricón."* It was typical of ballplayers to assume that only homosexuals were vulnerable to HIV infection. Since they were heterosexual, they were safe. Not really sure which I was, I didn't know what to think.

When it came to sex, ballplayers were a pretty ignorant bunch. In all my years in training rooms, I never saw a single condom or heard a single pitch for protected sex or abstinence. The mandatory health-education session for rookies, lasting one hour, made no mention of HIV or AIDS, even at the height of the epidemic in the mid-1980s. The main concern was to avoid getting "the girl" pregnant. STDs were an afterthought. Boys, they figured, will be boys.

"What's *that?*" guys would laugh when someone pulled out a condom.

It was all winks, jokes, and anecdotes. One morning during instruction league in St. Petersburg, Florida, in 1986, my rookie year, we were swapping stories of sexual conquests during stretching. The Detroit Tigers' famed minor-league coach Johnny Lippon offered some fatherly advice.

"Boys, if you're going *down* there, and it don't seem right, put a second rubber on" he said.

We laughed at Johnny's version of safe sex. This was the same man who would spit into his tobacco bag in front of everyone to insure that nobody asked to bum a chew.

But he was right. "I hate condoms," or "I can't feel a damn thing," or "Let her worry about it," was the view from the dugout. Players rarely considered, at least in front of one another, the consequences of that approach. Like my teammates, I was in a state of denial, and one dark day it was sure to come back to bite me.

~

IT WAS GREAT to be in the bigs—this time, I thought, for good, even though the 1994 campaign was pretty frustrating. During spring training, I owned the second-highest batting average in the major leagues (after Mike Piazza) among players with fifty or more at-bats: a cool .415. I started the season seeing a lot of playing time in center, and I went nine for my first nineteen. I was locked in, but then Tony Gwynn returned from the disabled list, and I was back on the bench.

I went a couple of weeks without so much as a pinch-hitting opportunity. Then Tony developed aother nagging calf injury, and our rookie first baseman, Dave Staton, started getting abused by big-league pitching. I got a bunch of starts against tough right-handed pitchers like Curt Schilling and Greg Maddux. I lost my stroke against their baffling stuff, and I must have gone something like 4-for-40 over the two-month period leading up to the all-star game.

I was in the dumps. I started pressing again, making things worse. My only solace were my pinch hitting stats. I went 12-for-28, a .428 clip, to lead the league. I hit pinch bombs off John Wetteland of Montreal and Steve Reed of Colorado.

But on August 11 the players voted to strike. The owners locked us out, and the season went down the drain. Just my luck. For the established players, losing a few months and a few million dollars was no big deal. But for a guy fighting to establish himself, it was a severe blow. I dreaded the uncertainty of waiting through the extra-long off-season for another shot at my goal. But what happened next reminded me once again that baseball is nothing more than a game.

~

AFTER THIS UP-AND-DOWN season, Sam made his usual trip home to Maryland for the holidays with his sister and her husband. I made the one-hour drive to Dana Point. I'd sneak upstairs after everyone had gone out or to bed just to hear his voice on the other end of the phone line.

Since Anna and I had officially separated, Mom started inquiring about girls. I was nearing thirty, so it was inevitable for her to want me to settle down and have a family—the happy life, as she saw it.

"Mom," I said. "I'm still getting over Anna. Give me a break."

After a few days of this, I was eager to get back home to greet Sam upon his return. But when he walked in the door, he looked a little haggard. Usually energetic and optimistic, he was suddenly lethargic and downcast. There were no specific symptoms, just a general sense of malaise. At first I attributed it to jet lag, or a lingering case of the flu. He'd had a hernia repaired a few weeks earlier. Maybe the operation had become infected. We became concerned a few weeks later when his thick black hair started falling out in clumps.

I made an emergency appointment with P. J. Mullanney, a local ear, nose, and throat specialist whom Sam knew through the local Middle Eastern community. An amiable guy with a bustling practice, the doctor could find no obvious cause for the illness. After drawing a vial of Sam's blood, he sat us both down in his office.

"Have you ever had an HIV test?" he asked Sam.

I froze. Up to that point, I'd imagined something manageable. Suddenly we were dealing with something of an entirely different magnitude, something I had only a dim awareness of from my basketball hero's diagnosis three years earlier. My first thought was that I'd given the virus to him. But I'd been vigilant about Mom's warning "not to get any girls pregnant" when I traveled the country playing ball. I'd always used protection with Anna. What little sex I'd had with men had always been "safe."

But when it came to Sam, I'd let my guard down. We were monogamous, and though we'd never spoken about HIV, it was clear that the last thing either of us desired was a latex barrier between us. In my naïveté it never even occurred to me that my new-found sex life could suddenly be considered risky. Could he have given the virus to me? That was unimaginable, too. He'd always been the picture of health.

Four days later, Sam and I were back in the doctor's waiting room. Dr. Mullanney greeted us right away.

"Come into my office and sit down," he beckoned. "I have something very serious to tell you."

Staring blankly at the floor, Sam said nothing, as if he'd already read the writing on the wall. I struggled to remain composed as the doctor explained that Sam's test had come back positive for antibodies to HIV. My mind went blank as Mullanney explained the treatment options. AZT, 3TC, T-cell counts, viral loads—it was all dismal. The doctor might as well have been speaking Arabic to Sam. When the truth finally hit me, I couldn't hold back the tears as they welled up in my eyes, and I held on to Sam's hand while he remained impassive in his chair.

Then the doctor turned to me: "William, I must ask you a question. Are you sexually active?"

Instead of worrying about my health, my thoughts turned to my demand for secrecy, the permanent obsession of the closeted ballplayer. I'd registered at the office as William Bean, and as far as I could tell no one who worked there had connected me with the ballplayer. As was our practice, we hadn't told the doctor that we were together, avoiding even the appearance of anything beyond friendship. But my reaction to the news had blown my already shaky cover.

My desire for privacy had caused me to misjudge Mullanney. People were usually more perceptive about these things than I gave them credit for, and he was no exception.

Through sobs, I blurted out: "Doctor, I have a very public job."

"Don't worry," he said. "The only people to know will be those you tell yourself."

The floodgates opened. I told him about my marriage to Anna, and that I'd always used protection when I stepped outside of our marriage.

"I just thought, that since it was just me and him. . . . "

I had no excuses for my risky behavior, only explanations. For the first time in my life, I could be both sexually and romantically uninhibited. The desire for that connection was so intense that it had overwhelmed my better judgment.

In truth, I was no different from my heterosexual teammates: in my physical prime, I felt somehow invulnerable to a disease associated with "promiscuous" homosexuals. I'd somehow put myself in another category, not bothering with the facts. There was little doubt, I confessed to Mullanney, that I'd been exposed.

~

THIS WAS BACK in the dark days when it took some time to get your results. It was as if I were holding my breath underwater the whole time. I tried to comfort Sam, holding him as we lay in bed at night. But he wouldn't even look me in the eye, and we barely said a word to each other. He refused to tell me what he was feeling, what, if anything, I could do to help. It was still January, and I got up each day and somehow went through the motions during morning workouts at the stadium. I stopped shaving; my appetite was gone.

I'd gone from denial to panic. Not only was I convinced I'd been infected, I was sure I would keel over the very next day. Every bruise or welt that showed up on my body—the battle scars exhibited by every player—*had* to be Kaposi's sarcoma, the skin cancer that was the scarlet letter of AIDS. My body had never disappointed me before. It terrified me to imagine this diabolical virus eating away at it from the inside.

As usual, I believed I had nowhere to turn for support. Talking to my parents would have meant coming out to them, and I was hardly ready for that, especially in such a dire context. I wasn't prepared to venture into Hillcrest, the San Diego gay mecca a few miles from our house, which abounded with support groups and counseling services. The idea of going to the Padres' trainer or medical staff was unthinkable, tantamount to career suicide when word went round in the organization about the ballplayer with the HIV scare. If one of the best basketball players in history had been forced to quit the game in his prime, what hope was there for a regular like me?

~

WHEN THE DAY of reckoning arrived, we made the twenty-minute drive in silence. It didn't take a brain surgeon to understand the ramifications of two years of unprotected sex with an HIV-positive partner. After what seemed like an eternity, Dr. Mullanney walked into the room and shut the door behind him. I was sitting on the examination table. Sam was perched on a chair in the corner.

"Billy, your test is negative."

Sam let out a wail, dropped to the floor as if he were praying, and put his hands to his face to cover his sobs. He had taken his own results stoically. Now he jumped up and hugged me. I think Sam's relief made me happier than the news itself.

Dr. Mullanney urged us to be more careful. Handing me a big bag of condoms, he told me to get tested every month. He was amazed by our ability to handle all of this on our own, and he recommended a good therapist. All I wanted to do was go home and catch up on all the sleep I'd lost.

For the moment at least, I could stop worrying about becoming baseball's poster boy for AIDS awareness. But Sam's infection cast a pall over everything. The pure joy of the early days of our relationship drained away. As hard as we tried to return to normal, it was impossible to ignore the fact that Sam had to pop these big horse pills of AZT all day long, and that he felt miserable.

Sam withdrew into a shell. He was so fearful of infecting me that it practically eliminated our sex life. I found myself dragging through the days. At night, I would toss and turn until I finally gave up and went to the living room to lie on the couch and stare at the stupefying blur of late-night television.

A couple of years later, I had a conversation with one of Sam's friends, and I learned that Sam had fallen into a similar depression sometime around 1984. He had lived the fast-lane gay life in Paris in the '70s and New York in the early '80s, when HIV spread like wildfire. Maybe he subconsciously knew something that he had found difficult to acknowledge. He was fanatical about his fitness, ate only the healthiest foods, and rarely drank anything but a glass of wine or champagne. It occurred to me that Sam might have knowingly put me at risk.

But one thing I knew for sure was that Sam loved me. His reaction to my negative diagnosis had shown me that. I knew it by the way he lit up around me, by his devotion to the life we had built together. If he'd risked my life, it had been because he feared the truth would drive me away. What he didn't know at the time is that nothing could've done that.

13 *In a Pinch*

BILLY ON THE SPOT ~ LET'S KICK THE FAGGOT'S ASS ~
STUNTMAN ~ SUNFLOWER-DEVOURING, GUM-CHEWING
MACHINE ~ A CLOSER'S WICKED STUFF ~ CHANCE AT
BASEBALL IMMORTALITY ~ HOOKED FOUL ~ CURSE OF A
LONG SWING ~ STRAINS OF MOZART ~ LITTLE PASHA

EVERYONE'S UNDEFEATED in spring" goes an old baseball adage. It's the one time of year when even bench players dream of a perfect season—hitting .300 and driving in the winning run in the seventh game of the World Series. In March, '95, my dreams included immortality for those I loved.

Back in D.C. for an extended visit with his family and getting plenty of rest, Sam was feeling stronger. The AZT Dr. Mullanney prescribed seemed to be having the desired effect. Much to my surprise, I'd been spared, and though the doctor warned me several times that I was still in the "window period" in which antibodies might not show up on the test, I stopped viewing every cough or runny nose as a death sentence.

Getting back out on the field for my second Peoria spring training and third with the Padres helped me put the trauma of the last three months behind me. The labor dispute had been truly nerve-wracking for a scrub like me, locked out for seven months at the age of thirty, helpless as opportunistic scabs crossed the picket lines. It was frustrating to watch the owners litter the fields with "players" who hadn't earned the right to be there.

Now the contract was signed, the team was back together and eager to contend, and there was not a cloud in the endless Southwestern sky. It was an enormous relief to stretch on the damp grass in the morning and to see everybody pile out of the dugouts onto the sun-drenched diamonds at the Padres' training complex.

Merv Rettenmund, my favorite coach, was back as hitting instructor. I had a lot of respect for Bruce Bochy, our laid-back manager with the trademark thick black mustache. Bochy and Rettenmund knew what I could do. If nothing else, I was a "gamer," a guy who could be counted on to stay healthy, show up on time, and get along with everyone. I was the guy who never screwed up on the base paths or overthrew the cutoff man, who came off the bench with a solid left-handed hack. Only the stars are allowed to be problem cases. I was the team's "Billy on the Spot," ready to go at a moment's notice.

Despite the trauma of Sam's diagnosis, I'd come on strong as camp approached. A few months earlier, I'd convinced myself I was on my deathbed. Now, as I walked shirtless through the trainer's room my teammates teased me about the definition of my abdominal muscles.

"Abs are for chicks," declared pitcher Doug Brocail, playfully whacking me in the stomach.

This was the same guy I'd heard shout, in jest, "Let's kick the faggot's ass," as we sat in the team bus driving past some poor soul who matched his preconception of a homosexual. I guess it never occurred to him that the faggot's ass might be perched on the seat next to him.

Just take a look at the bodies of most pitchers and you can understand why they make fun of the rest of us for working so hard to stay in shape. Brocail was a flame-throwing six-foot-six right-hander. He was easily one of the toughest, strongest guys I ever played with or against on a baseball field. But bare-chested in the locker room, he proudly showed off the hairy, bloated belly of a beer leaguer. He reveled in his girth, joking about how many beers it takes to develop a "body like this!"

"You're lucky God zapped that shoulder of yours with a bolt of lightning," I shot back. "Otherwise you'd be paying to watch me play today."

The truth is, appearances don't matter. Check out Gwynn, one of the game's all-time great hitters. Tony was batting an astonishing .394 when the lockout was ordered the previous year. Now he sauntered into the clubhouse at least thirty pounds over his ideal playing weight. We could only shake our heads in amazement at his ability to excel at such a high level in spite of his build. He managed to smoke the ball all over the park, *every day,* for two decades.

~

MY HEALTH SCARE helped me accept that the game wasn't just about conditioning. It was about learning to accept my ability—and its limits—and being able to feel good about what I could accomplish on the field, rather than focusing on what I couldn't. I reminded myself not to try to do too much, a recipe for failure.

My first few years I'd agonized about trying to keep up with stars like Gwynn, Barry Bonds, and Kirk Gibson. That, I finally realized, was simply not going to happen. It was a liberating notion, in a way, because I could still be a solid major leaguer. I was learning to embrace my role as a utility guy—otherwise known as a "stuntman," the baseball equivalent of the Hollywood double who does the stars' dirty work. We reserves took tremendous pride in our work, and when we weren't competing for a spot on the roster, we'd root each other on.

I'd nailed down my role as Gwynn's backup in right field. When Tony and I were in the starting lineup together, I hit third. This placed me in the crucial spot of protecting him in his annual assault on a batting title. Over the three years we had played together, we'd become pals. I took pride in seeing our nameplates, BEAN and GWYNN, side by side over our road lockers.

I was hitting off the batting T into a net one afternoon that spring when Tony happened by. Sitting down on an upside-down bucket, he threw me soft tosses while analyzing my swing, which had this big Ted Williams loop in it I was forever trying to eliminate. The secret to Tony's success was his ability to stay back on the ball as it approached the plate *and* the compactness of his swing once he committed.

"Dude, *relax*," he counseled. "Let the ball come to you. You're quick enough to catch up to it." The advice began to sink in, and I believed .300 was within reach, if only I could get enough at-bats.

At the same time, I was learning pinch hitting, a rare and coveted ability in the designated-hitter-free National League. This was my chance to be Superman again, swooping in to save the day by delivering the key hit when the team needs it most. It's precisely the infrequency of the pinch hitter's work that makes it so tough. Timing is everything, and when you're sitting on your butt for a couple of hours watching your teammates play, you can lose the "feel." Then the manager sends you up to the plate in the ninth inning to face a closer's wicked stuff without having seen anything that day but 70-mile-per-hour batting-practice pitches thrown by a grizzled bullpen coach with a sore arm.

The umpire, considering you a scrub, is unlikely to have any respect for your knowledge of the strike zone. Not only are you coming in cold, you are also forced to be more aggressive than a regular player because you can't afford to get behind in the count. Then you find yourself flailing at a slider or forkball in the dirt. *Strike three.* It's enough to turn you into a sunflower-devouring, gum-chewing machine.

A failed at-bat usually meant a loss because I was used when the game was on the line. After gathering my gear, I would slink back to a quiet clubhouse because I was out of the game. I'd grab a bite from the spread, then head to the showers, where the other guys would stand around hoping the hot water would melt away their frustration. We talked of the what-ifs and bad breaks and who was pitching tomorrow night. Forty-five minutes after the game ended, I would make my way out of the stadium, greeted by family in the parking lot.

"What happened?" they would say. The inevitable question-and-answer period would begin. The frustration of not producing a memory for them could eat you up.

After several of these lessons in humility, a funny thing happened. I actually started to get a feel for this uncanny art. I was a good fastball hitter who didn't strike out a lot. I studied pitchers closely. I was always hyper in the dugout, stretching, swinging a bat, and keeping loose. I yelled at umpires. I encouraged the regular guys. I traded barbs with the other reserves. I conferred with the coaches. Bochy knew I wasn't the type to be in the clubhouse eating ice cream. It helped that I'd played with some of the best pinch hitters in the game: Dave Hansen, Mickey Hatcher, Lenny Harris of the Dodgers, and Dave Bergman of the Tigers. Manny Mota, perhaps the best of all, had been my Dodgers hitting coach.

My Padres team record of five straight pinch hits—7-for-9 overall— started on a road trip early in the year. Like many streaks, it began with a blooper, in this case off the Expos' fire-balling closer Mel Rojas, in Montreal. Then I hit a pea against Mets lefty Eric Gunderson. My confidence was building. In Philadelphia, I bested changeup artist Doug Jones. Back home, I got my fourth off submariner Steve Reed of Colorado. The fifth hit came against Greg Harris of the Rockies.

I didn't learn that I'd tied the record until the start of the next game. That night, Bochy sent me to the plate against Harris again with a chance to break the record and achieve my own minuscule version of baseball immortality. I worked the count to three and one. Harris had to come in. He threw a strike that I nailed deep to right, but it hooked just in front of the foul pole and into the seats for strike two. I'd connected so solidly that on the next pitch I got perhaps a little over-zealous, hitting a frozen rope to second for an out. If I'd waited a fraction of a second longer, I would have driven it up the middle for a hit.

~

AFTER THE LONG LAYOFF, I was happy to reunite with my buddies Brad Ausmus, Trevor Hoffman, and Archi Cianfrocco. During the

Cactus League, we hung out, hit the links, and traded jibes. I could pretend-relax, but it was rarely the real thing. Fearing that my loopy golf swing would screw up my baseball cut, I'd learned to play golf right-handed. I wasn't going to win the U.S. Open, but I found a way to get around the course in pretty decent shape. For baseball players, golf isn't about golf. It's about hanging out, talking trash, betting a dollar a hole, and just being outdoors with your friends away from the pressures of the park.

With their positions assured, these guys knew spring was mostly about getting pitchers into shape for the season, but for me it was always my personal World Series. Younger, faster, less expensive phenoms were always coming up from minor-league camp and angling for my job. This year's version was Ray McDavid, a big kid blessed with a rare combination of raw speed, power, and arm strength. But it soon became clear that Ray, another lefty with the curse of a long swing, couldn't hit at the big-league level.

I missed Sam a lot, especially because we could speak by phone only when Brad, with whom I was rooming again, was out of the room. Or I'd make up lame excuses about needing to pick up something, then use the pay phone in the lobby to check in on him.

"I'm fine, baby," he'd say in his most reassuring voice. "Don't worry about me. The important thing is to get ready for the season. This is gonna be your year. I can just feel it."

I never pressed him further. Selfishly, I took his advice; I had to concentrate if I wanted to stay in the majors. Sam understood me well enough to know the truth—baseball was all I knew. I didn't have any notion how to support Sam on an emotional level, even after all he'd done for me over the last three years.

He was simply convinced I would succeed, and his unshakable faith in me, so naive it bordered on the superstitious, helped propel me forward. He seemed certain that the survival of our unlikely romance through our health crisis was a sign that I was ready for my breakthrough season. More than anything else, Sam, a baseball innocent, provided me with the grounding and reassurance I needed to survive the relentless, grinding pressure of a profession I couldn't imagine living without.

I chose to believe him. Having labored in Peoria for seven weeks, I couldn't wait to see him. I made the seven-hour drive to Del Mar in my Toyota 4Runner. As I hummed along to my favorite song, Jon Secada's "Do You Believe In Us?," I imagined sharing one of our candlelight meals with a Napa Valley Cabernet he'd picked out for the occasion. I looked forward to regaling him with the spring's worth of baseball stories.

And then I was home.

White apron wrapped around his waist, the strains of Mozart in the background, there he was, a smile spreading across his face. As I hugged him, it really did seem everything was going to be okay.

"Welcome home, my little *pasha*," he said, kissing me on the cheek when I was safely inside the front door.

14 *Baseball Players Don't Cry*

Burning with fever ~ Cardiac arrest ~ Pretty
girls your age ~ Playing with pain ~ My buddy Tim
Worrell ~ The star chamber ~ Ungodly sinker ~
A rocket up the middle ~ Humiliating torrent
of tears

TWO DAYS LATER I made the familiar turn into the driveway. I sensed something amiss. The front door was ajar, and I noticed the absence of Sam's ever-present music. In the middle of the white living room carpet was a pool of yellow vomit.

I called Sam's name. Racing upstairs, I found him lying in bed soaked in his own sweat and moaning incoherently. I placed my hand on his forehead: he was burning with fever. I held the back of his head as he gulped down cold water and which he immediately threw back up. I managed to help him out of his clothing and under a cold shower.

I couldn't get his temperature down. I called Dr. Mullanney, who told me to take him to the emergency room. After dressing him in clean clothing, I laid him in the backseat of the SUV and zoomed downtown. I passed the nearby University Town Center Hospital in La Jolla and drove an extra twenty minutes to another hospital, which I assumed would be more convenient for Dr. Mullanney.

You know those nightmares in which your cries for help go unheeded?

That's exactly how I felt once we reached the hospital, except I was wide awake. Sam was nearly comatose, slumped over the waiting-room bench, yet I couldn't get the medical staff to take his obviously deteriorating condition seriously. The nurses forced paperwork on me, fumbled with my insurance card, ignored Sam's obvious suffering. They wanted to know where his family was.

"I am his family," I insisted. Suddenly, I'd been transformed from closet case to gay-rights activist.

"DO I HAVE TO PAY CASH?" I barked.

When I finally secured him a bed, things were hardly better. Sam's temperature was sky-high. He was incoherent, his breathing labored. As I held his hand, I noticed he was turning yellow. Some guy purporting to be a medical doctor, clearly in way over his head, hovered as I adjusted Sam's reclining body. The guy ordered tests and looked puzzled as I pleaded with him.

"Sam, honey, hang on," I whispered in his ear, mimicking what I thought people said in these situations. "I'm going to take care of you. Everything's going to be fine."

I was so used to being on the receiving end of Sam's care that I struggled to comfort *him*. My jocks-are-invincible mentality made it nearly impossible for me to imagine the seriousness of the situation, or how vulnerable he really was. Where were the caped crusaders when I needed them? I willed him to pull through.

After I spent several agonizing hours pacing and fretting, Sam was still deteriorating. I again demanded that the staff "do something." The medical technician brought over a syringe, placing it in his IV tube.

"This will allow him to rest more comfortably," he said.

But Sam *was* calm, eerily so; I was the one who needed sedation. About fifteen minutes later, at about 6 A.M., Sam and I were alone inside the curtain when his breathing became labored. Then he bucked up and down. A beeper sounded.

The medical staff finally leapt into action, slamming his chest with electric panels and forcing a tube down his throat.

"What the hell is going on?" Now I was screaming.

"He's in cardiac arrest," the nurse said.

"What the hell does that mean?"

I knew Sam was gone when I saw the vacant look in his eyes. They kept trying to resuscitate him, but as time went on, their pace slowed. After they pronounced him dead, I sat in a chair next to him for what seemed an eternity. I hadn't even had an opportunity to say good-bye. The "doctor" had failed to take any decisive medical action before it was too late. He said something about an infection, or a ruptured pancreas, mumbled condolences, and went back to his rounds as if this kind of thing happened every day.

I made the trip back home through the morning haze, trying to digest what had just taken place. Cleaning up as best I could, I collapsed on the sofa. When I woke up, numb and exhausted, the only productive thing I could think to do was to call Mom. The most immediate problem was that I was expected at San Diego City Hall at 11:00 A.M. for one of the pre-season team functions players are required to attend. At this one, the lineup included the mayor, business leaders, and Padres boosters, who were just beginning to strategize about building a new downtown stadium.

Since I'd given Mom no reason to believe Sam was anything more than a friend, she had no way of grasping the depth of my despair. Hardened by years of hard work and an early marriage gone bad, she gave me the advice she'd lived.

"Take a deep breath," she counseled. "Call Sam's family. Then remember your obligation to the Padres."

Mom meant well. She drove the forty-five miles to my house to make sure I was okay. It pained me to conceal from her what Sam's death really meant to me. Everything was spinning around me, and I lacked the emotional wherewithal to express my true feelings. All the years of concealment and striving to live up to a phony ideal had stunted my ability to face misfortune.

As we sat on the couch, she wrapped her arms around me, stroking my hair like she had when I was a child.

"No use moping around the house, Billy," she said. "There's nothing you can do, and you'll only feel worse if you don't keep busy."

Apparently, baseball players were not the only ones to spout clichés. I wanted to tell her *everything*. But instead, disoriented by my shocking, sudden loss and stymied by shame, I followed her advice. As I showered and dressed, I couldn't escape the awful remnants of Sam's last hours—a sweat-soaked T-shirt, a half-filled water glass, a bottle of red wine he'd set aside for dinner. I sobbed at the sight of a framed photograph of us together in Las Vegas, where we'd risked exposure to enjoy one of our first vacations together. I had to get the hell out of the house.

~

BASEBALL BILLS ITSELF as the ultimate family sport. The television camera pans in on the players' perfect wives and cherubic kids cheering from the stands. If a player falls into some other category—divorced, gay, or, more likely, "playing the field"—the camera zooms in on his doting parents instead. Staged community events are no exception.

Padres fans fell into two categories, according to gender. The men all wanted to meet Tony Gwynn and Trevor Hoffman, who was blossoming into one of the most dominant closers in the game. Some bigwig city official was polite enough to mention my previous season's five consecutive pinch hits, before digressing into a meditation about whether Gwynn would make another run at .400. The older women boosters, who were usually dragged to such functions by their husbands, doted on and flirted with me. I was the speaker of choice for the San Diego Madres, the club founded by players' wives.

"Do you have a girlfriend, honey?" one woman asked, discreetly scanning my hand for a wedding band. "You're *so* cute. You look young enough to be in high school. I know plenty of pretty girls your age."

I usually enjoyed the attention, returning the flirtations with all the straight-boy charm I could muster. But now every exchange was an intolerable burden. I sputtered through conversations. As the mayor awarded Tony another plaque for his overflowing collection, all I could do was repeat my teammates' automatic response to each other when things got rough: "There's no crying in baseball."

It was a lesson I'd been telling myself for years, in my own version: *Ballplayers show up. A gamer like Billy Bean never gets injured or sick. He plays through pain, and he sure as hell doesn't mourn.*

I was determined to please everybody—Mom, coaches, fans. The world wouldn't have ended had I simply walked out and driven home. Once in a while, the team issues a statement that a player is excused for "personal" reasons or to attend to "family matters."

This had to be one of those situations. There was only one problem: How could I explain that my "family matter" was the AIDS-related death of my male lover with whom I'd been living secretly.

~

AFTER THE EVENT was finally over, my buddy Tim Worrell, a relief pitcher, asked if he could hitch a ride to Anaheim for that night's game, an exhibition against the Angels. I warned him I would be bad company. But I was also relieved at not having to make the long drive alone, even if I couldn't share my feelings. We chatted about the upcoming season. Tim had high hopes of earning a spot in the starting rotation.

About halfway there, the car sputtered and stopped. I looked at the dashboard—the gauge was below "E." In the anguish of the night and morning, I'd forgotten to fill the tank. This kind of thing didn't happen to me. If I was anything in baseball, it was a detail-oriented perfectionist, not some absentminded rookie with his head in the clouds. Running out of gas—one of the few things I could control—put me over the edge.

As the clock ticked toward game time, I broke into a sweat. Being on time to the park is the first baseball commandment, and I was about to violate it. As we waited for a tow truck, I focused on the cars as they whizzed by. Tim had no idea what my broken heart was feeling or where my screwed-up head was. But he could see I was unduly upset. He was so mellow that day, as though he knew I needed space.

"Don't worry about it, Beaner. We'll get there," he said.

We waited two hours on the shoulder of that freeway. Finally arriving at the field late, I let Bochy know it had been my fault. He was cool.

"Just get ready," he said.

Years of perfect citizenship had bought me a break. After all, this was still a spring-training game, even though we were back home. Opening Day at Jack Murphy Stadium was just forty-eight hours away.

It was the only time in my life I wasn't overjoyed to be in the starting lineup. Bochy had me hitting second and playing right. They say some guys are good enough to play in their sleep. I'm not sure that phrase ever applied to me, but that's what the game felt like. I drifted in and out of a nightmare, waking only when the ball came hurtling toward me at what seemed like the speed of light. Though I'm not sure I really focused on many pitches, I managed a bloop single to left and a four-pitch walk. I handled perhaps five putouts in the field without an error.

It was a relief to be toweling off after the game. Then one of our clubhouse kids said Bochy "wants to see you." It is the most hated line in sports. Every player knows exactly what it means. Given the events of the last twelve hours, I just couldn't believe it was happening to *me*.

I threw on a T-shirt and my long underwear. Then I made one of the longest walks of my life, toward the small star chamber in the visitors' clubhouse. Bochy and GM Randy Smith were waiting for me. After stammering through some pleasantries, Smith proceeded to spin out excuses about why he had to "send me down." Bochy was the kind of guy who hated delivering bad news. He stared at the floor the entire time. It seemed nobody could look me in the face that day.

~

SMITH SEEMED DISTRAUGHT. Two years earlier, he had personally congratulated me when I'd broken up a no-hitter with two outs in the ninth inning against Cincinnati. The Reds' pitcher, Tim Pugh, a big right-hander, boasted a blazing fastball. But on that night at Jack Murphy, he also had an ungodly sinker. In the eighth inning, Gwynn led off. We were losing 8-0, but the crowd buzzed with anticipation at the prospect of Gwynn spoiling the no-hitter. Everyone knew he represented our best shot. Tony worked the count but then flew out to center—his third out in a row. He was furious with himself, and the crowd fell silent. All was not well at the Murph.

But I'd noticed that the sinker had begun to flatten out, ever so slightly, and in the dugout Tony agreed it was suddenly hittable. The tension had reached into the dugout, where I was biting my nails. In the ninth inning, the fourth, fifth, and sixth hitters were due up. The first two batters made quick outs. Our manager that year, Jim Riggleman, sent me up to pinch-hit for Kevin Higgins, our left-handed catcher, who was called back while on his way to the plate. He wasn't too happy about being replaced, but he was a rookie so he couldn't say anything. It showed Jim's confidence in me, pinch-hitting a lefty for a lefty. Fired up, I took extra swings in the on-deck circle as the crowd noise built. The umpire yelled at me to get into the box. It was now or never. My heart was pumping furiously, yet I felt unusually calm.

It's me against him, and I'm better. I knew Pugh was coming right after me, so I was ready to hack at the first pitch. Since he'd been regularly painting the outside corner on his first pitch, I moved up in the box, crowding the plate. I guessed right but fouled that pitch straight back. The crowd groaned.

Whenever the ball slams off the backstop behind you on a line, you know you've taken a good hack. But I had missed the pitch I needed to hit. The second pitch was a breaking ball, outside. I was seeing the ball well, champing at the bit to get one I could handle. He threw his sinker low and away, making the count two and one.

The next pitch was probably a mistake, a sinker toward the outside corner. It caught too much of the plate, and my bat connected squarely, sending a rocket right back up the middle. I took the wide turn running to first, and I could hear the guys in the dugout hollering my name. The scoreboard lights exploded: *Bean-Er . . . Bean-Er . . . Bean-Er!*

The next batter, Craig Shipley, flew out. We'd lost the game. But with all the pats on the back for my "clutch" knock, it felt like a victory. Smith came down from upstairs to recognize me for saving the organization the everlasting embarrassment of being no-hit by a guy like Pugh, not exactly the Nolan Ryan of his day. Smith commented that day he admired my style of play, mentioning several times that he hoped I would consider teaching my approach to the game by pursuing a coaching career when my playing days were over.

~

THAT WAS YESTERDAY. Like any good GM, Randy wanted to know what I could do for him today.

"Billy, we're in a tough spot here," he told me. "This kid Tim Hyers has to stay on the roster or we lose him. If we send him down, the Blue Jays will take him back. This is the least destructive move for the whole team."

Easy for him to say, given that I was the one being ordered to sacrifice. Hyers had been a first-round draft choice of the Toronto Blue Jays in the late '80s. He had been left off the forty-man roster in 1993, and Randy had plucked him out of the Rule 5 draft. Randy didn't mention it, of course, but I'm sure it also didn't bother management that I'd be taking a $135,000 pay cut if I didn't make the opening-day roster.

The news made me feel like I'd been punched while already knocked out. Suddenly feeling exposed in my underwear, I insisted they were making a "huge mistake." In as steady a voice as I could muster, I told them that I brought something special to the table, that

I'd been productive for two years, never missed a day of practice, let alone a game, and that they would regret it, blah, blah, blah. Then I stopped in mid-sentence.

"You know what?" I said. *"Screw this.* Something horrible happened to me this morning. The worst thing *ever.* Nothing you can say to me right now can make me feel any worse than I already do. I'm getting out of here."

Expressing my anger felt better than groveling. And it had the added benefit of obscuring the pain of rejection. News travels fast in the locker room. Brad, Trevor, Archi, Phil Plantier, and pitcher Andy Ashby were waiting for me at my locker. They were pissed. They assured me I'd be back in a few days. Even though most of those guys were stars, they insisted I deserved to make the club as much as they did.

"Management doesn't know what the hell it's doing," Brad declared.

However predictable they may have been, these sentiments were the greatest gift I could have received: simple empathy from players who had stood in my cleats. Maybe they couldn't understand my personal life, but at least they could understand the hard knocks.

I let them know I'd had a "really tough day"—the understatement of the century—and that I loved them like brothers. Brad and Trevor reached over to hug me. Since I knew the gentlest touch was sure to unleash a humiliating torrent of tears, I pulled back and started jamming my gear into my duffle bag. I told them I hoped they would understand why I had to get out of there. I pulled on my jeans and favorite gray sweatshirt and flipped the clubhouse kid a $100 bill, telling him to make sure my gear found me wherever I ended up.

~

ON MY WAY to the parking lot, I wondered what else could go wrong. Not knowing whether to feel hurt or angry, I rode both emotions, alternately bawling and grinding my teeth. For a moment, I found myself consoled by the notion that I'd soon be in Sam's embrace, only to get hammered again by the grim reality. I ducked into a maintenance room inside the stadium so that nobody could see the tears that flowed down my face. I'd been awake for about thirty-six hours. I was exhausted, my head felt numb, and all I wanted was to hold Sam one last time.

Wiping the tears on my shirt sleeve, I remembered the group of people who'd shown up to watch me play—my family and friends. Weeks earlier, I'd secured a batch of tickets for this game at Anaheim Stadium, not five minutes from my childhood home. As I approached them, my eyes on the pavement, their smiles faded. Obviously something terrible had happened, something far worse than the defeat they had just watched.

As I struggled to regain my composure, Ed stepped forward and gave me a big hug. I whispered in his ear that I'd just been sent to the minors, and with that tears began streaming down my face again. I buried my head in his chest. Silence crept over the twenty or so people around us. My brothers were used to me being the impassive one, and for once I could see the pity in *their* eyes.

I did my best to explain my demotion. I was being sent down to the Padres' triple-A affiliate, the Las Vegas Stars. I had noticed that, just three days before the start of the season, the Padres were still carrying twenty-six players, one over the limit. Someone obviously had to go, but after years of living in fear of every roster move, this time around I'd been secure enough to dismiss the thought.

One of those twenty-six was a new acquisition, Fernando Valenzuela, once a Los Angeles Dodgers star, now fighting to hang on as a fifth starter, at a fraction of his former salary. Fernando was only a shadow of his former self. He'd lost a lot of arm strength. Nonetheless, the wily veteran had pitched surprisingly well in the Cactus League, fooling hitters with a variety of off-speed pitches and creating a difficult choice for management.

As a veteran, I had the right to demand my unconditional release and become a free agent. But being sent down the day before opening day limits a player's chances to find another team. I was out of options.

This was one more—but hardly the last—bewildering moment dealt by the great game of baseball.

Part Four

Closing the Door

15 *Nothing Left to Lose*

THE SWING OF THINGS ~ DREAMS OF FAME AND FOR-
TUNE ~ ED'S SNORING AND COUNTING THE CRACKS IN
THE CEILING ~ CLOSE MY EYES AND NEVER WAKE UP ~
BLOND, BLUE-EYED SURFER ~ A QUEER LIKE ME ~ SAM'S
NAME IN BLACK MARKER ~ A BULLET AIMED AT MY HEART ~
THE STREAK

FTER THE GAME at Anaheim Stadium, my parents urged me to sleep over at their house. Concerned about my emotional state, they wanted to keep an eye on me. The family consensus was for me to get back into the "swing of things" as soon as possible, but I wasn't sure I had the strength.

I'm no quitter, I told myself, but for once the words rang hollow.

It just didn't seem possible that so many horrible things could happen to one person, all at the same time. As I fell into a fitful sleep, I flirted with the idea of simply driving off into the sunset. Perhaps the best revenge was to disappear for a while.

But by the next morning, I was back to playing dutiful son, trying to make everyone happy by preparing for Las Vegas. As I was packing my car for the five-hour drive, Ed asked if he could ride along and hang out for a day or two. We'd never done anything like that together. I couldn't be sure what his thinking was, but his offer seemed like an unspoken recognition of Sam's place in my life. Because Ed was a former Marine and cop, a disciplinarian who believed in subjugating emotions to duty, his tenderness touched me all the more.

As we drove through the desert, I struggled to avoid the subject of Sam's death despite being consumed by it. We talked about baseball instead. Ed believed the Padres were screwing me.

"Don't let the bastards take away your love for the game," he said. "Don't give up your dream."

This advice resonated with my own intense competitiveness. It was the way I reacted to any setback, especially on the playing field. So for the moment, I went back to thinking I would simply set everything aside again for the game. Maybe I wasn't gay after all. Sam was the beginning and end of that part of my personal life, and I would never be involved with a man again. Without him around to remind me of my sexuality each day, it crossed my mind that maybe that part of me would wither and die along with him. I pretended to believe that for about two miles, but I knew it was bullshit.

The city's skyline appeared on the horizon. The orange and red light of sunset reflected off the sleek glass-and-concrete hotels and casinos. The multicolored neon that dotted the city cast a warm glow. I was reminded of a classic Hollywood movie scene—the hero arriving in the big city to pursue dreams of fame and fortune, except this time I wasn't counting on a happy ending. After all, in the cold-hearted terms of baseball slang, I was literally being sent *down*. It was hard to imagine ever being *up* again.

~

FOR ANYONE WHO'S MADE it to the majors, the minors are a brutal reminder of the real world. Having become accustomed to five-star hotels in major metropolitan hubs, I pulled into the parking lot of the inn where the Padres had reserved me a room. It was a fleabag motel on the strip, the kind of place where Nicolas Cage drank away his life in *Leaving Las Vegas*. From my room, I could see the new, glitzy Mirage

Hotel. I remembered the time Sam and I had stayed there together. It was the kind of place where you could lose yourself in the mesmerizing bustle of slot machines, roulette wheels, and glitzy shows.

As Ed and I walked around looking for a place to eat, I gazed at the landmarks, which I'd found so fantastic during my first tour but which now seemed to taunt me: wedding chapels, strip clubs, fast food joints—all full of lost souls wandering.

Back at the hotel near midnight, Ed and I lay down in small twin beds. Even though I hadn't slept for what seemed like days, my mind raced. I listened to the rhythm of Ed's snoring as I counted the cracks in the ceiling. No matter how hard I tried, I just couldn't accept the turn my life had taken.

Just two days earlier, things had finally begun to make some sense to me—a major leaguer in love with the man of his dreams who was on his way to beating HIV. Now I wondered how much Sam had suffered in those last hours of his life. I questioned whether I had been any comfort. I berated myself for choosing the hospital farther from our home. I tried to imagine what it would be like to have a sense of security again. I wondered what it would be like to close my eyes and never wake up.

~

As I SHOWERED the next morning, I realized I hadn't touched a base-ball in three days now, an eternity for a ballplayer during the season. The thought of getting back on the field—just playing catch and taking cuts in the batting cage—lifted my spirits. The truth was that the Padres really didn't owe me anything. I would have to earn another chance. Feeling sorry for myself while blaming it all on management was no way to get called back up.

Returning from a road trip, the Stars were preparing for an extended home stand. At least I would be getting right back into action. As Ed drove me to the stadium, we listened to Steve Winwood sing "I'll be back in the high life again." Telling myself it was a sign of better things to come, I grabbed on to that phrase and repeated it to myself.

I felt the familiar jitters of walking into an unfamiliar locker room. I'd witnessed good players quit just to avoid facing the prospect of starting over. Playing A ball can be fun, unless you have played in double-A. Playing double-A is exciting unless you've seen triple-A. But the biggest jump by far is between triple-A—the Stars' level—and the bigs. It's like the leap a performer takes in going from Reno to Vegas. There's no going back.

As usual, I was the first guy to show up at the park. After dropping my bags, I sought out my old friend Soup Campbell, the trainer. Soup had an irrepressible sense of humor. Despite being a fitness guru, he was forever fighting to keep the pounds off his own round frame. With his clean-shaven head and high-pitched voice, he was one of those unforgettable characters who seem to exist only in baseball. He reminded me of his good friend Tony Gwynn.

"It's bullshit you are down here, Beaner," he snorted, handing me a uniform with my name emblazoned on the back. "Fucking politics."

No doubt Soup was also thinking of his own slow, cruel ascent through the minors. "Just hang with 'em, and you'll be back in Diego in no time," he added.

I made an exception to my rule against heeding baseball clichés. Coming from Soup, these comments were like pats on the back from a big brother.

I walked next door to the manager's "office," a twenty-foot-square whitewashed closet with a light bulb hanging from the ceiling. Tim Flannery, a blond, blue-eyed surfer, sat at his brown Formica desk scribbling on lineup cards. A slick-fielding second baseman, Tim had played nine years for the Padres. He had been known as Mr. Padre until Gwynn took over that appellation. As overachieving Southern California boys who grew up on the beach, Flannery and I had bonded long ago. He'd retired from baseball at the age of thirty-two in 1989, when he landed a TV news gig in San Diego. After three years of that grind, he had returned to coach

A ball in Rancho Cucamonga. His team had won the California League title, and he had been promoted to triple-A manager. He was on his way to big things.

Our respect was mutual. I was his kind of player. Like Tim, I'd earned my opportunities. Now I had to do it again. I summoned a jocular exterior to cover the pain I was feeling. Tim gave me his version of Soup's "You really got screwed" speech.

"The Padres REALLY are calling you back up in a week or so," he said. *Yeah right. Heard that before.*

I unloaded all my experiences of the previous day—the death of my "best friend," my fear about talking about it, the blow of getting sent down. For once it didn't scare me that an authority figure was seeing my unfiltered disappointment and the rawness of my despair.

Tim was unlikely to have suspected anything unusual about my emotion. Unless he was extraordinarily attuned to these things, he probably saw it as the normal reaction of an athlete suffering from a crushing professional setback. After all, as a triple-A manager, he was used to dealing with exiled major leaguers, and he'd spent plenty of time on the bubble himself.

Tim tried to bring my focus back to the game. He brought me up to speed on the team, and my role on it.

"Billy, I want you to hit third and play center *every* day. Put everything else out of your mind, and just play so that we can get you back up to the show."

I wanted to hug him. He'd given me the familiar reassurance about my place in the world. Yet I hadn't been able to share all my feelings with him, and that in itself told me something. I walked out of his office with a new perspective on the game and its role in my life. I was becoming a bit more honest, at least with myself. Misfortune has a way of stripping away pretensions and delusions, and now I was seeing everything a little more clearly.

I'd begun to resent the silence about my personal life that baseball had imposed on me. It no longer felt natural or inevitable. For more than twenty years, I'd played by the hideous rules of acquiescence that competitive sports had forced on me as the price of success. And where had it landed me?

~

SOMETHING MAGICAL happened as I walked onto the lush green field in the desert heat early that afternoon, the athletic equivalent of my unburdening in Tim's office. My nearly obsessive fear of failure was beginning to recede, and I cared a little less about what other people thought about me. The stars keep their eyes on the prize no matter what happens on the field, in the papers, in the clubhouse, or in their personal lives. Although I was not without self-confidence and even occasional cockiness, something had always held me back. In times of despair, I blamed my sexuality. *Maybe what they say about gays is true. Maybe a queer like me really can't hang with the big boys.*

I owed it to Sam, who'd had such blind faith in me, to stop making excuses, especially ones that denigrated my love for him. I scrawled Sam's name in black marker on the lining of my Stars' hat. Whenever I felt choked with sadness, fear, or pressure, I'd take off my cap and repeat his name until a surge of confidence would course through my body.

Each game, every at-bat, took on an exaggerated significance, as if it were my last. I gained the enthusiasm of a person who survives a brush with death. I felt the freedom of someone who'd hit rock bottom, someone with nothing left to lose. Being unfamiliar to most of my teammates and feeling liberated from the "team player" image of a dutiful major leaguer, I became a far more selfish ballplayer. In the terms of the town, I was going for broke.

It is often said that baseball is the quintessential team sport, and in its purest form it surely is. But in truth players are judged individually. Even defending world champions jettison as much as one-quarter of their rosters before the next season's opening day to prepare for another run. Nowhere is this truth more evident than in the minors, where statistics are the god of all players. I simplified my games to combat my grief. *No more little Billy, unselfish team player, the sweet kid.*

Off the field, I spent a lot of time alone, living out of a suitcase. I needed the time by myself to rest, gather my thoughts, and come to terms with the turn my life had taken. When I left the room, I'd go to the movies with Archi Cianfrocco, who had been sent down shortly after I had. We roomed together on the road, and it was comforting to hang out with someone who knew what being demoted felt like. Mellow by nature, he was a reassuring presence on the long road trips, in the small towns of the Pacific Coast League, and during the endless hours in airports waiting for 7:00 A.M. flights in which we would be crammed into economy seats.

My younger teammates were harder to relate to. They either looked up to me because I had my own bubble gum card or regarded me as a has-been. Only a handful would ever be considered for a call-up, and most were aware that their careers would be short-lived. Over the years, I'd piled up some pretty impressive minor-league numbers, earning the nickname "Mentor." At the time, though, I was the one who needed guidance, at least off the field.

~

"The streak" began innocuously enough, during an ordinary day game in April at Vegas' sun-baked Cashman Field. I hit the ball on the screws my first four times up with nothing to show for it. In late innings we were down by several runs, and it looked like I wouldn't get another at-bat.

We mounted a rally in the ninth, closing to within a run, and I found myself walking to the plate with two outs and the bases loaded. I fouled off the first two pitches, falling behind in the count. I stepped out of the box. I started to say, *It's you against him, and you're better,* but stopped myself. I decided to place my faith in a new mantra—*This one's for Sam*—and I meant it.

The hitting conditions were perfect. I was both relaxed and taking every pitch personally, as if the ball were a bullet aimed at my heart. Fouling off several more close pitches, I worked the count to 2-2. Then the pitcher hung a breaking ball that seemed to float in front of my eyes for a fraction of a second. I recognized the pitch, stayed back, and then ripped a liner up the middle. Tony Gwynn would have been proud. Two runs scored, and I walked off the field with the winning hit. The crowd went wild.

After the game, Ed was waiting outside the locker room. We hugged—it felt good to have my father there. I thought I was going to start bawling my eyes out in front of my departing teammates, but they were too busy patting me on the back to notice. From then on, I was on fire, smoking the ball like Ty Cobb. I hit in twenty-two straight games. During my ten years as a pro, this was a personal best.

At the triple-A level, pitchers have talent and stuff. But they often lack command and control. I was seeing the ball really well, but mainly my streak was a matter of confidence. I went to the plate *knowing* that if the guy didn't pitch around me, I was going to make solid contact. My streak ended when I went 0-for-2, with two walks, one intentional. My last at-bat, I stroked a line drive the other way that the shortstop snared with a leaping grab.

I had been robbed of a hit, but that's baseball. I wasn't letting up. The next day, I went 2-for-4, starting another streak of twelve games. One-third of the way into the season, I had hit in thirty-four of thirty-five games, batting near .400 for that first month and a half. Yes, I was a major leaguer hitting minor-league pitching. But it felt damn good anyway. I was throwing myself back into the game that had inflicted so much pain. Now, for the first time in years, the game was providing me with a measure of consolation.

16 *Riding Pine*

WOES AND MOJITOS ~ TWO-MILLION-DOLLAR LEFT
FIELDER ~ NOTHING BOYISH ABOUT THIS MAN ~ WHERE
PLEASURE REGISTERS ~ THANK GOD FOR ROB DEER ~
GOING DOWN SWINGING ~ TIME FOR A CURVE ~ THE
LONGEVITY OF A BASEBALL CAREER ~ DOMBROWSKI'S
MARLINS AND THE WORLD SERIES

I WAS WAITING FOR my dinner, but what I was really looking for was a place to call home. My friend Carlos, whom I'd met on the last day of spring training that year, had taken me to Yuca, a swanky Cuban restaurant in Coral Gables. It was a sweltering summer night, and I spilled my woes out over a mojito, a Cuban drink made from sweet sugar cane, mint, and lots of rum.

This was during the 1995 all-star break. The Padres had just finished a three-game series in Houston, where I sat at the end of the bench in my perfectly starched road uniform. I'd spent most of the year after Sam's death yo-yoing between the minors and majors.

I'd skipped Sam's funeral four months earlier because I was afraid that if I missed even one game, someone might start asking why I cared enough about the guy to attend. The decision had left me overcome with equal parts despair and disgust, and I could not forgive myself for it. The very thought of Sam's family would send me into a tailspin. I couldn't forget the awful phone call I'd made to them, their utter disbelief, and the fact that I couldn't explain what he'd meant to me. We lost all contact after that week.

My teammates assumed I was suffering from the ordinary frustrations of big-league ball, which for me included riding the pine and never knowing my fate from one day to the next. Sitting on the bench had always gotten me down. Just when I was starting to feel good about my game, I would face a week of false-alarm pinch-hitting chances.

Until it's his turn to play, a reserve is the equivalent of a coach without authority. The demands on bench players include everything from watching the other teams' signs to monitoring opposing base runners and of course cheerleading for the regulars as they pile up big numbers and even bigger dollars. In my mood that summer, I wasn't up to my normal standards of attention and encouragement. I yearned for simpler days when all that mattered was my place in the batting order, getting some knocks, and playing solid defense.

In my fumbling efforts to deal with Sam's death, I'd reached out to Carlos, and over the summer we talked on the phone regularly. His therapeutic ear helped me through long nights alone on the road. Sensing my despair one night, he invited me to Miami, where he lived.

"You need to get away from the game," he said over the phone. "You need to smile. A friend of mine owns a great Cuban place where we can hang out and talk."

He was right. The Padres were scheduled to play the Mets in New York after the three-day break, so I booked a flight to Miami. If I wasn't going to be an all-star, at least I could try to have some fun. Carlos was my only gay friend, the one person with whom I could share my doubts and fears. Mom and Ed were in the dark. They were clearly worried, but for all they knew, I was simply struggling with the roller-coaster ride of professional ball. I hadn't been able to set foot in my Del Mar house since Sam had gone. I still felt I couldn't tell anyone the truth behind his death. AIDS was so out in left field, I still could barely say the word.

"I used to be the first person to show up at the clubhouse, and now I'm the last," I told my friend, nursing the drink.

The Padres had reneged on their promise. I'd done everything possible to earn a quick and permanent recall, including the twenty-two-game hitting streak, one of the longest in all of pro ball that year. During the first call-up two months earlier, I hadn't even been activated. I'd joined the team only to stand in the dugout collecting dust. The team needed me as an insurance policy because Phil Plantier, their two-million-dollar left fielder, had injured his hamstring. But he didn't think the injury was serious enough to be placed on the disabled list. I chewed a week's worth of bubble gum before the Padres shipped me back to Vegas.

It's funny how even privileged big leaguers with six-figure salaries can feel sorry for themselves. I'd seen guys bringing down high-seven figures act like a blown save was a matter of life and death. I wasn't any better, but now I wasn't just crying about my batting average or a demotion. I was carrying around the burden of the death of my partner.

"I know I have a lot of good ball left in me," I lamented to the patient Carlos while ordering another mojito. "I'm only thirty-one. I'm in my prime. What does it take to get a chance?"

As I explained the world of baseball, Carlos stared at me blankly. When I looked around the restaurant, I realized that, except to my parents, the sacrifices I'd made for the game were of little or no importance to anyone. That's just life. It wasn't personal. Everybody's life is hard. Baseball's just a game. I was young. I'd unknowingly played Russian roulette with a deadly virus, and I'd gotten lucky. My health was intact. But I missed my companion. Wallowing in self-pity seemed so much easier than dealing with reality. I had to get over myself, but I didn't know where to begin.

When we'd arrived at the restaurant, Carlos introduced me to his friend, Efraín Veiga, the owner. I noticed how handsome and mild-mannered he was. In fact, I couldn't keep my eyes off him. He was my ideal age—a decade older, I guessed. There was nothing boyish about this man.

Now he was approaching our table. To my surprise, he sat down and suggested I order the Chilean sea bass with purple Peruvian mashed potatoes—not exactly your ordinary ballplayer fare. But by now I'd given up the fiction that I was ordinary. Here I was at this chic eatery while most of the Padres were probably gorging on burgers and fries, washed down by beer.

Suddenly, my appetite was returning. Efraín ordered a special bottle of wine for the table. The three of us chatted about Miami, Cuban food, and the presidential campaign. The rum and wine were warming my insides, and baseball didn't seem so important anymore.

The game paled in comparison to my interest in the salt-and-pepper chest hair revealed by the open collar of Efraín's white linen shirt. I tried not to be too obvious about it. But the energy of the restaurant, the rumba music, the warmth of the Miami night, and that shirt against his tanned skin made him irresistible.

Efraín put me at ease with his easygoing manner and velvety baritone. For a moment at least, I was actually enjoying myself. I had no idea whether he even "played for my team," or what he thought of me. All I knew was that this was the first time I'd felt alive since Sam's death.

~

THE PADRES NEVER did re-activate me that season. Shortly after we finished the series in New York, they farmed me back out to Vegas. I took up residence at the Vagabond Inn.

My disappointment hardened into anger. The futility of my situation reminded me of a joke I'd heard my first year in triple-A. I was listening to a teammate bitch about spending the last decade in the bushes.

"Just keep playing well, and you'll get called up," I said, trying to be helpful.

"Beaner, the team charter would have to crash for me to get called up."

I wondered whether I'd fallen into that category. Tim Flannery did a bang-up job of handling the travel grind and keeping twenty-two guys from every corner of the globe from getting on each other's nerves.

Despite my dour mood, he never gave up on me and never let me give up on myself, not even for a second.

"Make them rip the uniform off your back," he said. "Now get out there and play!"

The bottom line was that the Padres weren't going to pay me a big-league salary to sit on the bench and eat sunflower seeds. Even at the age of thirty, a successful athlete can be considered washed up. Major-league franchises are forever thinking about the future. In most professions, thirty-year-olds are just beginning. But the body is not on the same schedule as the mind, and in sports the clock is always ticking, causing players to worry about every ache and pain. Potential is a very sexy thing, especially if a young guy with potential has been awarded a large signing bonus or a guaranteed contract. Veteran overachievers like me are considered a dime a dozen. When two players battling for a spot are even in the talent department, the younger one always gets the nod.

There was nothing to do except get back on the field. Thanks to Flannery's encouragement, I was soon locked in at the plate. Back in my third stint in Vegas, I picked up right where I'd left off with my twenty-two-game hitting streak earlier that season. I stepped into the ball like a man possessed, taking out my frustration on the hard white pellet. There is no better physical outlet, no better revenge on the cruelty life doles out, than the feeling of bat connecting squarely with ball, watching it soar on a line toward the outfield. The sensation of contact moves from your wrist up your arm and shoulder and into some nerve center in your brain where pleasure registers.

You know you're going well when your vision picks up the rotation of the seams as the ball hurtles toward you. It got to the point where the other team's infielders were taking a step back and shifting their defensive alignment toward my right-field power alley when I came up to the plate.

Thank God for Rob Deer. With more than 200 major-league home runs when he retired, Rob decided to revive his career with the Stars in his mid-thirties. He was betting that a bunch of round-trippers would earn him a September call-up. We quickly developed a mutual respect. I loved his gamer attitude, and he saw that I came to play every day.

Rob was one of the toughest guys I've ever known. Despite all his success with the Giants, Tigers, and Brewers, he never big-leagued anybody, setting a good example for the younger guys. He could tell that I was down in the dumps. He naturally thought the best way to lift my spirits was to take me out to the bars and clubs that dominated Vegas.

When I tried to beg off, he would lobby and cajole until I relented. He just wanted to have a few drinks, kick back, and talk baseball. He'd made quite a bit of money in the majors, and he was not afraid to lavish it on his friends. Straight bars weren't my scene anymore, but I really enjoyed hanging out with this old pro. His fun-loving optimism and passion for the game helped me forget my troubles.

His presence spurred me on the field as well. He and I battled for the home-run lead on the team, and no one was surprised when he edged me out in the last week. At six-foot-four and 235 pounds of solid muscle, he would dig in at the plate and take a tremendous swing at anything resembling a fastball, practically twisting himself into the ground. When he connected, he hit the ball so hard it took your breath away. He used a thirty-six-ounce bat, one of the heaviest around, which is also why he piled up Ks at an astonishing rate. He was an inspiration. Here was a guy nearing the end of his career, giving it his all, to hell with the results. Rob Deer was determined to go down swinging.

~

As THE SEASON wound down, I found myself daydreaming about that good-looking restaurant owner from Coral Gables. We had met only once, and I figured he wouldn't even remember me. I wasn't going to just call him cold. As luck would have it, Carlos phoned to invite me to his own birthday party after the season, in late October. I said yes before he'd finished asking.

I began to feel comfortable among Carlos's gay friends, and I was falling hard for Miami and the tropical climate. I was amazed at how matter-of-fact everyone seemed about sexuality. Here were businessmen, lawyers, architects, and hotel managers who didn't waste precious time and energy hiding. These ordinary guys were the real superheroes, not the frustrated athlete in their midst.

If they could be honest, why couldn't I? Pro athletes are the most pampered people on earth, yet when it came to being openly gay they have much less freedom than everyone else. It just didn't add up. Maybe I should have listened to Mom and become a police officer after all.

The only downer came when Efraín didn't show up at Carlos's party. I was hoping to see him, and I was looking for him around every street corner and every time the door opened, but it was always someone else.

The day before I was to return home, I found the courage to visit his restaurant, Yuca. I arrived late in the afternoon, hardly the best time to catch the owner. I nervously asked the host if I could talk to "Mr. Veiga." I was informed that he wouldn't be in until later that evening. My heart sank. I left a vague message asking him to call. I realized that when we had met four months earlier, I hadn't even asked if he was involved with anyone.

Back in Southern California, I found myself preoccupied with this Cuban who I wasn't even sure remembered me. Indifference wasn't something I was used to. I pretended it didn't matter whether he called me or not, but it did. A week passed. I'd just about given up when the phone rang. Apologizing for not getting back to me sooner, Efraín explained that he received nearly thirty messages a day, and it had taken him a while to get to mine.

I could tell he was trying to place me.

"Billy?" he repeated. I hadn't left my last name because I was afraid someone might notice it. This was pretty stupid because he easily could have disregarded the message.

"Billy the baseball player! How could I forget you? It was nice of you to stop by. I'm sorry I missed you."

I stammered through some small talk. Then I told him I had been going through a hard time, and that evening at his place had helped me heal. I'd been rehearsing this conversation for some time. Despite my nervousness, I was ready to convey what I felt in my heart.

"I don't want you to take this the wrong way," I began. "I have no idea whether you're already involved with someone else, or even interested in me, but I haven't stopped thinking about you since the night we met. I don't want to complicate your life, but I need to tell you that I have very strong feelings for you."

That was my best fastball. Now it was time for the curve. "I'm going to hang up now," I concluded. "I apologize if I'm out of line. If you are interested, please call me back. If not, I appreciate your time. I hope you do. Good-bye."

I hung up. My hands were shaking, but I felt relieved. I'd said it. I stared at the phone. A moment later, it rang.

~

I KNEW I COULD never live in the home Sam and I had shared. It had been *our* house, and the memories were still too raw. I had to get a for-sale sign up. Seven months after Sam's death, I finally cleared out our belongings.

I tiptoed across the carpets as if Sam's ghost had taken up residence. His scent lingered everywhere. His clothes from his last night were still lying on the floor, next to the bed. I lost it all over again at a photo of the two of us that was sitting on the dresser.

During our three years there, Sam and I had become friendly with our neighbor Carol. She had seen me pull into the driveway after the long absence. She knocked on the front door.

We'd never discussed our relationship with Carol, a divorced mother. But Carol knew instinctively how much Sam and I cared for each other.

I could trust her. The moment she walked through the door and gave me a big hug, I started bawling. Before long, she'd joined in.

"I just can't believe how much I miss him," I said.

"I know, honey," she said, holding my hand.

Carol probably had no idea how important that moment was for me. For the first time, someone understood what Sam meant to me. As I drove back to Mom's, I took comfort in the fact that there were people who could treat me just like they would anyone else who'd suffered a loss.

Yet I still couldn't confide in my own parents. Why had it been easier to talk to a neighbor? They guessed something was wrong. Mom would inquire as gently as she could, and I would shut her down with a curt "I'm fine, Mom."

She and I had always been so close it was hard to keep the truth from her. But I'd become accustomed to secrecy, and even though it was clearly the right time to open up, I feared letting her down. How on earth could I tell her that her "golden child" was gay, and his male lover had just died of AIDS-related complications? With my tenuous hold on the only career I'd ever known, I was hardly in the position to risk losing her love.

~

EFRAÍN DIDN'T KNOW what to make of this kid's interest in him. A well-known figure in the Miami area, he was also a very private person. Most people weren't quite sure if he was gay or not, and he certainly wasn't going to volunteer the answer. At the same time he was comfortable with himself.

He could probably tell that my gay identity was still pretty shaky. He knew absolutely nothing about baseball, and he couldn't have cared less that I played professionally. For all he cared, I might have been one of the busboys at his restaurant. This had an odd appeal at a time when I was burned out, and down on the game.

We lived on opposite sides of the country. There was nothing convenient about our mutual interest. But after dozens of late-night phone conversations, we decided to give it a shot. In the first week of November, Efraín picked me up at the Miami airport and drove me to his simple Mediterranean house in a quiet Coral Gables neighborhood. I immediately felt at home there. I enjoyed long runs through streets lined with lush foliage and palm trees. The warm, brilliant days that never seemed to end were paradise.

Efraín offered a kinder, gentler way of looking at the world. He had an unflappable bearing, and his manner of speech soothed me. He told me about the finer things in life I'd missed out on while playing ball. After graduating from Georgetown University, he had spent four years in New York City and five in Costa Rica. He traveled often to Europe, where he spent time in Paris. Along the way, he'd learned to speak French and Italian. As with Sam, it was fun to be around someone who didn't talk baseball twenty-four hours a day.

Efraín forced me to stop driving myself around the bend, to slow down, enjoy life, and let others around me do the same. I would talk a mile a minute, ticking off a long list of things I wanted to accomplish, and he'd insist that we sit down and enjoy a home-cooked meal together with a bottle of wine. The next morning, we'd wake up, put on a pot of rich Cuban coffee, and sit by the pool for hours, enjoying each other's company. I told him about the politics of baseball, and he taught me about Cuba and art and how he'd turned a passion for entertaining and cooking into a thriving business.

In January, I decided to stay put in Miami until spring training started. I jumped into my baseball workouts, training with a bunch of ballplayers at the University of Miami, which had a spacious complex of fields and batting cages.

~

THEY SAY PRACTICE makes perfect. But hitting is one of those challenges so vexing it resists perfecting. You must master the strike zone, and how the home-plate umpire interprets it. Over the years, you begin to understand your limitations. You learn the strengths and weaknesses of pitchers. Then you must bring all these skills together into one package.

When you get it right, turn on a fastball, lacing it down the line, it's one of the greatest feelings on earth. When you screw up, flailing helplessly at a ball in the dirt, it's one of the worst.

The arduous challenge of hitting a round ball with a round bat is what keeps most hitters from coming into their own until their late twenties or early thirties. The potential longevity of a baseball career, compared to almost every competitive sport except golf, is one of its greatest draws. While your body might not be what it once was, hard work and wisdom compensates for the slow decline of physical ability. Some terrific hitters have played until the age of forty. Hank Aaron hit forty-four home runs at the age of thirty-nine. Darrell Evans, my Tigers teammate in '87, hit thirty-four at the ripe old age of forty.

In January of 1996, four months before my thirty-second birthday, I firmly believed I was poised to have my best season. I was in great shape. I felt confident, strong, and quick as lightning. I was a proven pinch hitter, a versatile outfielder who could also hold his own at first base. I was deemed the consummate professional. I had mashed the ball at triple-A. And, compared to the huge salaries guys were bringing down, I could be had for a song.

But now none of that seemed to matter. I had an awkward and painful conversation with my agent, Dennis Gilbert, about my playing future. I was reluctant to accept another minor-league deal, fearing another long season in the bushes filled with silences and secrets. Settling in Miami, I'd begun to see the possibilities for a new life. I wasn't going back.

Dennis had no way of grasping my dilemma or fighting for my career the way I could fight for myself. He'd been loyal to me over the years, working hard for me through the ups and downs of a journeyman ballplayer. But in the back of my mind, I had a sneaking suspicion that he worked even harder for his rich and famous clients like Barry Bonds and Mike Piazza. He had a business to run, and it was a lucrative business with little room for guys not bringing in big fees.

Certainly ballplayers had personal struggles, and he dealt with them all the time, but mine was pretty unique. It wasn't one of the typical stories fans read in the papers about athletes: broken marriages, rumors of steroid use, a DWI. This one, I feared, would blow Dennis' mind. In fact, I was pretty sure it would turn the baseball world upside down.

Dennis wasn't the only one who couldn't surmise the stakes. My parents accepted my decision with surprising equanimity. Efraín, always reserved anyway, was noncommittal. He told me he would support me "no matter what," a strange echo of Dennis' advice to "do whatever makes you happy."

In weighing the decision, I was withholding crucial information from the people who could help me most. At that time, Efraín didn't know enough about my passion for the game. He didn't understand the sacrifices it had entailed. Mom and Dad hadn't a clue I was struggling with my sexual orientation. And Dennis didn't know I was trying to juggle both.

I made one last stab at bridging the gap between my life and my career. I picked up the phone and called Dave Dombrowski, the respected general manager of the Florida Marlins. If I could catch on with the only team in south Florida, perhaps I could have the best of both worlds, just like it had been in San Diego.

Dombrowski told me he loved my game and that I'd be an excellent addition to the club. However, he'd just signed Joe Orsulak, another veteran utility guy, to play the role I would have filled.

"Would you consider going to Charlotte?" he asked. This was the home of the Marlins' triple-A team. "If you play well enough, you'd be the first guy we call up."

Thanking him, I told him I'd mull it over. Charlotte was only a short flight away, but I just couldn't summon the enthusiasm. I never called him back. I felt trapped between two mutually exclusive words. At the age of thirty-one, I was calling it quits.

A year and a half later, Dombrowski's Marlins won the 1997 World Series.

17 *Safe at Home*

BASEBALL HAD OWNED my imagination since I was a shirtless kid shagging flies in the Southern California sun. What happens when the dream is gone? What would occupy its place in my imagination? After my retirement, I didn't know what to do with myself. I spent the days grappling with these questions.

The dream may have been over, but the nightmare lived on. I was still having the same one I'd had since I started playing competitively: Alone in front of my locker in the clubhouse at game time, I'm about to lead off and play center. Pulling on my uniform, I realize something is missing—cleats or shoelaces or stirrups. I rummage around in my locker, gear flying everywhere. I race around looking for the final piece of my outfit. I hear the announcer call my name. Recognizing that I can't make it to the field in time, I shake and weep, falling apart right there on the carpet.

I wake up in a sweaty heap of blankets and pillows, my heart pounding. Something was missing in my life, all right. But it was a lot more than a piece of equipment. Baseball had been my everything: my physical outlet, my mental challenge, my source of income, and my social life. It wasn't just my reason for being. It *was* my being.

~

I ROLLED OUT of bed on what should have been the first day of spring training in 1996, empty and lonely. I'd heard the stories about retired athletes, old warriors who struggled with drug and alcohol abuse, chronic pain from injuries, and the lack of financial and professional skills to exist outside the game.

I didn't have these problems. But I could relate to the struggles. Here I was, thirty-one, in the best shape of my life, with no vision for my future. What was the use of being able to hit a small white ball with a wood bat in the real world? Did it matter that I had the ability to rifle a ball from right field to second base on a line? On the other hand, what on earth could match the intensity and passion of pro ball? What could replace the adrenaline rush of competing with and against the best players on earth?

Like a bitter aftertaste, my past wouldn't go away. I was angry with my parents for not understanding what I was going through. I remained pissed off at Dennis for not urging me to keep playing. I'd wanted a life raft even though I hadn't warned anyone I was drowning.

I was even angry with Efraín for raising the possibility of a better life. He was cautious with his feelings. I wanted him to say, "I love you and I'm going to spend the rest of my life with you. Go ahead and play another year or two or three, and make sure you're ready to move on before you quit." He never suggested anything resembling that, and I felt too vulnerable to suggest it for him. I'd chosen my love of him over baseball, and now I resented him for it.

Watching baseball on TV or listening on the radio only made things worse. *I could do that,* I repeated to myself, again and again until it drummed out every other thought in my head. *I could still do that!*

~

THE TROPICAL PARADISE became a constant reminder of just why I'd exchanged a lifelong fantasy for the lure of another. The wide boulevards, art deco architecture, and warm blue-green ocean lapping against white-sand beaches evoked the pleasure principle I'd never allowed myself to appreciate. The residents' indifference to sexual distinctions couldn't have been more different from my preoccupation with them.

It felt strange to be in a place where men could hang out—or check each other out—without worrying about who might notice. The necessity of pretending had ruled, and sometimes ruined, my life. The first time Efraín took me to Lincoln Road in South Beach, I watched men holding hands, and I felt nervous for *them,* even though all around me were indications that it was okay to be yourself.

"La playa está caliente," Efraín said as we drove around the area.

And he was right—the beach was hot, in more ways than one. It was wild to think of myself as a sex object for other men, and it took a while to feel free to enjoy their glances and the incredible openness of desire.

As always, exercise lifted the darkness. I jogged on the beach, lifted weights, found pickup basketball games at the gym. No longer worried about screwing up my baseball swing, I played a few left-handed rounds of golf for the first time in years. I finally had the time to work on tennis—a sport I'd always enjoyed but lacked the opportunity to pursue. I began to recapture the innocence of sports, and it felt good to play for fun. Over the years, the trappings—from contracts to statistics—had become more important than the game itself.

Efraín and I spent all our time together, and after a while we started checking out the town as a couple. About a year after I quit, we headed to the Barroom, a huge club that catered to a mixed crowd. It was one of those trendy places where sexual orientation took a backseat to looks and money.

As we were about to enter the club, a stretch limo pulled up to the curb. Out popped David Wells, who'd recently signed a huge new contract to play for the Yankees. A posse of three or four guys followed, no doubt on the hunt for the beautiful women Miami is famous for.

I'd gotten to know David when we were both playing in the International League, where he was toiling for the Toronto Blue Jays organization. He was a lefty with a mean hook and an even meaner demeanor on the mound. Off the field, he partied with the best of them. He was a throwback to the Mantle days when guys caroused all night and played all day. In fairness to Mantle, though, David was a starting pitcher, with four days off between starts. It's hard to compare him to a position player, who must be ready to play every day.

His wicked sense of humor was legendary. When I got a rare start at first base for the Mud Hens in 1988, David happened to be coaching at first base. (In the minors, starting pitchers coach first base when they aren't on the mound.)

It was a humid summer night in Ohio, and the moths and mosquitoes were swarming. Between innings I was tossing grounders to the infielders when David snuck up behind me. By rubbing his thumb and forefinger together in my ear while standing behind me, he managed to create the exact sound of a moth's hum. I practically jumped out of my cleats dodging that oversized "bug." I looked around, and the whole Syracuse Chiefs' club, standing in the first-base dugout, was hooting and hollering at me. David flashed me a shit-eating grin as I doubled over in laughter myself.

Having added about thirty pounds since his minor-league days and sporting the buzz cut he'd made famous, David sidled right up to me.

"Billy Bean!" he said. "What's up, dude? Where have you been?"

Introducing Efraín as my "friend," we chatted for a while. It was the first time another player had seen me with a male partner. I mumbled awkwardly about growing tired of traveling for the game and a desire to go into broadcasting.

I had nothing to fear from a guy like David. But even though I was retired, I clung to the secrecy of my playing days. In truth, he probably couldn't have cared less. So why did I?

~

I WASN'T JUST cut off from my teammates and everyone associated with my baseball life; I was in only sporadic touch with my family. I felt like an exile.

But the men in my life, past and present, gave me some perspective. Sam's family had escaped from the Iranian revolution of 1979. He'd immigrated to America to find the political freedom he had been denied.

Efraín's family had left Cuba to escape the oppressive regime of Fidel Castro. It was humbling to be among people who'd sacrificed so much. Both families had left their homeland behind because they wouldn't accept a life that was dictated to them, one that did not include freedom and democracy.

I found it inspiring that Efraín's parents, Esther and Efraín Veiga, Sr., had sent their only child ahead to the United States in 1960. Efraín's father had run a lumber company that was confiscated by Castro's government. At the time, they didn't know whether they would ever see their son again, but they would do anything to make sure he was not brainwashed by the new regime. He was sent to Miami to live with relatives he'd never met.

On the last flight out of the country on October 21, 1962, two years before I was born, the Veigas escaped and reunited with their only child. They left everything behind, including their life savings. Efraín, Sr., who'd learned the butcher trade as a young man, went to work for a large meat distributor.

I was an outsider in this community, too. Even though I spoke Spanish fairly well, I found myself closed off from conversations because I wasn't fluent. The Veigas were kind, but it took a while before I was accepted. The formal Latin culture made it difficult for Efraín to discuss his orientation with his conservative parents.

As a ballplayer, I didn't fit neatly into the gay community, which had long been shunned by the sports world. I'd never met so many people who felt they had no business being on a playing field, a lesson they'd been taught since childhood. Most people I met had no idea I was a former big leaguer.

I tried to avoid drawing attention to myself. I'd always had an interest in broadcasting, and I worried that being "out" would kill my chances.

It was odd going from pro ballplayer, in the driver's seat, to sitting in Efraín's backseat. People saw me as his young plaything, his little sidekick. Most Cubans love baseball. But his friends, gay and straight, had no interest in the sport, or any sport for that matter. For a long time I felt they assumed I was with Efraín only for a free ride. I was in a weird limbo, trying to please people I didn't even know. Where, exactly, did I belong?

~

ONE THING I KNEW for sure was that I needed to make things right with my own family. When I returned to Dana Point for the holidays in '96, my mother was clearly upset with me. Since she'd always doted on me, I felt her withdrawal intensely. After a day or two of mounting tension, she grabbed me by the shirt sleeve.

"We need to talk," she said. "Can we go get some coffee?"

We sneaked out of the house and drove to a cafe. Sensing a confrontation, my heart skipped a couple of beats.

"Billy, I can't understand why you've been so distant," she said.

My silence was causing her pain. As we sat in the car in the parking lot, I fumbled for the right words.

Mom found them for me.

"You're *gay*, right?"

I held my breath.

"As your mother, I just want you to be able to tell me anything, no matter what," she said.

"How'd you know?"

"You're my son. How couldn't I?"

It wasn't my sexuality that bothered her. She felt wounded because I hadn't trusted her enough to turn to her for support, instead of suffering in silence all those years.

I assured her that none of this was her fault. "If I had to do it all over again," I said, "I would've told you a decade ago. I couldn't even admit it to myself."

We sat in the car as I poured out what I'd bottled up for the last decade. The facade just melted away. The poor woman's jaw dropped with every revelation. I told her everything except the cause of Sam's death, which I wasn't sure she was ready to hear.

I had barely scratched the surface by midnight. We decided we had better get back home so Ed wouldn't worry. I was ready to go to bed, but Mom felt we shouldn't wait until the morning to tell him. I'd finally calmed down a bit, and now I was being sent back to the wolves. Then I realized that Mom deserved this moment, so up the stairs we went.

As usual, Ed was snoring loudly. It felt awkward to wake him up with such a personal revelation. I stood over him as Mom tried her best not to cry.

"Ed, I've something to tell you," I said, tapping him on the shoulder. I was embarrassed to use the word "gay," so I found another way of saying the same thing. "Sam and I were more than friends—he was my lover."

"I hope you know that I'll always love you, Billy," he said. "Now can I go back to sleep?"

We laughed out loud. Talk about diffusing tension. I think Ed had suspected for a while, but out of respect for my mother and me, he'd held his tongue. I leaned over and gave him a hug. All of my brothers and sisters were visiting for the holidays and it felt good to be near everyone. I slept more peacefully that night than I had in a long time.

Apparently, there was another person I hadn't fooled. The next day, when I informed my sister, Colette, she told me that in 1994, after a family visit with Sam and me at our house in Del Mar, her daughter Leia had asked, "When can we visit Uncle Billy and Aunt Sam again?"

At the time Leia was four years old.

~

I SET OUT to find a suitable occupation to replace my preoccupation. I modeled for Sports Authority, Office Depot, and several other businesses. I did sports reporting and producing at Channel 6 News in Miami. I did updates and served as a guest host for WQAM Radio's sports talk show. I spent a lot of time back in the locker room interviewing baseball stars, including the Marlins' Gary Sheffield, a disgruntled slugger who'd arrived in a trade with my old team, the Padres, in 1993. I'd have given anything to be on the other side of the microphone.

I'd been paid to play a game. Kids had begged for my autograph. Friends and family had picked up the newspaper each day to read about my work of the day before. Now my former career was nothing more than a conversation piece. Unlike a lot of retired ballplayers, I didn't have the luxury of millions of dollars sitting in bank accounts, real estate, and stock portfolios. I had to learn to make a living like everyone else.

It would be a good thing for pro athletes to experience ordinary life while they are still playing. They'd find new respect for their sport and the fans who make it possible for them to earn an incredible living while running around manicured playing fields. I was working long hours for little money and barely seeing Efraín, who was spending a minimum of twelve hours a day in his restaurant. I'd quit doing what I loved in order to be near him, and now I hardly ever saw him.

I was bemoaning our plight one day when Efraín piped up, "Why don't you help me run Yuca?"

He'd moved the place to Lincoln Road, and business was booming. He needed all the help he could get. It sounded like a good idea, except I didn't have the faintest idea how the business worked. He taught me the ropes, A to Z, and before long I was managing the place, freeing him up to work on quality control and the creative side, which he loved.

This fast-paced business appealed to me. It gave me a chance to be in a social workplace, something I'd always enjoyed as a player, and the job called on a variety of skills and calm under fire. I lacked management training, so I relied on a simple sports metaphor to create a positive atmosphere for the fifty employees: teamwork. Speaking Spanish was also a big plus with the primarily Latino staff.

Efraín and I had become business partners as well as a couple. We tried to maintain a low profile, not an easy thing to do when you are serving lunch and dinner to hundreds of people every day. The town began to notice that the famous restaurateur had a companion.

In early 1998, we decided to open a new, bigger place. After years in the trade, Efraín had socked away a little bit of money. I had some baseball savings, so we pooled our resources. We came up with a business plan and sold Yuca, a difficult move for Efraín because it had been his livelihood for eleven years. The remainder of the investment pool came from a small group of limited partners, among them the fabulous Spanish-language talk-show host Cristina Saralegui.

I threw myself into the preparations as if I were training for an upcoming season. We found a central location that required a complete makeover, next to the main floor of the fashionable Albion hotel on Lincoln Road. It had two levels connected by a huge staircase, floor-to-ceiling windows overlooking the street, and a long, stainless-steel bar on each floor. The open kitchen was an architectural masterpiece.

We hired a star chef from Charlie Trotter's restaurant in Chicago, where I spent two weeks studying their operations. We planned an upscale menu highlighting the flavors of Mexico that were largely overlooked in the Southeast. We named the place Mayya and planned every detail down to the penny and the inch.

I barely found the time to fit in my sacred runs along the beach, sometimes delaying it until 3 A.M. before turning in for a few hours of shut-eye.

~

A FEW WEEKS before Mayya was scheduled to open, I received a jolt out of the blue. I still had one foot firmly in the closet. I still hadn't told anyone from my ballplaying days. I missed the guys from my college years—Tim Layana, Jim Bruske, Damien Bonenfant, and Jim McAnany. I had given them only my work number from the old restaurant, Yuca. At home, I made sure the answering machine had my name and voice alone.

Since I'd retired, I wasn't sure why I was holding on so fiercely to my secret. It wasn't that I feared rejection since I now had a lot less to lose. I was pretty confident these guys could handle the revelation. It was partly habit. It was partly a desire to get back into the game of baseball in some capacity. On top of it all, I was ashamed of all the lies and silences I'd subjected them to. Coming out would mean owning up to my cowardice.

After graduation, Layana and I had stayed in touch, talking by phone about once a week. We followed each other's careers as closely as possible. After being drafted by the Yankees, he bounced up and down between the minors and majors. He played parts of two major-league seasons plus one day of a third.

His big break came in 1989, when the Cincinnati Reds plucked him off the New York Yankees' triple-A roster in the Rule 5 draft. Manager Lou Piniella had gone from New York to Cincinnati that season, and he thought highly of Layana's arm. Tim spent the whole year with the Reds in 1990, compiling a 5-3 record with a 3.49 ERA and two saves in fifty-five innings as a middle reliever. He was disappointed when he was left off the playoff roster and the Reds went on to capture the World Series. But I'm sure the hurt eased when he was voted a full share of the World Series bonus, which ended up being more than his entire regular season's salary.

After his stellar rookie year, I was excited about his prospects. But he never really established himself in 1991, when he went 0-2 with a 6.97 ERA in two months with the Reds. Called up by the San Francisco Giants in 1993, he got hit pretty hard in two innings of work and was sent back that same day. He never played in the majors again, ending his career with the triple-A Rochester Red Wings the next year. Tim was one of those guys who'd gotten by on his God-given talents. But he let himself get out of shape, and after throwing so many innings in college, in the minors, and in the bullpen, his once golden arm lost its pop.

We stayed in touch until I quit the year after he did. Without baseball to keep us together, we drifted apart. It didn't help that I avoided the topic of my personal life, and despite our youthful escapades together, he never asked. His own life was an open book: he finally settled down in Culver City, where he'd grown up, and got married to the mother of his second daughter in 1998. I couldn't attend the ceremony even though he'd been at mine. Like me, he felt lost without baseball. He hoped to become a coach at Loyola, and he had a good chance of ending up there.

On June 26, 1999, Tim was in Bakersfield for a charity golf tournament. After a long day on the course, he was at the wheel of his Chevy Blazer, driving his brother, Mike, and two buddies home from the links. Tim decided to stop at a convenience store during the two-hour trip home on the Pacific Coast Highway.

He slowed to turn into the parking lot. From the oncoming lane, a Mercedes-Benz, speeding at seventy-five miles per hour, passed another car on the right. Tim never saw the Benz as it slammed into the passenger side of his car.

With seat belts securely fastened, the passengers came out unscathed. Tim, however, was not strapped in. He was thrown out the driver's side window. He probably would have survived had the unstable SUV not rolled over and landed on him. Bleeding internally, Tim somehow managed to ask if Mike was all right. When the paramedics lifted the car off of Tim, amazingly he stood up and ran over to the side of the street, where he sat on the curb before collapsing. He was DOA at the hospital at the age of thirty-five.

~

TIM LAYANA had been my best friend, yet I'd missed the news of his death. My buddies had no way of reaching me. Jim McAnany left a message at Yuca the day after Tim's death, but the new owners never forwarded it. The news of Tim's death had been on ESPN, on the radio, and in the newspaper. But in my walled-off world, it didn't reach me. Nine days later, Anna, with whom I'd remained close, sent a fax to the restaurant passing along her condolences. Finally, someone at Yuca thought to forward the fax to me.

I couldn't believe it. Tim was gone—one of the strongest, most vital men I'd ever known, an imposing force on the mound and in life. When I got in touch with Jim, he told me he had assumed that since I'd been out of touch, I wouldn't have wanted to attend the funeral anyway.

Once again, the closet—self-imposed, this time—had caused me to miss the funeral of one of the people I loved most. I felt ashamed, and now I didn't even have the excuse of a baseball career. I'd been hiding from my buddy in Miami Beach, 3,000 miles away, for no reason other than fear and self-hatred. What, exactly, would it take for me to wise up?

In a few weeks, Efraín and I were set to launch Mayya. The *Miami Herald* prepared a story about the opening. I was friendly with the reporter, Lydia Martin. Over lunch one day at the new place, she casually asked whether she could identify Efraín and me as a couple as well as business partners.

Before Tim's death, I would have declined. But in my disgust, it took me about two seconds to give her the answer she wanted. I was an idiot for being so distant from everyone I loved. Maybe this would force my hand. Maybe Lydia, a journalist I trusted, would save me from myself.

"Why not?" I said. "It's time to grow up."

~

I DIDN'T THINK all that much about the disclosure, assuming it would amount to little more than one line in what I hoped would be a big story about the chic new eatery in town. It didn't occur to me that anyone outside of Miami would care about the sexuality of a baseball scrub like me. I'd known about the baseball player Glenn Burke, who told the world in 1982. I'd heard of Dave Kopay, the Redskins' running back who somehow summoned the courage to come out way back in 1975. Then there was the great Martina Navratilova, arguably the best women's tennis player of all time, and the unrivaled Olympic diver Greg Louganis. I certainly didn't see myself as belonging in this august company.

After the interview, Lydia went back to the office and rewrote the story to underscore the irresistible "ballplayer comes out" angle. The night before the story was to come out, I got cold feet all over again. I called Lydia to feel her out about killing it.

"The story is written," she said decisively. "There's no going back."

I got up early the next morning to find the *Herald* in the driveway.

"Billy Bean was a closeted gay outfielder in the macho world of big-league baseball, then the silent life-partner of a famous name in South Beach Cuisine," began the story, buried in the Lifestyle section. "Now as an equal partner in a new restaurant, he is finding his own voice."

Even Lydia was caught off guard by the sensation that ensued. The story went out on wire services and CNN. By that afternoon, the phone was ringing off the hook at home and at Mayya, which hadn't even opened yet. Everyone wanted to talk to the player who, as Lydia put it, "had given it all up for love." They wanted a guided tour of the homophobic world of pro sports.

I'd spent every second of my life trying to stand out on the field while blending in off it. My world suddenly was upside-down. I wasn't sure what people expected of me. I kept picturing my coaches, wondering what they would think. *What would Coach Meiss say?* As an athlete, lots of people help you find your way to your goal. I wanted to say to them, "Hey, it's just me, little Billy Bean, same guy as before, except no more lies."

I'd always been comfortable talking to reporters, chewing the baseball fat with them long after the other ballplayers had gone home. I prided myself on being one of those ballplayers who could face the press even after a bad game. But I was rarely their first choice of interview subjects. Now I had *my* choice of interviews. After receiving many requests, I decided to do only a few.

I hung out with Robert Lipsyte, one of the most respected sports reporters in the country, who'd taken up the cause of gay athletes in a thoughtful manner. His story, "A Major League Player's Life of Isolation and Subterfuge," appeared just under the fold on the front page of *The New York Times,* on September 6, 1999. I also agreed to do a story and be photographed and interviewed for the cover of the December 6 issue of *The Advocate.* I thought the photo spread looked great, but Mom complained about the layout—in which I posed in a tight shirt and jeans holding a baseball in my left hand, saying it was too sexually provocative. Thank God she didn't know about the centerfold request from *BlueBoy.*

A few days after the *Times* story appeared, my cell phone rang, and I heard a familiar voice.

"May I please speak to Mr. Billy Bean?" I knew it wasn't a close friend because nobody calls me "Mr." anything, although my new gay friends might, in a moment of camp, refer to me as "Ms. Bean."

"My name is Diane Sawyer, and I am a journalist for ABC News," the elegant voice announced.

"Ms. Sawyer, believe me, I know who you are!"

All the national news shows were interested, but Diane Sawyer was the only television personality who bothered to pick up the phone herself. It didn't hurt that I'd seen so many of her sensitive reports on gay causes.

I was honored, and she made my decision easy. She put me at ease, allowing me to tell my story without fear. (The interview aired December 8, 1999, on *20/20.*) It was a revelation to me, after so many years of fearing media exposure, that so many journalists were sympathetic to my struggle and eager to share it with the country. What I'd feared would be a shameful revelation had become a source of great pride.

~

THE MEDIA ACCOMPLISHED what I'd failed—getting me in touch with my old friends. My Padres teammate Scott Sanders heard the news and then informed my buddies Trevor Hoffman and Brad

Ausmus. After speaking to me, Brad told *The New York Times* that he'd never questioned or wondered about my sexuality before I'd gone AWOL in Miami Beach. It was only then that rumors began to circulate on the ballplayer grapevine, and now the story had confirmed it.

It "wouldn't have made any difference to me when we played together," Brad was quoted as saying, "and it doesn't matter to me now."

One of my Padres managers, Jim Riggleman, called me a "class act," adding "everyone loved Billy on the club." Jim Bruske, my college buddy and a major-league pitcher, said the revelation would have "no impact on our friendship." Lenny Harris, my Dodger teammate, called Mayya to offer his encouragement, as did Benny "The Wiz" Ruiz, a minor-league shortstop turned fireman, whom I had played with in the Detroit Tigers organization. I had many long conversations with Chris Donnels, who was also still a big leaguer.

Trevor cared so little about my homosexuality that he barely made mention of it when he, Brad, and I got together for a reunion dinner in Del Mar.

"The next time you're in town, dude, let's go surfing," he suggested. "Just like the old days."

Dude, let's go surfing. That simple sentence was music to my ears, the reassurance that nothing really had changed in the minds of the ballplayers I respected, these icons of masculinity and traditional values.

But their kindness also reminded me of what a fool I'd been. After all, I'd roomed with Brad for two years. I remembered all the times I'd wanted to tell him only to back off for fear that he wouldn't know how to handle it. Why had I insisted on imputing the worst possible motives to the people I loved most?

The reflexive connection between homophobia and athletics had been hard-wired into me since I stepped onto the football field at the age of eight. Now the anti-gay attitudes I'd been subjected to for so long were dying like broken-bat flares on the outfield grass. The bonds of teammates, I was learning, were far stronger than prejudice.

Not every player was so happy about it. Former Yankees outfielder

Chad Curtis said that most players "wouldn't want the thought of a teammate possibly checking them out. You have a lot of guys in this room who are fairly uncomfortable with the idea of women in the media coming in here—even at the notion they're being looked at." His teammate, pitcher Andy Pettitte, agreed: "There would be the question of being comfortable."

I'm glad Curtis and Pettitte had the guts to say what they thought, but I have a feeling their words would have been less pointed had they known a gay teammate. Whatever problems they have with diversity are their own. Female sports writers were routinely subject to harassment, including guys exposing themselves to them in the locker room when these brave women were just trying to do their job.

It infuriates me to think that players would actually believe that a gay teammate would be any less serious about his job than they are. It takes a huge amount of work to reach the majors, and I wonder if they really believe a player would sacrifice his career for a cheap thrill. Being gay doesn't mean you lack self-control. On the contrary, gays and lesbians have had to suppress their natural desires far more often than heterosexuals. Restraint comes with the territory, and anyone who thinks otherwise is just plain ignorant.

The silence from other quarters was deafening. I didn't hear from Tommy Lasorda or Sparky Anderson. I didn't hear a word from Dennis Gilbert, my agent of ten years. The baseball powers-that-be could not be bothered to call or issue a statement. Bud Selig, the baseball commissioner, and Sandy Alderson, the highly regarded number-two man who built those great A's teams in the liberal Bay Area, didn't seem to give a damn about the questions my stories raised. On the other hand, I was merely describing my experience. I hadn't voiced my concerns. At least not yet.

~

THE ENTIRE PERIOD was something of a blur. I couldn't really focus on the media or the political fallout. I was working long hours at the restaurant, which began to falter almost as soon as it opened. The food won praise (*The New York Times* and the *Herald* gave us excellent reviews). But Mayya never quite caught fire in a way that would justify the expense of operating a place with such high overhead.

We'd made mistakes. For one thing, the Mexican cuisine did not go over well with the local Cuban population, partly, I suspect, due to Mexico's disregard for the embargo with Castro's Cuba. The tourists tended to be more interested in Cuban and other Latin flavors. Whatever the case, it didn't work, though not for lack of effort. Some nights, while I helped my staff clear tables and clean bathrooms, the big leagues seemed awfully far away.

Early the next year, Efraín and I shut down the restaurant. We were forced to sell our house to satisfy creditors, and we moved into a smaller one, off the waterfront and down the street. I'd lost all my savings. My first post-baseball venture had ended the same way my career did, disappointingly. The stress from these dark days took a toll on our relationship. Succumbing to the strain of financial uncertainty, the two of us went days without speaking.

I was consoled, however, by the reaction to my public declaration. After three years of anonymity in South Beach, all of a sudden I caught people staring at me, and many came up to say hello. I had autograph-seekers for the first time since my retirement. Letters, phone calls, and e-mails poured into Mayya and the *Herald*'s office.

"Mr. Bean's success in the sport proves that a gay man can achieve the same level of proficiency as a heterosexual man," one e-mailer declared. Apparently, the writer had not noticed my lifetime batting average!

"Perhaps your readers will begin to understand the struggle gays and lesbians face every day, fearing they will lose their job," wrote another.

A gay man e-mailed Lydia to say that Javy Lopez, the Atlanta Braves' catcher, was "hotter" than I am. Oh, well. Easy come, easy go.

Predictably, several people confused me with Billy Beane, the savvy general manager of the Oakland A's who spells his last name with an "e."

Beane, two years my senior, grew up in San Diego, where he was a high school phenom and a first-round draft pick of the New York Mets in 1979. We actually played together in 1988, when we started in the outfield for the Toledo Mud Hens. Our beat reporter dubbed us the "Rice and Beans" outfield because our left fielder was named Pete Rice. The joke would've been much funnier in Miami.

Billy Beane's major-league career ended in 1989 at the age of twenty-seven. He and I became friends the year we played together, but as is often the case in pro sports, when we changed teams, we fell out of touch. I remember being frustrated at the constant confusion when I was with the Padres. Sometimes I played along when a fan would say he remembered me from Patrick Henry High School in San Diego.

Billy went on to build a perennial contender on a shoestring budget in Oakland, which has a large gay population. I always knew he would be successful "upstairs." He was one of those players who are too smart for their own good.

With the situation now reversed, I wondered if *he* rued the confusion, a good test for the younger generation of baseball leadership. Did being mistaken for a gay man bother him? Does it help him understand the stigma of homosexuality? Would he stand up for a gay ballplayer on his carefully constructed squad?

~

ONE DAY I received a letter that helped put everything in perspective. A young man wrote that his best friend had committed suicide because he was despondent over his homosexuality and tired of living in fear that his parents would disown him.

"If he had known about your story," the man wrote, "I know he would still be alive today."

I was moved, even though this wasn't a burden I was fully prepared to bear. But there were some small things I could do. I had invitations to speak at political rallies and at fundraisers for gay and lesbian youth groups. Professional athletes have always ignored such groups in their youth outreach efforts, and I wonder how my life might have been different had I heard openly gay and lesbian athletes tell their stories.

In April 2000, I was asked to address the "Millennium March on Washington" for gay and lesbian rights. As I looked out over the half-million people gathered on the Washington Mall that sunny spring day, playing before 42,000 screaming fans at Dodgers Stadium suddenly seemed easy. But I felt more confident now than during my playing days, with no fear of failure, and at last I could speak from my heart.

"When I played baseball, I was all alone," I said, surveying the crowd. "Today I'm a member of a big family—one I'm proud to represent."

Part Five

Extra Innings

18 *The Level Playing Field*

TIM LAYANA AND BAFFLING KNUCKLE-CURVES ~ THE
FAGGOT'S GONNA PLAY! ~ MCGWIRE'S 61ST HOME RUN ~
THE FLAMBOYANT SHINJO AND BARRY BONDS IN
A KIMONO ~ JACKIE ROBINSON AND TURNING THE OTHER
CHEEK ~ STRIPES LIKE A FUCKING ZEBRA ~ PEE WEE
REESE ~ IF FRED LYNN WERE GAY ~ JOHN WETTELAND'S
HALL OF FAME ~ THE LORD DIDN'T HANG THAT SLIDER ~
JOHN ROCKER AND THE 7 TRAIN ~ BOBBY VALENTINE AND
MIKE PIAZZA ~ HEAD HELD HIGH

FTER WATCHING THE last out of the 2002 World Series from
my couch in Miami Beach, I returned home to Santa Ana to
attend my twentieth high school reunion as I began work on
this book.

Baseball was in the air. Bolstered by an amazing comeback in game
six, the Anaheim Angels, who play just a short drive from my childhood
home, had just defeated the Giants in a seven-game series. A new labor
agreement had decreased the disparities between small- and large-
market teams, returning the game to where it belongs—the field—and
undermining George Steinbrenner's attempt to purchase—rather than
earn—yet another trophy for the Yankees.

Here were two overachieving, fundamentally sound teams that got
by on guile, teamwork, and clutch performances. With the exception of
Barry Bonds, whose ability is out of this world, there were few stars,
but two excellent strategists in managers Dusty Baker and Mike
Scioscia.

Watching Tim Worrell in a Giants' uniform brought back memories of our days together with the Padres. He was the pal I'd given a lift to the ballpark on that awful day when Sam had died and I was sent down. As a Padre, he'd struggled to find a role on the pitching staff and lived in the shadow of his older brother, Todd Worrell, who had been one of the game's top relievers.

I was happy for Tim. He'd established himself as the Giants' set-up guy late in his career without a single overpowering pitch. He was making hitters look foolish, painting the corners with darting fastballs and change-ups. Except for the eighth inning of game six of the World Series, when he gave up a couple of key hits, he was masterful. Watching him work with his catcher, Benito Santiago, made me want to grab my mitt and play catch in the front yard, just to remember that magical feeling of ball smacking into glove. What I wouldn't have given for a simple game of catch with Tim again.

The morning of my reunion party, I stopped by Loyola. The sun was shining as I drove through the front gate of the lush campus of my alma mater. I wandered around, reminiscing, before heading to the baseball stadium. It blew me away to see my name and number emblazoned on the wall over the entrance, alongside those belonging to my dearly departed buddy Tim Layana and the pitcher whose records Timmy had broken, Jerry Stone. I walked inside the park where we'd spent four years together.

I sat down in the bleachers between home plate and first base. There were the giant eucalyptus trees beyond the fence in left-center where Chris Donnels had launched some of his massive round-trippers. In my mind's eye, I could still see Timmy on the mound from my vantage point in center field, rocking into his windup and unleashing that baffling knuckle-curve, displaying his big-league stuff for the scouts. It was as if we'd played here only yesterday, not a decade and a half ago.

Since my retirement, I'd struggled to make sense of the arc of my career and its sudden ruin. In less than one year, I'd lost both the partner I loved to a dread disease and also the game that had been my savage, lifelong preoccupation. I told myself that everything happens for a reason. I was privileged to have played in three great big-league cities, as well as Venezuela, Mexico, and Japan. Many of my teammates became my close friends.

I had emerged from the ordeal of a public coming out as a better, happier person. Living in Miami Beach with my partner, Efraín Veiga, I had the trauma of those dark days behind me. I'd shed enough tears for a lifetime, and now I was finally moving on. It was an enormous relief finally to be myself, surrounded by people who love me for who I am rather than who they want me to be. I'd reunited with my family, and life made sense again.

But there were still some nagging questions rattling around the back of my mind. Returning to my old stomping grounds of high school and college clarified them. Where had my career gone wrong? What had become of my childhood dreams? Was there anything I could do to help level baseball's playing field so that gay kids wouldn't suffer some version of my own fate? What, exactly, did it all mean?

~

WATCHING COLLEGE PLAYERS scamper across the field below me and hearing the crack of aluminum bat against ball reminded me of the pure joy of baseball, the innocence of varsity athletics. For a moment, I imagined myself back at the plate during my senior year, my average hovering around .400, *knowing* I was going to hit the ball hard—somewhere fair and out of reach. Wielding that thirty-two-ounce bat made me feel invincible, my future limitless. I imagined glorious years as a hitting hero ahead of me.

Had my real career measured up? I'd certainly started out on the right foot. "Talk about too good to be true," began the news report of my debut with the Tigers in 1987, at the age of twenty-two, when I'd gone 4-for-6, tying a big-league record. In the end, maybe it *was* too good to be true. In six years of big-league ball—four additional years were in the minors—I hit .227 in 475 at-bats over 272 games. Ouch. The numbers don't lie. Perhaps nothing sums up my career better than my five consecutive pinch hits in 1994 with the Padres—no small feat, but one that easily goes unnoticed and one that only a bench player can accomplish.

All athletes believe they can become stars given the right circumstances. I'll never know for sure exactly what kind of ballplayer I could have been. Like a lot of retired athletes, I wonder every day how I would have performed with 475 plate appearances in *one* season. Some players are handed opportunities, but I wasn't so lucky. Not being a power hitter, I needed to hit for high average. Instead, I was merely average. I was a deadly low-ball hitter with a quick bat. I could handle breaking pitches and off-speed stuff. But I had a long swing that I was forever trying to shorten.

Even today, at-bats flash through my mind like videotape. Pitchers went after me with high fastballs, which reach the plate a fraction of a second faster. Unless you possess exceptional power, they are a recipe for lazy fly balls. I needed to adjust by laying off them, but when you only get a couple at-bats every few days, that's easier said than done. In the warped perspective of a pro athlete, it seemed like my whole world hinged on making solid contact in just a few at-bats.

By focusing on the stuff I *could* handle, I adjusted to the grinding pressure of a game dominated by failure. I loved playing defense, where I excelled, and my managers always tried to get my glove into the game as early as possible. It was a pleasure just to get a chance to run the bases, lay down a bunt for the team, or dive for a ball heading for the gap. Before games, I ran extra wind sprints, shagged flies, and took grounders until the laces of my glove split. I roamed the dugout, rooting for the everyday players. I prided myself on my clubhouse presence and efforts to boost morale, a perpetual problem on losing teams. I tried my best to be the "Billy on the Spot" everyone expected.

As a Padre, I offered my teammates haircuts, which soon became known as "Beanies." It got to a point where I had to keep an appointment book. Trevor Hoffman trusted me enough with shears to have me cut his hair a couple of days before he married his wife, Tracy. Andy Benes, our star pitcher, nicknamed me "Floyd" after the barber on the *Andy Griffith Show*. This was great fun, but it also says a lot about my career. One of my nicknames came from my haircuts, not my exploits on the field.

~

IT SEEMS LIKE I spent those ten years with one foot in the major leagues and the other on a banana peel. Looking back on my career, my friend, former pitcher Jim Bruske, was kind enough to tell a reporter, "Billy could have been a great player, but he tried too hard to make everyone happy, and he put too much pressure on himself."

Jim was right. The closer I got to a breakthrough, the more I pressed and doubted my ability. I went after success on the field to compensate for my unhappiness off it. Great players stay in the moment, but I worried about the results before the opportunities came my way. "Keep it simple," my manager Sparky Anderson used to remind me. But I found a way to complicate everything.

It's you against him, and you're better, was the guiding philosophy of my early days as an athlete. But the reality of my big-league career was more like *It's you against yourself, and you both lose.* My biggest flaw had nothing to do with my stroke or those rising fastballs. In the show, everyone has skills. Some have more than others, but mental toughness differentiates the great from the merely good. I spent far too much time wondering whether I measured up to the guys around me, whether I could match their toughness, ferocious competitiveness, and even their masculinity.

From my earliest days on the playing fields of Southern California, my coaches and teammates equated homosexuality with weakness and failure. From my Pop Warner football coach's warning not to "run like a faggot" to Tommy Lasorda's "cocksucker" jokes, the drumbeat of homophobia was as relentless as the roar of a capacity crowd urging on the home team. It never occurred to me that there might be something wrong with these crude and dehumanizing comments. They would've been a lot easier to ignore if I hadn't looked up to the men who made them.

With the dawning realization in my twenties that I was gay, I began to internalize this equation. When I'd strike out or roll over on a fastball, tapping a weak grounder to second, I berated myself on my way back to the dugout. *You're a fucking pussy. Get some balls. Swing the bat like a man!*

In baseball, it's believe in yourself or pack your bags. I wanted to be happy and content more than I wanted to be great and famous, and that's why I made the decision to leave the game behind. Only with the advantage of hindsight did I realize that perhaps I could have been both good *and* happy. If only I could have been judged on the quality of my game, not the gender of my partner.

~

Baseball is a game. But it is also much more—our national pastime, a metaphor for values, a moral undertaking, an international language. It has always reflected, as Nicholas Dawidoff wrote, "the contours of the nation." It's the means by which guys in business suits and guys in construction hats bond over a beer. Gay guys and straight guys can sit elbow to elbow at the sports bar watching the World Series.

But when it comes to gay ballplayers, baseball has not lived up to its promise of equality and opportunity. The greatest game on earth should be leading the way for equality, as it did in the days of racial integration, not lagging behind every other industry in the treatment of gay athletes.

I grew up believing the diamond was the fairest, most just place on earth. It was a place where poor kids could get ahead, where white, brown, and black players had an equal chance to succeed, where the scrawny son of a single mother would be judged on performance alone. It was a shock when I realized, in my late twenties after nearly a decade of service, that simply being myself was considered incompatible with pro ball. The malicious, anti-gay climate of the game forced me to make a cruel choice between personal and private life, between love of the game and love of a man.

After all I sacrificed for the game, it pains me that MLB still refuses to take even the most basic steps to help and support its gay players. Harassment and discrimination are allowed to run rampant, forcing many big leaguers to remain closeted. A few straight players have made it known they don't want to share the clubhouse with openly gay team-mates. Baseball has allowed the discomfort of these narrow-minded guys to trump the right of gay ballplayers to work in a safe environment.

Because young gay athletes have never seen a role model in male team sports, they assume quite logically that they would be unwelcome in that arena, that the competitive disadvantage would be too great and too unpleasant. They've read the comments of athletes such as Reggie White and John Rocker. They've seen the leagues drag their feet when it comes to improving the atmosphere. Baseball, football, hockey, and basketball offer no hope for gay kids looking for heroes.

~

WAS IT POSSIBLE that I could become a voice for these young men and women? After thirty-five years of hiding, to be asked to lead the charge seemed overwhelming. I'm just one retired ballplayer, hardly a star with clout. So it was surreal to watch the letters pile up when my story became public in 1999—three years *after* my career had ended. To be honest, the writers weren't expressing the kind of accolades I'd dreamed about as a kid. I'd unwittingly tapped into the demand for gay images in sports. All of the mail I received was moving, but there was one that gave me goose-bumps as large as the ones I had during my first big-league at-bat.

"I am 34 years old and have been lucky enough to see firsthand a number of the great moments in baseball—an Aaron home run in late 1973, Jim Abbott's no-hitter, McGwire's 61st home run—along with scores of Mets games," the writer from Brooklyn said. "Yet I have never been compelled to write a fan letter before this week. I'm sure that as you were growing up and fantasizing about playing in the majors, you dreamed that your fan mail would be for your fielding or hitting. But the milestone that you have passed is ultimately of far greater importance than the marks of 3,000 hits, 755 home runs, or a 1.12 ERA. I hope that you truly are proud, not only for who you are, but of your decision to help others."

At first, I had trouble accepting these sentiments. The attention I was getting felt something like a consolation prize or a moral victory, the kind of thing you latch on to as you cope with a tough loss or a poor performance. I'd been programmed to believe that all that mattered was the outcome. I thought the meaning of my life was to be a .300 hitter, become rich and famous, an ambassador for the game of baseball. Like Roy Hobbs, I wanted fans to say, "There goes Billy Bean, the best there ever was." It took me a while to wrap my mind around, "There goes Billy Bean, the guy who spoke his mind."

I'd somehow stumbled across the one thing that could match the intensity of pro baseball—a cause. I'd always avoided anything more than dinner-table conversations about politics. But here was something I could do that might make an impact. The gay community has plenty of role models, in nearly every profession, but only two from pro team sports, the former football players Dave Kopay and Esera Tuaolo.

Dodger owner Walter O'Malley once called Sandy Koufax "the great Jewish hope." African-American and white kids alike idolize Alex Rodriguez, Sammy Sosa, and Barry Bonds. These role models prove that prejudice can be overcome. When the Giants acquired Japanese outfielder Tsuyoshi Shinjo, the organization rolled out the red carpet for him, including a welcoming party in San Francisco's Japantown. Even Bonds, the elusive slugger, showed up, donned a kimono, and toasted his flamboyant new teammate with sake. Sure, it was a smart marketing move by the club, but it also was a respectful nod to a community that hasn't been represented very often in the bigs.

I look forward to the day when the Giants and other clubs extend the same courtesy to a young gay outfielder. I can almost see it now: a round of Cosmos, on the Giants, at the Midnight Sun bar in the Castro. (In the brutal world of sports, however, hope must eventually give way to reality. By mid-season, Shinjo was hitting .240. The Giants benched him in favor of a new acquisition, Kenny Lofton, who helped lead them to the World Series. After the season, Shinjo was cut. Even in Japantown, few missed the prospect who didn't produce.)

Had I heard of a Billy Bean when I was younger, maybe I wouldn't have shed so many tears. When I was growing up, I had little guidance in my attempts to understand who I was off the field. Baseball spent years teaching me how to hit a curveball, but not one second on how to be an adult.

Had I known better, perhaps I wouldn't have married, unknowingly subjecting my wife to so much pain. Maybe I wouldn't have banished my parents from my life for the entire time I was in baseball. Maybe I would have demanded time off from the Padres to attend my partner Sam Madani's funeral—just like any other employee.

I would have sat solemnly but proudly in the first row, dignifying my love for that man and our short time together, instead of pretending he didn't exist and that our life together never happened.

~

THERE'S PRECEDENT FOR social change in baseball. After my incidental outing, fans and sportswriters rushed to anoint me the gay Jackie Robinson. Let me make one thing perfectly clear: I'm no Jackie Robinson.

Like other early black major leaguers, Robinson overcame enormous obstacles that I can grasp only from reading history books. He was subjected to barbaric racism. He received death threats. Fans called him "nigger" and "watermelon boy," and ordered him "back to the jungle." By turning the other cheek and focusing on the game, he survived with dignity.

Baseball didn't integrate solely out of a humanitarian concern for opportunity and equality. The change didn't occur because management had the best interests of black athletes at heart. It occurred, like most changes in pro sports, because of competitive pressures and business considerations.

In 1945—nearly a decade before the end of legal segregation—Robinson signed a contract to play for the Brooklyn Dodgers. Laboring in obscurity for the Dodgers' Montreal farm team, he may not have set out to create social change, but he sure did. Like any other ballplayer, he wanted the chance to compete. He wanted to be judged for the quality of his play rather than the color of his skin.

The Dodgers' general manager, Branch Rickey, was looking for an opportunity of another kind. In Robinson, he saw the cornerstone of a dynasty, a draw at the gate—and a man with the character it would take to create change during an ugly time in American history. The other owners, fearing backlash, passed on Robinson. Rickey took advantage of their cowardice.

Asked why he signed Robinson, he gave a simple answer that sums up the way to social progress in the game: "I want to win." Featuring Robinson's rare combination of speed and power, the Dodgers proceeded to win six out of the next ten National League pennants. In 1955, the "Bums from Brooklyn" finally beat the Yankees to capture a World Series title.

Faced with similar hostility, I had retreated, lied, and hid. Even though it took a tremendous toll on me, not to mention everyone around me, I could pretend to be something I wasn't—I ducked the kind of conflict Robinson and Rickey confronted. Like Robinson, I wanted a shot at living up to my potential. But carrying a torch was the last thing on my mind. I was simply doing my best to realize my lifelong dream without drawing attention to or raising questions about my personal life. The way I thought about it then, it would have taken a player with a Ruthian record behind him to carve out a gay-rights legacy in baseball.

~

WHO'LL BE THE first active major-league ballplayer to take on this challenge? Who'll risk it all for immortality? It might just happen by accident. Keeping a secret is not only emotionally consuming, it makes a lapse in concentration likely. The occasion could be as simple as a major-league player slipping into a gay bar only to be greeted by a local baseball reporter. With the media ready to pounce on any revelation, it's only a matter of time before something like this happens.

Or imagine a varsity pitcher who enjoys the game but doesn't anticipate a future in it. During his junior year he comes out to his friends and family and joins the high school's gay-straight alliance, as kids routinely do these days. Growing up in a liberal suburb, he finds that his coaches and teammates accept him fully. The school paper profiles him.

No one pays much attention until his senior season, when he grows three inches, fills out, adds a few miles per hour to his fastball, and develops into a star, racking up strikeouts like a young Randy Johnson. Scouts and GMs are so impressed by his ability that his sexual orientation becomes a non-issue.

Then comes the hard part. He must prove he belongs, every practice and every game, against daunting odds. The simple truth is that for a player to be open, he's going to have to be better than his peers. He may have to duck under a few beanballs and be prepared for some serious heckling. Like Robinson, he's going to need a ton of support. When Dodger manager Leo Durocher received a petition from players who objected to Robinson's presence on the team, he launched into one of the great anti-racism speeches of all time.

"I don't care if this guy is white, black, green, or has stripes like a fucking zebra," he declared. "If I say he plays, he plays. He can put an awful lot of fucking money in our pockets. Take your petition and shove it up your ass. This guy can take us to the World Series, and so far we haven't won dick." Now that's what I call *leadership*.

Most of all, the kid will need a Pee Wee Reese moment. During one game, Robinson, playing second base, was being booed mercilessly. The captain of the team, shortstop Pee Wee Reese, a southerner who had initially resisted a black teammate, strolled over and put his arm around Robinson. The crowd fell silent. Reese had made an unspoken demand: give the man a chance.

By the end of the season, the team had actually united around Robinson against the hostility showered on him by opponents.

Who will be the Branch Rickey, Leo Durocher, or Pee Wee Reese to this young gay pitcher? Could it be Dusty Baker, who was so good to Glenn Burke, the talented young outfielder who was driven out of baseball because he wouldn't keep quiet about being gay. A-Rod? My classy Padres manager Bruce Bochy?

Baseball is ready. I truly believe a lot of players would vie to do the right thing. It was heartening to discover the guys I had played alongside being generous in print when the reporters descended upon them. They made it clear they wouldn't have any problem with a gay teammate as long as he was a solid ballplayer.

In my experience, the vast majority of pro athletes are decent, hardworking guys who'd never hurt anyone. It's only the bad apples and head cases that get all the press attention. When pro football's Reggie White made his famous speech to the Wisconsin legislature, in which he blasted every minority group with every imaginable stereotype, he got weeks of press coverage. Such incidents make the sports world look like a bastion of bigotry.

There's little doubt the majority of ballplayers could handle a gay teammate. We're laying the groundwork now. I recall my excellent Padres teammate Doug Brocail making disparaging comments about everyone, all the time, including gays. He was simply young, strong, and loud.

"I'm not gay so I can't say much about it," he told a journalist after learning of my coming out. "I don't know if it's because of a feeling or if it's related to a gene. But I'll tell you what: Billy was a heck of a teammate, he always got the hit when we needed it, and that's the way I look at it."

Now that's progress. Thank you, Doug.

~

FEW BALLPLAYERS ARE choirboys off the field, but that doesn't make them bad guys. Unless you play beside them, it's very difficult to know what they are made of. I saw plenty of players lovingly kiss a wife or girlfriend good-bye only to spend the next two weeks on the road screwing around. It was nobody's business but theirs. Yet it seems hypocritical to turn our heads away from heterosexual mischief, while the mere thought of the most committed same-sex companionship is still taboo.

I played with John Wetteland in the Dodger organization for three years. He was a hell-raiser with one of the best heaters around, one of those zany characters right out of *Bull Durham*. He drove other players nuts with his practical jokes. Since he was a blue-chip prospect, he could get away with just about anything. I'll never forget the night he came bounding into the hotel room I was sharing with Dave Hansen in Albuquerque. A bunch of us were seated around a table playing cards. He proudly showed off what other players termed his "brown trout hall of fame," an album of photographs he'd taken the previous season of his, and some of his teammates', most impressive contributions to the Texas sewer system while he was playing in San Antonio.

So imagine my surprise when I picked up the July 27, 1997, edition of *The New York Times Magazine* to find a big photo of Wetteland in the locker room. "How Can A Moral Wrong Be A Civil Right?" read the T-shirt he was wearing, a disparaging reference to gay-rights causes. John had become a born-again Christian. "Jesus Christ is my point man," he said.

I'm happy John found religion. I'm a spiritual person myself. The world is full of beauty, and I believe that we were all created for a reason. But John is a classic case of a ballplayer who forgets where he came from and what got him to the top. The idea that Jesus would have scorned equality is an antiquated manipulation of scripture. As far as I'm concerned, the ultra-right-wing Fellowship of Christian Athletes, which has campaigned against gays and never asks athletes to take a hard look at their own values, deserves a place in Wetteland's old photo album.

I admired Will Clark for his comment in that same article. "Hey, I congratulate you on doing something for your life," the sweet-swinging lefty told a teammate who gave up a home run and attributed it to God's will. "But this is about baseball. And you'd better go out there and do it yourself. The Lord didn't hang that slider."

~

JOHN ROCKER is a left-handed relief pitcher with nasty stuff. He zoomed to fame with his unpredictable 97-miles-per-hour fastball, showing his stuff on national television during the National League play-offs three years in a row when he played for the Atlanta Braves.

Rocker also has some nasty attitudes. In 2001, he told *Sports Illustrated* that minority groups were despicable, complaining about "all the queers with AIDS who ride the 7 train in New York City." America is a free country, and John Rocker has a right to speak his mind. But it's just plain wrong for ballplayers to encourage prejudice, and Rocker has paid a heavy price for his venomous words—he was fined, suspended, and banished to the minors. Many people called him an idiot. They may be right.

At the same time, he simply got caught saying what some people think but are afraid to say. Ballplayers, worried about their reputations, have learned to spout politically correct lines fed by agents and handlers.

It's easier for baseball to blame the outburst on the player than look in the mirror. Wouldn't it be more productive for Major League Baseball and its thirty clubs to include sexual orientation in its anti-discrimination clause? I'd rather MLB do what virtually every other industry does today: institute more aggressive diversity-awareness training that includes sexual orientation. They need to make it clear that harassment won't be allowed on the field or in the locker room. As it now stands, a case could be made that all thirty big-league clubs and dozens more minor-league ones are in violation of Title VII of the Civil Rights Act.

The Major League Baseball Players Association, of which I'm a member, should make the case for sexual orientation non-discrimination, as other unions routinely do. As the association has made clear, baseball is a workplace, not a playground. In states and municipalities with gay-rights laws on the books, baseball clubs may actually be violating anti-discrimination statutes by allowing a hostile workplace.

John Rocker and I could have coexisted on the same team. I played long enough to know that a baseball clubhouse is one of the most diverse places on earth. There are as many prejudices as there are players. Most of the differences have nothing to do with race, religion, or even sexuality. As Doug Brocail put it so well, it's all about character—whether a guy's a team player, whether he plays through injuries, whether he comes to play every day. Everything else is irrelevant. Baseball must make it so.

~

BASEBALL TOUTS ITSELF as a game without borders, when in fact it is filled with obstacles both obvious and invisible. There are plenty of players locked in the baseball closet. During my playing days, there were always guys I got the "vibe" from, some of whom were among the game's greatest players. With more than 750 big leaguers at any one time, it's not difficult to imagine a dozen or so gay ballplayers.

In the summer of 2002, Mets manager Bobby Valentine told *Details* magazine that the big leagues are "probably ready for an openly gay player. . . . The players are a diverse enough group now that I think they could handle" a gay teammate. The media took this to mean that Valentine was clearing the way for one of his own players to come out. They zeroed in on Mike Piazza, the team's slugging catcher. No evidence was offered for this rumor.

Over a decade ago, Mike and I played together in the Dodger organization. We got to know each other in part because we shared the same agent, Dennis Gilbert. I enjoyed watching him go from a sixty-second-round draft pick to a sure first-ballot Hall of Famer. The guy can rake.

Overall, I thought Mike handled the rumors like the pro he is. Yet I was disappointed with his response to questions about his sexual orientation. "I'm not gay. I'm heterosexual," he declared. Then he added, "In this day and age it would be irrelevant. If the guy is doing his job on the field . . . I don't think there would be any problem at all."

Aside from the redundancy in that first part of his statement, Piazza missed an opportunity to send a message. He could have refused to answer or asked, "Why does it matter?" Once again, young gays and lesbians were reminded how important it is for a superstar to be outspokenly straight, whether he actually is or not. Even so, it was nice to hear that one of the game's best and most respected players wouldn't have a problem with a gay teammate.

Shortly after this episode, I started getting interview requests to talk about Valentine and Piazza, which I did. The informative Web site Outsports.com criticized me for speaking about the career-threatening dangers of coming out publicly at the major-league level, saying that I was encouraging players to stay closeted. I even made a guest appearance on a July 2002 episode of the HBO series *Arli$$* built around this premise. (Dennis Gilbert was the inspiration for the Arliss Michaels character, which was created by Robert Wuhl. Doing the show was like going back in time, only now everything was better. I actually got to act out the kind of supportive, sensible conversations about being a gay ballplayer I wished I could've had with Dennis.)

It's asking a lot for a ballplayer, having devoted his life to the game, to shoulder the burden for a cause, no matter how worthy. The stakes are extraordinarily high. Who protects him—or her—from bigoted fans? And from the manager, or the free-rein front office? All you have to do is look at what happened to Glenn Burke. Times have changed, sure. But how much?

The speculation about who will become the first active player to openly identify as gay remains a hot topic for sports talk radio. Until that happens, MLB is off the hook; it doesn't have to bother with creating the conditions that would make it possible for gay players to be themselves.

After I came out, commissioner Bud Selig received complaints from fans upset about the prejudice I described in the game. In an August 2000 letter to Outsports.com, Selig responded, "Everyone who wants an opportunity in Major League Baseball, and is deserving of that opportunity, should have that chance."

To me, this sounds like boilerplate. In the 2002 labor negotiations, ownership won major concessions from the formidable players union and Selig stared down George Steinbrenner. But when it comes to making the locker room and the diamond safe for gay players, he ducks and heads for cover.

~

THE RESPONSIBILITY should not fall to MLB alone. The gay and lesbian community must also share the burden for integrating baseball, and it's not enough to scream discrimination from ballpark parking lots. We need to get involved in the game on every level. If the teams themselves aren't mature enough to handle a gay player yet, there are plenty of other places to start. There still isn't a single openly gay scout, front-office exec, coach, or even umpire.

My own experience shows that the game can indeed handle a qualified gay person in a prominent position. There are plenty of baseball people, both on the field and off, who can be relied on in this mission. Shortly after *The New York Times* article appeared in 1999, I received a call on my cell phone. I was surprised to hear from John McHale, Jr., who at the time was the chief executive officer of the Detroit Tigers.

"Billy, I just want you to know that you were once and will always be a member of the Tigers," he said. "You have my support and the support of this organization. Once you wear the Old English *D* on your chest, it can never be taken away."

McHale, who went on to take a similar post with the Tampa Bay Devil Rays, invited me to be his guest at the next opening day at Tiger Stadium. I wasn't able to take him up on his offer, but it meant a lot to hear from this respected baseball man on the team I broke in with.

Once again, the message was clear. The loyalty of a team supersedes almost everything that divides human beings.

A few months later, after Efraín and I sold our restaurant and I'd had some time to digest my coming out, my desire to get back into baseball returned with a vengeance. For years my coaches had encouraged me to pursue a coaching career after I retired. But that seemed a little too close to the field for comfort. The last thing I wanted was to make players edgy or to become a distraction. I'd always wanted to work in a front office, so in August 2000 I wrote a letter to the Marlins' Dave Dombrowski, one of baseball's brightest minds. I hoped that McHale's words would serve as a good omen for my comeback.

Dave and I were acquainted. I had worked with his wife, Karrie Ross, at Channel 6 News in Miami Beach. Karrie was a pioneer in her own right, a female sportscaster in the early days of ESPN. But I had no idea how he had reacted to the news of my coming out, and I had no recourse because the state of Florida does not include sexual orientation in its nondiscrimination law. I was aware that ownership might be nervous about being the first organization to place an openly gay man in a prominent position. After laying out my experience in pro baseball and the business world, I finessed the gay issue.

"My national exposure," I wrote, "which was an accidental occurrence, will ultimately have to be considered by you, but it can also be an opportunity for the Florida Marlins to make a national statement, and will bring the organization a whole new legion of fans. I will tell you that it has never, nor ever will, be an issue. I respect and love the game of baseball. It was a privilege to play it for 10 years. The game has survived the departure of all of its great names and personalities, and will certainly survive without me. It is our national pastime, and it will always be in my blood. To feel like I cannot be a part of it because of my orientation is frustrating. I am qualified, I have the experience, and I only want the opportunity to prove myself each day, by the content of my character, and my ability to produce for my employer. I am prepared to begin work in a position that is behind the scenes, and will draw attention only to my abilities, not my personal life. The last thing I am seeking is more recognition."

Dave generously invited me to his office at Pro Player Stadium after that season. Over the course of eight months, we discussed several positions, including one that would involve marketing to gay and lesbian fans. But before we could reach an agreement, Dombrowski, frustrated by the Marlins' budget woes, resigned to take a similar post with my old team, the Tigers. The discussions ended with his departure, putting my quest to return to the great game on hold. Since then Efraín and I have formed a real estate partnership—and we're living happily in Miami Beach. Every day, I realize how fortunate I am to have found this wonderful man.

~

AFTER I CAME out publicly, I worried, more than anything else, about the reaction of my college teammates. Something about the bonds forged in your first time away from home becomes a part of you and lasts forever. Though I'd been out of touch, I dreaded losing their respect and friendship. I'd heard from several of them, but not all, and I hadn't seen most of them in person. In the spring of 2000, I'd returned for an alumni game.

There was an air of sadness about that spring day. Being together reminded us all of Timmy, our lost teammate, the one whose fun-loving nature and dominance on the mound had made possible all we'd accomplished, the guy who'd helped give me the confidence to fulfill my major-league aspirations.

I hadn't planned on playing because my left shoulder was bothering me. But I'd suited up just in case I changed my mind. So with the game tied in the seventh inning, Jim McAnany and Chris Donnels urged me to grab a bat. There was a runner on third base with one out. The situation clearly called for the old standby, the sacrifice fly.

The players, who'd been jawing at each other, went silent. As I approached the plate, Jim McAnany, the starting catcher on that 1986 championship team, broke the ice.

"All right, the faggot's gonna play," he shouted.

Everyone laughed. As usual, Jimmy wasn't afraid to say what everyone else was thinking. Tim's loss had a way of putting everything in perspective.

"This faggot's gonna drive in that runner from third," I shot right back.

I was still in good enough shape to roam center field, but I hadn't seen live pitching in over four years. The slow pitches I faced while playing for the Ft. Lauderdale Storm, my gay softball team, didn't exactly count.

It really didn't matter what I did. The point was just being there among old friends after a long hiatus. But old habits die hard, and I was determined not to fail. *It's you against him, and you are better.*

I dug in. I fell behind 0-2 and then worked the count full. The next pitch was a fastball, low and inside, right where I like it. I ripped a towering drive toward the center field fence. The ball fell into the fielder's glove on the warning track—I'd gotten under it just a hair. But the runner tagged and scored easily. I'd done my job, sacrificing for my home team.

~

TWO YEARS LATER, looking around the stadium's familiar confines as the Loyola student team scrimmaged on the day of my Santa Ana High reunion, I wondered what it would be like to be a college athlete in 2002. I remembered the amazing energy and bustle of collegiate play, the eagerness to learn everything about the hardest of games all at once.

I wondered if any of these kids struggled the way I had. Would the straight guys accept and stand up for a gay teammate? Despite all the social changes over the last decade, there was still the possibility they'd be uncomfortable with a "fag" like me, and that my sexual orientation would negate everything I'd accomplished for the school during my four years there. Had my coming out robbed me of all credibility? Was my sexual orientation all anyone would remember?

Dave Snow long ago had moved on to Long Beach State, where he had guided the team to five College World Series berths. The new Loyola coach, Frank Cruz, was a worthy successor who led the Lions to several conference titles. He was standing in the dugout observing the scrimmage when he spotted me in the stands. I was getting ready to leave when he motioned me over and called the players off the field.

"Guys," he said. "I don't interrupt practice for many things. But we are honored today to have a legend among us. This is Billy Bean, one of only three players in the school's history to have his number retired. He went on to have a big-league career. I'd like him to say a few words."

I was surprised by Frank's request. I certainly didn't feel like a legend. But for once, I let myself enjoy a compliment. After all, I was proud of what we'd accomplished together here. I'm not exactly Knute Rochne, but I was moved by the gesture, so I took a few moments to compose my thoughts.

"When I was here at Loyola, we learned that the team was only as good as the last guy on the bench," I began. "Until then we were just a bunch of guys wearing the same jersey. Whether you're a bullpen catcher or a bonus baby, the team comes first. We called ourselves the 'mules' because we worked hard, played fundamental baseball, and nobody got star treatment. Whether you make it to the next level or not, this is the most fun you're ever gonna have. Baseball's a lot like life—you can't control the bounces, but you can give it everything you've got. Respect the game, make your school proud, and kick some ass!"

When I was done, the players looked me in the eye and nodded. I leaned up against the backstop and watched them run back onto the field. I imagined the ragging Timmy would've given me for my little pep talk, smiled, and walked out of the stadium, head held high.

Billy Bean's Glossary of Baseball Slang

Activate ~ To make a player available for play, usually from the disabled list.

Advance scout ~ Talent evaluator who gauges a major-league team's future opponent.

All-star break ~ Three-day break at the halfway point of the season coinciding with the All-Star game. The most popular players in baseball—thirty from each league—are selected for the game by fans or named by managers.

At-bat ~ Plate appearance by hitter.

Bat speed ~ Quickness with which a batter swings at a pitch.

Batter's box ~ Rectangular area in which a player is allowed to stand while at bat.

Battery mates ~ Pitcher and catcher.

Batting practice ~ Period before a game when each team takes swings against live pitching.

Batting T ~ Hitting device that allows players to work on their swings without live pitching. The ball sits on a tube about two feet off the ground and is usually hit into a net.

Beaned ~ Hit by a pitched ball.

Benchwarmer ~ Player who sits on the bench more often than he plays.

Big Red Machine ~ Nickname for the great Cincinnati Reds teams of the 1970s.

BlueBoy ~ Magazine of gay erotica.

Box score ~ Statistical breakdown of a game, listed in the sports pages of most daily newspapers.

The bushes ~ Term for minor leagues; also known as the bush leagues.

Cactus League ~ Spring training league in Arizona.

Call-up ~ Player's promotion from the minor leagues to the majors.

Camp ~ Another term for spring training.

Chalk ~ White substance used to demarcate the foul lines that radiate from home plate to the outfield fence.

Chew ~ Long-leaf tobacco rolled into a ball and placed in the mouth like chewing gum; makes a player look as though he has a golf ball in his cheek.

Choking up ~ Placing one's hands a few inches up on the handle of the bat to allow a faster swing with more control.

Cleats ~ Shoes worn by baseball players. Metal or rubber spikes provide traction.

Command ~ Pitcher's ability to place the ball precisely.

Cy Young Award ~ Named after baseball's all-time winningest pitcher, who had 511 victories, this annual award goes to the best pitcher in each league.

Dip ~ Smokeless tobacco that comes in a round tin and is placed between the cheek and gum.

Disabled list ~ List of players injured and unable to perform. Placing a player on it allows his team to replace him with another.

Double-play combination ~ Second baseman and shortstop cooperating on a play that results in two outs.

Duck fart ~ Softly batted ball that lands safely. Considered a lucky hit.

Dugout ~ Area in which each team sits during the game, usually below the surface of the field. My primary residence during my big-league days.

ERA (Earned run average) ~ Average number of runs a pitcher gives up per nine innings, not including runs caused by fielders' errors, which are unearned.

ESPN's *SportsCenter* ~ Cable television show that revolutionized the way fans follow sports by providing continuous coverage.

Eye black ~ Paste placed under players' eyes to absorb the glare of the sun and improve vision.

Faggot bomb ~ Derogatory term for homosexuals, ued when a player makes a mistake or shows weakness or lack of determination on the field.

Fenway Park's Green Monster ~ Boston's left-field fence, which stands thirty-seven feet high.

Flair ~ Soft hit, usually off the end of the bat.

Forkball ~ Pitch that manifests a sharp downward movement in the last stage of its arc.

Forty-man roster ~ List of the total number of players a major-league team may protect at one time—twenty-five on the major-league team and fifteen from the minors.

Frozen rope ~ Hard-hit line drive that stays low to the ground.

Fungoes ~ Batted balls intended for fielders' practice, usually conducted by coaches. A long, thin bat is used to hit these fly balls and grounders.

Gamer ~ Player who works hard every day, never gives up or loafs, and can be counted on in the clutch.

General manager ~ Front-office executive who makes personnel decisions.

Getting in on him ~ Fastball on the inside of the plate. If the ball is hit, it is usually with the handle of the bat.

Going the other way ~ Hitting the ball to the opposite field of a batter's natural power alley. Also, to follow a different path.

Grapefruit League ~ Spring training league in Florida.

Great stuff ~ Used to characterize a player who pitches with speed and movement.

Hall of Fame ~ Museum in Cooperstown, New York, where the greatest players are enshrined, as voted by sportswriters.

Heat ~ An excellent fastball.

Hitter's count ~ When a batter is in a favorable position concerning balls and strikes.

Hook ~ Curveball.

Hot Stove League ~ Off-season talk among fans about the prospects of their favorite teams.

Instructional League ~ Post-season training of approximately six weeks for minor-league prospects.

K ~ Strikeout.

Knock ~ Base hit.

Leadoff ~ First batter in the lineup or starting a new inning.

Light-hitting catcher ~ Term applied to backstops who struggle offensively but are valued for their defense and ability to work well with pitchers.

Line drive ~ Hard-hit ball that's neither on the ground nor a pop fly.

Lineup card ~ Listing of the order in which players appear at-bat and their defensive positions.

Little League ~ Baseball association for children.

Lock out ~ When the owners of major-league teams do not allow the players to come to work. Typically a tactic used in labor negotiations.

Long toss ~ Throwing drill to strengthen arms by playing catch from long distance.

Mickey Mantle syndrome ~ Describes a player who parties often at night and still finds a way to play well the next day. Great slugger Mickey Mantle had a reputation for often staying out late and drinking with friends during the season.

MLB (Major League Baseball) ~ Business association that organizes thirty teams into two leagues and six divisions.

Mound ~ Solid pile of dirt from which the pitcher throws.

Mudville ~ Mythical town of Ernest Thayer's *Casey at the Bat.*

MVP (Most Valuable Player) ~ Player who is judged to have contributed the most to his team in one season, as voted for each league by sportswriters.

Nasty ~ Describes a pitcher who has such good movement that the ball is all but unhittable.

Off-speed pitch ~ Pitch other than fastball or slider, usually a curve or change-up used to keep a hitter off balance.

On the screws ~ To hit a ball squarely.

Opening day ~ First game of the regular season.

Option ~ One of various clauses in a baseball player's contract giving teams the right to send the player to the minors three separate times before he can choose to become a free agent.

Overpowering ~ Describes a pitcher who is hurling the ball quicker than batters can respond.

Pacific Coast League ~ Triple-A league affiliated with major-league clubs based in the West.

Painting the corner ~ Pitching the ball so as to consistently hit the edges of home plate, eighteen square inches of white rubber with a one-inch black border.

Pea ~ Hard-hit ball.

Phenom ~ Young player with potential.

Pinch hitter ~ Batter who substitutes for a player in the game. Most commonly employed when a light-hitting pitcher is scheduled to bat late in the game.

Pinch runner ~ Faster runner who is substituted for a slower one who has gotten on base.

Pine tar ~ Sticky substance that players put on the bat to improve their grip.

Pitching around ~ Walking a dangerous hitter.

Pop Warner ~ Football league for young people.

Pull hitter ~ Batter who hits the ball to his natural field and tends to be a power hitter.

Rake ~ Ability to hit well.

RBI (Runs Batted In) ~ Credit given to a player whenever he enables a baserunner to score through a hit, sacrifice, or walk with the bases loaded. An RBI cannot be awarded when a run scores as a result of an error.

Riding pine ~ Another word for sitting on the bench, which is often made of wood.

Round-tripper ~ Home run.

Rubber ~ White rectangular anchor at the top of the pitchers' mound.

Rule 5 draft ~ Mechanism by which one team obtains a player left off another team's forty-man roster.

Ruthian ~ Of mythical proportion in baseball terms; derived from Babe Ruth.

Scouts ~ Talent evaluators who travel the globe searching for new talent.

Scrub ~ Player who does not approximate a star.

Sent down ~ Demoted from the majors to the minors.

.300 ~ Batting percentage considered a mark of excellence, computed by number of hits divided by at-bats.

Single-A, double-A, triple-A ~ Three ascending levels of the minor leagues; triple-A is the level before the bigs.

Sinker ~ Fastball that descends as it reaches the plate, often causing hitters to swing over it or ground it into the dirt.

Sitting on a pitch ~ Anticipating what a pitcher will throw next.

Slider ~ Pitch that bears in on or away from a hitter.

Slugger ~ Hitter with home-run power.

Slump ~ Extended period of poor performance.

Spring training ~ Preparation for a baseball season. Generally starts in the third week of February and lasts until opening day in early April.

Starting rotation ~ Four or five pitchers designated to start consecutive games. A player uses the rest between starts to rebuild strength in his throwing arm.

Stroke ~ Swinging the bat.

Submariner ~ Pitcher whose throwing motion is from the side.

Suicide squeeze ~ Bunting a runner in from third base.

Trade ~ Exchange of players.

Utility player ~ Versatile backup.

Winter ball ~ Off-season competition, usually in Venezuela, Mexico, Puerto Rico, or the Dominican Republic.

World Series ~ Best-of-seven-game series between the American League and National League champions.

Wrigley Field ~ Chicago Cubs' historic park, where majority of Cubs games are still played during the day.

Acknowledgments

Billy Bean and Chris Bull acknowledge: This book could not have been published without some exceptional teamwork. Marlowe & Company editor and publisher Matthew Lore rescued the manuscript from the minor leagues and coached it all the way back up to the bigs. Matthew's sharp editorial eye, rare combination of patience and persistence, and vision for what this book could be made all the difference. We'd also like to thank all the folks at Marlowe/Avalon who helped out: Ghadah Alrawi, Karen Auerbach, Maria Fernandez, Peter Jacoby, Shona McCarthy, Michelle Rosenfield, Donna Stonecipher, Simon Sullivan, and Mike Walters. Thanks to Howard Grossman for the cover design and David Vance for the cover shot. Thanks also to Jed Mattes and Fred Morris of the Jed Mattes Literary Agency.

Billy Bean acknowledges: Linda and Ed Kovac put up with my determination as a kid, sat through hundreds of baseball, basketball, and football games, and tolerated my shooting a basketball in the driveway at 1 A.M., well after they'd gone to bed. My parents inspired me by their ability to understand, accept, and love each other and all their children. It is an honor to be their son.

My brothers and sister—Joe, Brian, Tommy, Jason, and Colette—have always been there. My grandma, Dottie Arnett, a strong and proud woman, passed along her stubborn will and much love. I have seen her cry only once in my life—the day she learned that my partner Sam Madani died.

My coaches—Bill Ross, Hershel Musick, Tom Meiss, and Dave Snow—changed my life for the better, and inspired a passion for the right way to play sports. To Gina: I grew up with you and will always cheer, admire, and love you. I'm sorry it was so difficult. Sam taught me so much about life in the short time we had together. I miss you.

Chris Bull's devotion to baseball inspired me to tell a story that proved alternately humbling, exhausting, and exhilarating. This book would not have been written or published without his collaboration, faith in my story, and determination. His dedication pushed me to places I never thought we would find, and I am forever grateful. He is not only a special writer, but my friend.

Elizabeth Birch and the Human Rights Campaign in Washington, D.C. awakened me to how my experience could help others. These dedicated activists gently showed me the responsibility we all have to our communities. The Hetrick-Martin Institute in New York City has shown me the way in reaching out to gay youth, whose suffering is too often overlooked. To every kid who loves to compete in sports: I salute you.

Martina Navratilova, Billie Jean King, Greg Louganis, Dave Kopay, Tom Waddell, and others paved the way. This book is written in honor of Glenn Burke, a man and ballplayer who was ahead of the curve, died before his time, and paid a terrible price for refusing to lie. Esera Tuaolo, bravo!

Brad Ausmus had the patience to put up with the media requests about my story, in the process showing the strength, maturity, and wisdom to speak his mind on an unpopular cause when it would have been so easy not to. Thanks. Jim Bruske, Chris Donnels, and Jim McAnany, who knew me from Loyola to the majors, let me know that nothing had changed.

Loyola Marymount University helped me realize my dream. Carol Layana and the entire Layana family provided my home away from home during my college years. I will never forget my friend Tim Layana, another good man who died too young. Jim and Rosemany McAnany provided a family atmosphere in my college days.

My Miami friends helped me rebuild my life and make the city my new home.

To my best little buddy, my dog Paco. Our long runs together are the best therapy.

And most of all, to my partner and companion, Efraín Veiga, whose patience and understanding over the past seven years have been astonishing. Your unconditional love makes every day special. Thank you for putting up with the endless tennis, hoops, marathons, Laker games, *SportsCenter,* and everything else. I hope you will share the rest of your life with me. *Te quiero mucho!*

Chris Bull acknowledges: Jeffrey Escoffier, Tom Mallon, and Gerry Lore read early drafts of the manuscript and started us on the right track. Bob Gray introduced me to Billy at a party at his splendid house in Miami Beach. Judy Wieder of *The Advocate* sent me to profile Billy and then put the story on the cover. My editors at the magazine, Jon Barrett and Bruce Steele, generously allowed me the time off to work with Billy to finish the manuscript. Jon's ability to turn out his own book on a short deadline reminded me it was possible.

My buddy David Check made possible one of my best baseball experiences as a fan: the 2002 World Series. His unqualified acceptance and support made all the difference. Mike Korengold, also there when it mattered, loaned me a smart line at a crucial time, lots of good conversation, and dry humor. Paul Amato drove me around L.A. and made me laugh. Michael Bronski, as always, provided intellectual sustenance. John Gallagher, my friend and collaborator and editor on *The Advocate* profile, is unfailingly generous with editorial feedback. My squash partner and friend Andrew Holleran dispensed insights between lobs and drop shots.

Billy's parents, Linda and Ed Kovac, provided details as well as steak and apple pie. Efraín Veiga opened up his and Billy's home to me for several visits and shared his cooking and his wisdom. Thank you, Ethel. My own parents fostered my appreciation of baseball as a child and tolerated this book's writing schedule over the holidays in my father's sun-filled studio. The music of Pete Yorn and David Gray inspired late-night work sessions.

Hans Johnson pored over every line. Hans is everything I could want in a partner—amazingly, even a deft and thoughtful editor. His dictum, "Even when you think you've told enough stories, tell another one," helped guide the development of this book. I love you, Hans.

Finally, I'd like to acknowledge my double-play partner, Billy Bean. By trusting me to help him put together his remarkable story, Billy granted me the privilege and pleasure of living through the ups and downs of a major-league career as well as a study in the courage it takes to be yourself and inspire a cause. In the process, I went from fan to friend and back again.